D1569419

A Local Habitation

Essays on Poetry

JOHN FREDERICK NIMS

Ann Arbor
The University of Michigan Press

Copyright © by The University of Michigan 1985
All rights reserved
Published in the United States of America by
The University of Michigan Press and simultaneously
in Rexdale, Canada, by John Wiley & Sons Canada, Limited
Manufactured in the United States of America

1988   1987   1986   1985   4   3   2   1

Library of Congress Cataloging in Publication Data

Nims, John Frederick, 1913–
   A local habitation.

   (Poets on poetry)
   Includes bibliographies.
   1. Nims, John Frederick, 1913–   —Aesthetics—
Addresses, essays, lectures.   2. Poetry—Addresses,
essays, lectures.   I. Title.   II. Series.
PS3527.I863L6   1985   809.1   84-21938
ISBN 0-472-06356-1 (pbk.)

The poet's eye, in a fine frenzy rolling,
Doth glance from heaven to earth, from earth to heaven;
And as imagination bodies forth
The forms of things unknown, the poet's pen
Turns them to shapes, and gives to airy nothing
A local habitation and a name.

Acknowledgments

I am grateful to the University of Illinois at Chicago, and particularly to the Institute for the Humanities there and to its director, Professor Robert V. Remini, for the generous fellowship that afforded me the time necessary for the completion of this project.

I am grateful too to Donald Hall for encouraging it, and to Linda Howe for her intelligent and helpful copyediting.

—J. F. N.

Grateful acknowledgment is made to the following authors, publishers, and journals for permission to reprint previously published materials.

Agenda for John Frederick Nims's translation of "Lo ferm voler qu'el cor m'intra" by Arnaut Daniel, *Agenda* (March 1984). Reprinted by permission from *Agenda*, Albert Bridge Road, London, SW114PE.

Doubleday for excerpts from *The Book of the Courtier* by Baldesar Castiglione, translated by Charles Singleton. Copyright © 1959 by Charles S. Singleton and Edgar de N. Mayhew. Reprinted by permission of Doubleday & Company, Inc.

Harper & Row for "On Making an Anthology" from *The Harper Anthology of Poetry,* 1981. Reprinted by permission from Harper & Row.

Houghton Mifflin for "Tide Turning" from *The Kiss: A Jambalaya* by John Frederick Nims. Copyright © 1982 by John Frederick Nims. Reprinted by permission of Houghton Mifflin Company.

University Press of Virginia for "The Greatest English Lyric?" from *Studies in Bibliography*, edited by Fredson Bowers, vol. 20. Also for "Yeats and the Careless Muse" from *Learners and Discerners*, edited by Robert Scholes. Copyright © 1964 by the Rector and Visitors of the University of Virginia.

Contents

Ovid, Golding, and the
Craft of Poetry

"The most beautiful book in the language"—so Ezra Pound salutes Arthur Golding's translation of Ovid's *Metamorphoses.* Not an offhand opinion either: in *Notes on Elizabethan Classicists* of 1915 or '16, Golding, "no inconsiderable poet," came in for high praise; Pound even found it necessary to specify that he was *not* saying "Golding is a greater poet than Milton." A 1929 footnote to the article says, "His *Metamorphoses* form possibly the most beautiful book in our language." By 1934, in the *ABC of Reading,* even the "possibly" is dropped; and by 1964, in *Confucius to Cummings,* an anthology of poetry edited by Pound and Marcella Spann, no writer except Browning is accorded such extensive representation: there are twenty-eight pages of Golding to twenty-four of Shakespeare (and to less than three of Chapman's *Odyssey*); a note reminds us that it is "a volume that has been called 'the most beautiful book in our language.'"

But how carefully had Pound read Golding? He seems to have looked at the pages of Professor Rouse's edition of 1904, seen that the language was livelier than much translator's English, found a few bright passages, and exalted his discovery into a lifelong enthusiasm. There are signs of imperfect reading in the passages he quotes. He gives us, as from Golding, this line about Proserpina gathering flowers:

And while of Maidenly desire she fillde hir Haund and Lap

From *Ovid's Metamorphoses: The Arthur Golding Translation* (1567), edited by John Frederick Nims (New York: Macmillan, 1965).

But Golding's word was not "Haund"; it was "Maund." Pound apparently thought it a misprint, which he took on himself to correct. "Maund" means a wicker basket; Golding uses the word several times. Here it translates Ovid's "calathos." (In *Confucius to Cummings,* p. 56, the word is correctly glossed by one of the editors when it appears in VIII, 853.) "Haund," in any case, is an improbable spelling for "hand" in Golding, who wrote "hande" only ten lines above the line quoted. In the selection Pound calls "Address to Bacchus" he quotes Golding as writing

. . . throngs of Fownes and Satyres on thee tend.

"Fownes" arouses our suspicion as an unlikely way to spell "Fawns," which is normally "Faunes" in Golding. What he wrote here was "Frowes," quite a common word in his translation. "Frow" (Dutch, *vrouw*) meant first a Dutch woman, later any woman; it was applied especially to the Bacchantes and in this passage translates "Bacchae." There are other misreadings in the lines Pound quotes; it is surprising that they still appear in *The Literary Essays of Ezra Pound,* published some forty years after the piece was written.

It is true that few critics have shared Pound's enthusiasm. C. S. Lewis, in *English Literature in the Sixteenth Century,* says that the poem, in "ugly fourteeners," "ought to be unendurable, and it almost is. . . ." A cooler judgment is that of F. O. Matthiessen, who, in his *Translation: An Elizabethan Art,* writes: "The barriers of meter are not easily crossed from one language into another, and it requires a poet to translate a poet. Such works as Golding's Ovid and Harington's Ariosto neither suggest the qualities of the original, nor possess exceptional poetic merit in compensation." My own opinion is that while Golding's work is not "beautiful"—if that word has any critical utility—it has other claims on our attention. It is certainly the most famous translation of Ovid into English. It was the English Ovid from the time of its publication in 1567 until about a decade after the death of Shakespeare in 1616—the Ovid, that is, for all who read him in English during the greatest period of our literature. And in its racy verve, its quirks and oddities, its rugged English gusto, it is still more enjoyable, more plain fun to read, than any other *Metamorphoses* in English.

An odd collaboration, that between the sophisticated darling of a dissolute society, the author of a scandalous handbook of seduction, and the respectable country gentleman and convinced Puritan who spent much of his life translating the sermons and commentaries of John Calvin. Hardly less striking than the metamorphoses the work dealt with.

Ovid—Publius Ovidius Naso—has given us his own autobiography in *Tristia* IV, 10. He was born in 43 B.C., the year which closed the Ciceronian Age with the death of the great orator. The poets of that age had been Lucretius and Catullus, both dead about ten years when Ovid was born. Vergil, whom Ovid saw only once, was then about twenty-seven; Horace, whom he heard recite, about twenty-two. Propertius and Tibullus, who died long before Ovid, were in their childhood. He himself lived through the whole period of the Augustan Age: Augustus began to reign in 27 B.C., when Ovid was fifteen; he died in 14 A.D. Ovid, banished from Rome in 8 A.D., survived the emperor by four years—the only poet of the great age who lived on into the Christian era.

Like most of the Roman poets, he was born outside of the city itself, at Sulmo, now Sulmona, about 100 miles to the east. His family was prosperous if not affluent. His practical father, who once complained that not even Homer had left any money, sent him to Rome and later to Athens to be given the kind of education, largely rhetorical, that a prospective lawyer and public official should receive. Ovid's interests, however, lay elsewhere; poetry, he said, had always come naturally to him—though no poet has kept a craftier eye out for the artistic effect. At few times in the history of the world can an environment have been more congenial for poetry. The work of Vergil, Horace, Propertius, and Tibullus was beginning to circulate when Ovid was a young man; rich and powerful figures were willing to sponsor and encourage literary talent.

Ovid's earliest work, the *Amores*, consists of rather light-hearted amorous elegiacs, which, especially in the translation of Christopher Marlowe, sound rather like the *Elegies* of the young John Donne. These were followed by the *Heroides*, a series of letters from "heroines" to their absent lovers. The *Ars Amatoria*, or *Art of Love*, a sort of tongue-in-cheek guide for philanderers, which some have seen as disenchanted or satiric, created something of a scandal; it may well have been one of the reasons why Ovid was banished by an emperor concerned about the morality of his people. There seems to have been a mysterious other reason too: Ovid refers to it sometimes as a mistake he made, sometimes as an inadvertence like that of Actaeon, who suddenly found himself staring on Diana while she bathed. Scholars have speculated ever since, often lewdly, on the exact reason for the banishment; John C. Thibault's *The Mystery of Ovid's Exile* (1964) finds none of some thirty-three theories satisfactory. The punishment was severe for a poet who loved Rome and its society: he was sent to Tomi on the shores of the Black Sea, a savage outpost in a grim landscape of bitter winters, whose inhabitants spoke a barbarous dialect, and whose very survival was threatened by the wild tribesmen around them. Here he spent the ten years of life remaining, his poetry of complaint and appeal ignored by the authorities in Rome. Ovid was married three times; his only child, a daughter, was probably a wife at the time of his banishment.

Ovid's most famous English translator, Arthur Golding, was born in Essex in 1536 of a family of prosperous land-owners whose name went back beyond the Conquest. One of his sisters married John de Vere, Sixteenth Earl of Oxford; she was later lady-in-waiting to the queen. Strongly Protestant, even Puritan, in his convictions, Golding probably dropped out of Cambridge when the Catholic Queen Mary came to the throne in 1553. But, in the university or out of it, he must have read the classics thoroughly as a young man. Translating from the Latin and the French became the chief work of his life. His *Preface* to Ovid explains why he could translate a poet so exuberantly pagan, and why at the same time he could be working on John Calvin's *Treatise on Offenses,* which he followed with several volumes of Calvin's sermons and commentaries. In all, Golding published over thirty volumes, most of them religious. But with them were a translation of Caesar's *Commentaries* (a work which Longfellow mentions as among the books Miles Standish owned), an account of a sensational London murder of 1573, later dramatized as *A Warning for Fair Women,* and an account of the London earthquake of 1580. Golding, who during the happiest period of his life was on speaking terms with many of his great contemporaries, was married and had eight children. From the time of his elder brother's death in 1575 until the end of his life he was harassed by a series of lawsuits over mortgaged property. For all of his famous friends and wealthy relatives, he spent a year or two in debtors' prison; when he died in 1606 he left debts so large that only a man once rich could have accumulated them.

When Ovid was ejected from Rome in 8 A.D., his most ambitious work, the *Metamorphoses* (Golding uses the singular *Metamorphosis* of some manuscripts) had not been given its final revision. Ovid, in despair, threw his own manuscript into the fire. Friends who had copies did not join him in this symbolic suicide, and before long he was sending back instructions for its publication. The fifteen books are a collection of some two hundred and fifty stories which involve the theme of transformation, though sometimes, as in the stories of Phaethon and Proserpina, the theme is incidental. The transformations are generally of men and women into something else—animal, vegetable, or even mineral. Sometimes the change is a means of escape, sometimes a reward, sometimes a punishment. Some stories are only a few lines long; some several hundred. There is an order roughly chronological from the change of original chaos into the universe up to the development of Rome from a humble village to world capital—and even on to the apotheosis of Julius Caesar as a star. There are many tones, from the homely sweetness of Philemon and Baucis to the frenzy of a girl's incestuous love for her father or her brother; from the little idyll of Pan and Syrinx to the rape, mutilation, and cannibalism of Tereus, Procne, and Philomela. The tales follow each other with marvellous rapidity—*senza tirar fiato,* says an Italian editor—and are connected in all sorts of ways, some so ingenious that Quintilian objected to the cleverness. Such compilations of *epyllia* (short narrative poems) had been made before; some had even dealt with the same theme or a more specialized one: transformation into birds, for example. How much Ovid borrowed from lost originals of course we do not know; we know that he did borrow, and we know that it was the custom for ancient poets (as for such modern ones as Pound and Eliot) to allude deliberately, even by quotation, to other literary works. Ovid's gallery of narrative exuberance has been called baroque, even "violently baroque," yet the language itself, for all of its rhetorical elegance, is simple and "classic." Ovid is a sensuous poet; he sees in pictures that have reminded some readers of those at Pompeii. Little wonder that in the Renaissance his book became a sort of "painter's bible," so that one can hardly go through a museum of Europe or America without seeing picture after picture of Ovidian inspiration. The sophisticated poet says elsewhere that such transformations as he describes are impossible. But if they were possible, he seems to say, this is how they would happen to such people as we know in such a world as that around us. "His book sings," says A. G. Lee, one of his recent editors, "of the manifold variety of life, telling us that the world is full of beauty and wonder, that life is good and to be enjoyed."

Mere escape literature, some might say. Yet perhaps the most delightful escape literature we have: off into an enchanted world very much like the one we know, except that sorcery and miracle are as real as gravitation. Any bird by the roadside may be the comrade or enemy of another day, encouraging or reproaching us; the tree in the yard may be last year's girl friend, the same sheen on the bright leaves as the golden hair had once.

Yet if not serious in the kaleidoscope of detail, the *Metamorphoses* have a serious philosophical undercurrent, brought to the surface in the long discussion of Pythagorean philosophy in XV, which sees change and growth as fundamental and eternal laws of the universe. As we know they are: over the years, if not before our faces, we have seen men turn into wolves or weasels, seen them turn to rocks of this kind or that. We have even seen them turn, last of all, into flowers and trees. Valéry is Ovidian when he writes:

> L'argile rouge a bu la blanche espèce,
> Le don de vivre a passé dans les fleurs!

> (The red clay has drunk the white kind;
> the gift of living has passed into the flowers!)

Time is telescoped in Ovid: the girl is a tree in seconds, so that Apollo's palm on the warm bark can still feel the beating heart beneath. These transformations are like the time-lapse films of a flower developing—the process of weeks, perhaps, in a few seconds. Poets have always been fascinated by mutability; some have seen the meaning of life in passionate surrender to the spirit of change. We think of Goethe in *Dauer im Wechsel* or *Selige Sehnsucht;* of Rilke in the "Wolle die Wandlung" of the Sonnets to his Ovidian Orpheus—the phrase itself from a sonnet (II, 12) that ends with Daphne, now laurel, yearning for her pursuer to change into wind:

> Und die verwandelte Daphne
> will, seit sie lorbeern fühlt, dass du dich wandelst in Wind.

> (And the transformed Daphne,
> since she feels [changed into] laurel, wants you to change
> into wind.)

Lines like these remind us that in reading later poetry we cannot be quite sure we are not reading the classics, perhaps Ovid himself, metamorphosed. Goethe, in one of his noblest poems, the *Trilogie der Leidenschaft,* says that the hours went by like sisters, alike yet not identical:

Die Stunden glichen sich in zartem Wandern
Wie Schwestern zwar, doch keine ganz den andern.

(The hours resembled each other in their gentle passage, like sisters indeed, yet none exactly like the others.)

We know he is thinking of Ovid's palace of the sun, where the engraved sea nymphs are described as having

facies non omnibus una,
non diuersa tamen, qualem decet esse sororum.

(a face not one and the same for all, and yet not dissimilar, but such as [the faces] of sisters ought to be.)

Goethe probably knew Ovid better than he knew any other poet. So, we suspect, did Dante, though he was obligated to take the more orthodox Vergil for his guide. So too did Shakespeare. One wonders if any other poet can claim so many devoted followers among the great?

It would be hard to come on a more striking illustration of Ovid's theme than the posthumous fate of the poet himself. Banished from pagan Rome for—we can almost say—immorality, he was enthusiastically gathered to the allegorical bosom of the Christian Middle Ages. Though earlier centuries had been hostile, the twelfth and thirteenth centuries have been called an Ovidian Age. In allegorized versions of his *Metamorphoses,* he became even a sort of Christian theologian. Extracts were made for convents: the goddesses were presented as nuns, the gods as their clergy. The amours Ovid described become their pious meetings. Although moralized versions of erotic stories were expressly banned by the Church, they remained long in vogue. In the most important, the endless *Ovide moralisé* of just after 1300, the whole of Christian morality is discovered in the *Metamorphoses.* Three-personed Diana, who was not only the huntress but also the Moon and Hecate, stood for the Trinity. Cupid, with halo, was the Infant Jesus. Ceres seeking Proserpina represented the Church looking for the strayed souls of sinners, her two torches the Old and New Testament. Another allegorizer took the story of the lewd nymph Salmacis, who flung off her clothes to leap into the water after the bathing Hermaphroditus, to be about the True Church soliciting Protestants to return to her ardent breast. Golding, in his *Epistle* and *Preface*, reprinted in this present edition after the fifteen books as an example of Ovid moralized, does not permit himself these absurdities. The Salmacis story for him merely shows that idleness encourages lust, which can be enervating. Golding is sensible in a century deluged by allegorical commentaries, which thinkers such as Rabelais derided. The allegorical tradition is alluded to in R. R. Bolgar's *The Classical Heritage and Its Beneficiaries* and in E. R. Curtius's *European Literature and the Latin Middle Ages,* but is more fully treated by Jean Seznec in *The Survival of the Pagan Gods:*

> . . . this pseudo science, which teaches us to hide, or to discover, the most serious precepts beneath the most frivolous outward appearance, offered a providential means of reconciling the pagan and the Christian worlds . . . basically, allegory is often sheer imposture, used to reconcile the irreconcilable— just as we have seen it lending decency to the manifestly indecent. . . .

But in Golding's two pieces, which may have been only a gesture toward his conscience and any censorious official eye, it is not the "dangerous fraud" Seznec calls it. Ovid, says Golding, is not merely telling stories; he is giving

> pitthye, apt and playne
> Instructions which import the prayse of vertues, and the shame
> Of vices, with the due rewardes of eyther of the same.

He proceeds to certain common-sense examples from each of the books, with some practical advice for the conduct of life. As the jingle on his title page insists, there is more here than meets the eye:

> With skill, heede, and judgement, this worke must be read,
> For else to the Reader it standes in small stead.

Ovid's importance in the Elizabethan Age can hardly be overemphasized. In his *Mythology and the Renaissance Tradition in English Poetry,* Douglas Bush holds that "a history of mythology and the Renaissance tradition must be largely an account of the metamorphoses of Ovid." And he finds Golding's translation "all-important" in England.

But, in these years of Shakespeare commemorations, we may wonder what Golding meant to that dramatist. We know what Ovid meant: L. P. Wilkinson, in the best book we have on Ovid, reminds us that Shakespeare echoes him about four times as often as he echoes Vergil, that he draws on every book of the *Metamorphoses,* and that there is scarcely a play untouched by his influence. Golding's translation, through the many editions published during Shakespeare's lifetime, was the standard Ovid in English. If Shakespeare read Ovid so, he read Golding.

It seems certain that he did. Yet for Professor Rouse to call his 1904 edition by the title of *Shakespeare's Ovid* is misleading in its implications. T. W. Baldwin (*William Shakspere's Small Latin and Lesse Greeke*) has brought his impressive knowledge to bear on this and other problems; his conclusion is that Shakespeare quite possibly used Golding in the Stratford school along with the Latin. This would account for the way Shakespeare now and then seems to blend the two together: "the evidence now seems to be conclusive that [he] habitually used both." Of one passage in Shakespeare Professor Baldwin writes: "The nuclear greatness which Shakspere sees is in the original, not in Golding's awkwardly obscure translation." His general conclusion is that Shakespeare knew Ovid's stories and treatment, and that when he was working on a situation that recalled Ovid he would turn to the *Metamorphoses* for suggestions: "There is no indication that he does more than run through Golding's translation. . . ." Shakespeare's Ovid, we might say, was Ovid.

All writers on Golding and Shakespeare adduce Prospero's famous speech in *The Tempest,* which begins:

Ye elves of hills, brooks, standing lakes and groves

and quote Golding's

Ye Ayres and windes: ye Elves of Hilles, of Brookes, of
   Woods alone,
Of standing Lakes . . .

                                                    (VII, 265)

Baldwin, after a close study, concludes that "at first sight the
relation . . . appears a great deal stronger than it is." We can
hardly claim that Shakespeare got his elves from Golding,
since he had had elves of his own in the earlier plays. Baldwin
points out that for the Elizabethans certain Roman minor
gods (*dii*) were "elves," and he reminds us that if Golding and
Shakespeare, looking at the same Latin text, had used the
same Latin dictionary, they would have come up with the
same English words. Pound may be overconfident when, after
saying that Golding's work is "the most beautiful book in the
language," he adds, "my opinion and I suspect it was Shake-
speare's."

   In the burlesque of the Pyramus and Thisbe story in *A
Midsummer Night's Dream* (V, i), Shakespeare seems to be pok-
ing good-humored fun at Golding, whose version has one of
the lovers thanking the wall for its "courtesie" in leaving the
chink they can talk through (Ovid had said: "Nec sumus in-
grati"), and has Thisbe ("thy Thisb") die with such lines as

This said, she tooke the sword yet warme with slaughter of
   hir love
And setting it beneath hir brest, did to hir heart it shove.
                                                    (IV, 196–97)

At the silly pitch of passion in the burlesque, it is curious that
the lovers break into what are really Golding's fourteeners,
complete with inversion and tautology, though in Shake-
speare the line is printed as three short lines, made ridicu-
lous by an overuse of rhyme:

Thy mantle good, / What stain'd with blood? / Approach, ye
    Furies fell!
O Fate, come come! / Cut thread and thrum; / Quail, crush,
    conclude, and quell.

Though Golding's translation of Ovid is the most enjoyable
we have, the enjoyment is not, I think, in the poetry. Ovid was
a great poet; Dante put him among the four greatest he knew.
Golding was a respectable literary gentleman, with a thor-
ough knowledge of Latin (he does not make the boners that
Marlowe does), with a sharp eye for the life about him, and
with a keen ear for racy English. But to read Golding with the
original is to be in for continual disappointment. First, we
notice how wordy Golding is. Latin is of course terser than
English, but no difference between the languages can excuse
Golding's writing twenty words for Ovid's three, or turning
one line into two, three, or even four. Marlowe, a craftsman
of genius, was able to render Ovid line for line; Golding adds
over 2,500 lines to Ovid's 12,000. Ovid himself has been
found long-winded, even if musically so, but the general ef-
fect of his writing is one of conciseness. Single lines and
phrases have been ringing in the literary memory of Europe
for two thousand years. He combines terse elements, with
little reliance on modifiers; whereas he can introduce his Iron
Age with "de durost ultima ferro," Golding has to write

> of yron is the last
> In no part good and tractable as former ages past.

Ovid calls gold the incentive to evil, "irritamenta malorum";
Golding, who tends to say things twice, calls it

> The spurres and stirrers unto vice, and foes to doing well.

Ovid says Lycaon is the very image of savagery, "eadem feri-
tatis imagost"; Golding says

> and every kind of waye
> his cruell heart in outward shape doth well itself bewraye.

Even the simple "ibimus illac" ("we'll go there") becomes

> To make my passage that way then my cunning will I try.

Showpiece lines suffer the most. When Apollo warns his human son that he wants too much in asking to guide the solar chariot, he tells the boy that his state is mortal, what he asks is not:

> Sors tua mortalis; non est mortale quod optas.

A line memorable in its phrasing and in its melancholy application to so much in our experience. But who would remember, or care to remember:

> Thy state is mortall, weake and frayle, the thing thou doest
>   desire
> Is such, whereto no mortall man is able to aspire

When the spiteful old hag Envy flies over Athens, she is said almost to weep because she sees nothing to weep at:

> Vixque tenet lacrimas, quia nil lacrimabile cernit.

Perhaps the line is too clever. Golding, who loses the important word play of *lacrimas-lacrimabile*, makes it clumsy:

> And forebicause she nothing saw that might provoke to
>   weep,
> It was a corsie to hir heart hir hatefull tears to keepe.

A last example, from thousands possible, of Ovid's polished conciseness and Golding's gangling diffusion, is in the dying words of Thisbe, who tells Pyramus that she—unfortunate!—will be called the cause and companion of his death:

> letique miserrima dicar
> causa comesque tui.

> And wretched woman as I am, it shall of me be sed
> That like as of thy death I was the only cause and blame,
> So am I thy companion eke and partner in the same.

Golding has a special weakness for adjectives, the handiest means of stretching out a line metrically deficient. Ovid uses no adjectives when he has the wolf swimming among sheep in his great flood. Golding contributes three:

> The grim and greedy Wolfe did swim among the siely
> sheepe.

Ovid first mentions Phaethon without an adjective; Golding contributes three overlapping ones: "a stalwart stripling strong and stout." Sometimes it seems that Golding—as Plato has Socrates say of a bad poet—seems to be trying to show in how many ways he can say the same thing, or how many synonyms he knows. Ovid: "pugnes"; Golding: "Strive, struggle, wrest, and writhe."

Golding, who in his prose can write perfectly natural English, in verse permits himself inversions that have never existed in our normal English speech patterns:

> She staide without, for to the house in enter might she not

or

> . . . names that . . .
> To thee O Liber wonted are to attributed bee.

The meter also forces him to patch out lines with such dull putty as "even so likewise," "howbeit yet of all this while," "conditionly that when that I," "by means whereof away without," and "immediately without delay." He uses "for" with the infinitive ("for to go"); says "the which" and "for because"; uses "the same" for "it." Pound defends one of his faults: "his constant use of 'did go,' 'did say' is not fustian and mannerism; it was contemporary speech, though in a present-day poet it is impotent affectation and definite lack of technique." But it was not contemporary speech; lack of technique is precisely what it was. Golding's prose is straightforward, without inversions, almost entirely without the *do*'s and *did*'s unless they are emphatic, as we still do use them. Here are some lines from his report of the earthquake, in modernized spelling: these, and not what we find too often in his verse, are the patterns of English speech.

> Again, whereas in earthquakes that proceed of natural causes, certain signs and tokens are reported to go before them, as: a tempestuous working and raging of the sea, the weather being fair, temperate, and unwindy; calmness of the air matched with great cold; dimness of the sun for certain days afore; long and thin streaks of clouds appearing after the setting of the sun, the weather being otherwise clear; the troubledness of water even in the deepest wells, yielding moreover an infected and stinking savor; and lastly, great and terrible sounds in the earth, like the noise of groanings and thunderings, as well afore as after the quaking—we find that not any such foretoken happened against the coming of this earthquake. And therefore we may well conclude (though there were none other reason to move us) that this miracle proceeded not of the course of any natural cause, but of God's only determinate purpose, who maketh even the very foundations and pillars of the earth to shake, the mountains to melt like wax, and the seas to dry up and to become as a dry field, when he listeth to show the greatness of his glorious power, in uttering his heavy displeasure against sin.

This is English, and we can amuse ourselves by thinking how less English it would be if he had versified it:

> And whereas earthquakes, which that eke of causes naturall
> bee,
> Afore the same are signs thereof, and tokens for to see

The rhythm was an old-fashioned one when Golding wrote. "To most sensitive contemporary ears," says T. S. Eliot, in writing of the Senecan translators of that decade, "the fourteener had had its day." It may seem curious to us now, who talk of poetry of "the fifties" or "the sixties," that Pound, so fond of making it new, should admire a behind-the-times translator. And yet who remembers if Catullus wrote in the manner of the 60s or the 70s B.C.? Villon in the

manner of the 1460s or the 1450s? And if Golding was be-
hind the times, Chapman, in his translation of the *Iliad*, was
even more so.

If Golding's fourteeners do not take us, with Chapman's,
into the realms of gold, yet they have considerable narrative
merit. Except for the wordiness and the inversions, they are
clear and fast-moving—more readable than the lines of
Studley and Jasper Heywood that Eliot quotes for their "vig-
orous vocabulary and swinging meter." For one thing, Gold-
ing's lines are not clotted with excessive alliteration: one finds
almost never such a line as Heywood's

> Whose growing guttes the gnawing gripes and fylthy foules
>   do fyll.

One of the merits of Golding as verse writer is the casualness
with which he lets the syntactical pauses fall. The fourteener
tends to break into two half-lines, one of four beats, one of
three, with a strong pause after each. Richard Edwards's fa-
mous *Amantium Irae* begins:

> In goyng to my naked bedde, as one that would have slept,
> I heard a wife syng to her child, that long before had wept

Every line in this eight-line stanza, almost every line in the
five-stanza poem, has the pauses in exactly the same places.
But in Golding, though his basic line is like Edwards's, the
pauses may come anywhere, as in Juno's complaint (II, 647–
51):

> I have bereft hir womans shape, and at this present howre
> She is become a Goddesse. Loe this is the scourge so sowre
> Wherewith I strike mine enimies. Loe here is all the spight
> That I can do: this is the ende of all my wondrous might.
> No force. I would he should (for me) hir native shape
>   restore

Golding can so far disregard the end-stop as to have an "and"
there:

> Here now I Arethusa dwell: here am I setled: and
> I humbly you beseche . . .

He can so far disregard the pause after the fourth beat that he can have a word straddling it:

> The horie Sallowes and the Poplars growing on the brim

Equally carefree is his use of rhyme. He has no objection to drawing on unusual forms that happen to fit. "Breast" he generally spells "brest," but when he needs a rhyme for "fist" he is willing to spell it "brist." "Such" is his usual spelling, but as a rhyme for "whiche" it can turn to "syche." "Stand" is "stand" or "stande," but as a rhyme word for "pond" it can be "stond." "Like" and "well" become "lieke" and "weele" to go with "shrieke" and "keele." His normal form is "before," but to rhyme with "borne" he uses "beforne." No doubt these forms existed, but they are not the ones he uses naturally— say in midline, where no need for a rhyme affects his choice. No more natural are the archaic infinitives he uses only for rhyme, "to saine" for "to say"; "make me donne" for "make me do." Generally he rhymes in pairs, but often he uses triplets, and he feels quite free to run on to four or even five rhymes in a row.

Perhaps all Golding needed to write fourteeners well was a couple of sessions on meter and natural speech with so canny a teacher as Mr. Pound. His lines then might have sounded like Samuel Daniel's in *Ulysses and the Siren,* if we take the liberty of writing its four- and three-beat lines as one:

> Come, worthy Greek, Ulysses, come, possess these shores
>   with me;
> The winds and seas are troublesome, and here we may be
>   free.
> Here may we sit and view their toil that travail on the deep,
> And joy the day in mirth the while, and spend the night in
>   sleep.

Here is something of the elegance so often ascribed to Ovid. As there is in the modern fourteeners that Yeats has occasionally written:

> The old brown thorn-trees break in two high over Cummen Strand . . .

or

> "You but imagine lies all day, O murderer," I replied

Golding's inability to dominate meter meant that most of his verse was not as well written as prose. If he failed in rather obvious matters, it is not surprising that he quite missed the kind of subtlety that Ovid tried for, and succeeded in, time after time. Examples are more interesting for the light they throw on poetic craftsmanship and the problems of translation than for what they tell us about what Golding failed to do.

Ovid, when writing about the Iron Age and its evils, mentions the frightful stepmothers mixing up their "lurid" poisons:

> Lurida terribiles miscent aconita nouercae.

"Lurida," transferred from the pale faces of the victims to the poison itself, its juxtaposition with "terribiles," and the suspense about what is "lurida" and what "terribiles" give the line its effect. This is entirely a matter of how words are put together. In Golding the eerie line comes to nothing except a couple of inversions and a wrong last word, for the rhyme:

> The stepdames fell their husbandes sonnes with poison do assayle.

In XIV, the Sibyl tells Aeneas that nothing is impossible for human worth to achieve: "Invia virtuti nulla est via." The point is in the words: no *via* (road) is *invia* (impassible). If one believes, with Goethe and Valéry, that what one wants from a translator of poetry is not mere paraphrase of thought but a rendering of equivalent effect, then one will not be satisfied with a translator who ignores such points, as Golding does with "No way to vertue is restreynd."

In VIII, Ovid describes how Daedalus built the labyrinth, confusing its structure so deliberately that no one once in could find his way out. "It leads the eye into going astray by the riddle of its various ways," to give a loutish paraphrase of

> lumina . . .
> ducit in errorem variarum ambage viarum.

Variarum, viarum—these look and sound so alike that one seems a blurred image or echo of the other: the very diction dramatizes the confusions of the maze. Golding simply passes over such virtuosity. He even ignores a line as obvious as the one about the horses of the sun beating their hooves against the barriers in their eagerness to be away: "pedibusque repagula pulsant." Christopher Marlowe, faced with a similar problem in the *Amores,* did what he could by turning Ovid's four *p*'s into three *b*'s (the closest letter to *p* in effect) in translating

> Ite, piae volucres, et plangite pectora pinnis

as

> Go, godly birds, striking your breasts bewail

Sometimes Ovid is indeed too clever. He was told so in his own time, and his ghost has been hearing it ever since. Should a translator then correct Ovid's taste, if indeed he offends in such passages as the one in which Jove is decreeing that mankind shall be destroyed by flood? The other gods lament the loss, the *iactura.* In the next three lines are heard the sounds *-tura, -turus,* and *tura*—not to speak of *terrae, terras,* and other echoes. The muffled repetition is supposed to represent the way the gods mutter among themselves, dwelling on the theme *iactura.* For the Roman ear, the effect may have succeeded or it may have failed. What is important is that Ovid, like most good poets, is well aware that it is not enough to express thoughts—that what the poet tries to do is somehow mimic, as far as possible in the medium of language, what he is saying, instead of *just* saying it. Ovid cares about this, and he is a poet; Golding does not—he is a good honest man.

Professor Bassett once decided that the most beautiful line in Homer was

πὰρ ποταμὸν κελάδοντα, παρὰ ῥοδανὸν δονακῆα

in the representation on the shield of Achilles of the cattle moving from barnyard to pasture "along the murmuring river, along the slender reed." Most of us might feel that a great line ought to have more human content; we want the rage of Achilles, the grief of Andromache, or at least the bright hair of Helen above the embattled walls. Bassett's line is a miniature abstraction in words; it has little reference to any reality beyond a musical one—though one can say, if he wishes, that he "hears" the ripple on the pebbles, the wind in the reeds. What we have here is a delicate musical pattern: the two halves of the line have almost—that important *almost!*—the same vowel pattern:

a oao eaoa
aa oao oaēa

A Hawaiian charm, if one singsongs it with the rhythm. This is a kind of effect that Ovid likes and works for. Describing the Golden Age, he says that there were rivers of milk, rivers of nectar, and that "golden honey was trickling from the green oak."

> flumina iam lactis, iam flumina nectaris ibant,
> flauaque de uiridi stillabant ilice mella.

Abundance is mimicked in the repetitions of the first line. The *fl*, twice associated with that abundance, is picked up in *flauaque;* that line begins in profusion. *Flaua* means *golden;* it modifies *mella* (*honey*) at the very end of the line. Honey is everywhere in this opulent world. But *flaua* is put next to *uiridi*, which means *green* and modifies *ilice* (*oak*), on the far

20

side of the long word that means a continuous flowing. So we get gold against green, the pure idea of color, before we know what is gold, what is green. (Gold and green are the thematic colors used throughout *Fern Hill,* Dylan Thomas's poem of his own golden age.) The rich trickle begins in *stillabant,* with the *-bant* of continuity a bit more emphatic after the *ibant* of the line before. The liquid *ill* is sounded again in *ilice* and again—for the sound too trickles—slightly varied in the *ell* of *mella.* Of the eight central vowels, six are *i*'s, which, as Plato long ago observed in the *Cratylus,* is (as the quickest of the vowel sounds) "expressive of motion." Almost a patter of honey, gold on green. This, I suppose, is "beauty" in poetry, if anything is. (It is not the highest value; we can all think of lines in Dante or in Shakespeare far more piercing than these.) Golding gives us

> Then streames ran milke, then streames ran wine, and
>   yellow honey flowde
> From ech greene tree whereon the rayes of firie Phebus
>   glowde.

The first line is the better, though sibilant. Except for the long *e*'s of "greene tree" (whatever they stand for there), not much happens except bumbling in the second line. Golding loses the specific "oak" and gets in some unnecessary mythology with an obvious adjective. Ovid's line, without mentioning Phoebus, is full of warmth and clarity. In I, 708, Ovid gets a similar effect when he describes how Pan, grasping for the nymph Syrinx, finds that she has turned into a sheaf of reeds, from which comes a "thin sound like one lamenting": ". . . sonum tenuem similemque querenti." Thin vowel sounds, many querulous nasals; the line itself is as *similem querenti* as sound can make it. Golding again only states: "which made a still and mourning noyse."

A parenthesis: thinking of such "trifles" when one composes, noticing them when one reads—all this seems, especially to those who do not write, to madness near allied. One can only say that the testimony of poets and the researches of their critics have shown that the poets have had such effects in mind, and have bent their expression in these directions when they had call to and could. No effort has been too great—provided it does not show. And no discipline has been too severe: Stravinsky in *Poetics of Music* approves of Baudelaire's "never have prosodies and rhetorics kept originality from fully manifesting itself. . . ." It is not only such poets as the magnificent Góngora who are craft-conscious in lines like

> le dejó por escondido
> o le perdonó por pobre

> (left it [in peace] as being hidden,
> or pardoned it as being poor)
>> ("Angélica y Medoro")

but even—perhaps especially—such "spontaneous" poets as Catullus and Villon. The former's

> litus ut longe resonante Eoa
> tunditur unda

>> (poem 11)

> (where the shore is beaten by the far-echoing eastern wave)

did not come about by chance. John Fox's *The Poetry of Villon* shows by example after example that "it would be quite wrong to think of him as the vagabond poet, dashing off his verse in careless fashion, without a thought for the finer points of versification" and other technical matters even more subtle. Ovid, like most good poets, was fascinated by such problems. Professor Bush quotes Gilbert Murray on Ovid: "He loved the actual technique of the verse." Which reminds us of the remark of Robert Frost to a lady who remonstrated that when he was writing his "beautiful poetry" ("beautiful" was a word he avoided) he surely wasn't thinking of technical problems, and he couldn't really like *those*. "Like'em!" growled Frost. "I revel in 'em!"

The shape of sentences, for example. Frost also liked to say that to write poetry was to "go a-sentencing." It would be hard to find a poet who "sentences" more satisfactorily than

Ovid does. Words are placed precisely where they will have the greatest effect; we are led through the suspensions and fulfillments of his syntax as through a Mozartean music. As one example of his precise placing: in VII he tells the sad but all too human tale of the love of Cephalus and Procris. Cephalus, after the heat and effort of the chase, calls out again and again for *aura,* for the fresh woodland breeze. His sighs are overheard and misunderstood; a zealous eavesdropper reports to Procris that her husband is meeting a certain Aura in the woods. Procris too misunderstands, and her misunderstanding is her death. The whole chain of circumstances depends on how the word *aura,* or *Aura,* occurs. Ovid places it carefully. When first used, it is separated from the *Et* that introduces it by a long *inciso* that keeps us waiting for the noun. Once uttered, it is repeated immediately; it is the first word of the next three lines, though varied by being never twice in the same case:

> repetebam frigus et umbras
> Et, quae de gelidis exibat uallibus, auram.
> Aura petebatur medio mihi lenis in aestu,
> auram exspectabam; requies erat illa labori.
> "Aura," (recordor enim) "uenias," cantare solebam

(I was looking for coolness and shady places and for the air that came from the cool valleys. Mild air is what I was looking for in the midday heat; I was longing for air—that would be a relief after my striving. "Air," [for I remember] "please come," I used to sing)

Of the seven times Ovid uses the word, here and later, five times it is placed with special sensitivity. Golding uses his "Ayre" nine times, but he lets it fall where it happens to.

Why then read Golding, if, as Professor Bush says, he "often missed or blunted Ovidian points" and was only "moderately faithful"? At least for the stories, if not the poetry; stories translate when poetry does not. But Golding also has something very engaging of his own to give us.

He begins by metamorphosing Ovid: by turning the sophisticated Roman into a ruddy country gentleman with tremendous gusto, a sharp eye on the life around him, an ear for racy speech, and a gift for energetic doggerel. If the Latin mentions Midas's "tiara," Golding calls it a "purple nightcap." The exotic "harpé" of Perseus, the curved blade so special it had a special name, becomes a good English "woodknife." The classical ilex, instead of being called a holm-oak, becomes the English "Sugarchest" tree. Instead of saying that Io sleeps on the ground, he says that what she lacks is a "good soft featherbed." When a skeptic sneers at the story that Perseus's father was Jove in a shower of gold, Golding has him call Jove the "forged Dad." He sees the ancient world in terms of his own. Instead of "nec supplex timebat / Iudicis ora sui" (nor did a plaintiff fear the face of his judge), he says, "There was no man would crouch or creepe to Judge with cap in hand." Mercury, on his way to kill Argus, does not merely drive "ut pastor, per deuia rura capellas" (as a herdsman his goats through isolated rural areas); he strides right into an Elizabethan countryside, and

> Retayning nothing but his staffe, the which he closely helde
> Betweene his elbowe and his side, and through the common fielde
> Went plodding lyke some good plaine soule that had some flock to feede.

Golding does not translate quality or tone, but he infallibly "Englishes" the stories. When Jove has a council of the gods, Golding says that he summoned his "Court of Parliament." When the Cyclops arranges his hair, with rakes, in the hope of pleasing Galatea (or "Galat," as Golding calls her) he "marcussottes" it—which meant to leave Turkish mustachios, the kind that would be exotic in England, though what one might expect of a Cyclops, who was Sicilian anyway. More than once Golding modernizes military equipment, frankly turning an ancient siege engine into a gun. Even proper names may get their English equivalent. The Aegean Sea becomes the Goat Sea; Parthenium Nemus becomes Maiden Wood. Picus's wife,

Canens, is called "Singer." Hyllus becomes plain English "Hill," and Elis, "Ely." He suggests in a marginal note that Vertumnus and Pomona might be interpreted as "Turner" and "Applebee." When he doesn't translate names, he de-classicizes them with jaunty Elizabethan abbreviations. Pentheus, Theseus, Orpheus, and others lose a few inches of their heroic stature when they are called "Penthey," "Thesey," and "Orphey." Thisbe tells Pyramus she is his darling "Thisb." Augias is "Augie." Morpheus loses all dignity when he turns into plain "Morph."

Golding is at his best in describing places and people. Ovid, who has some celebrated place descriptions himself, has of course given the hints—I doubt anyone would say that Golding is doing it better. But he is doing it freshly and with a view to his world and that of his readers. Take the terrain of the great Calydonian boar hunt:

> A wood thick growen with trees which stoode unfelled to
> that day
> Beginning from a plaine. . . .
>   Now there was a hollow bottom by,
> To which the watershots of raine from all the high grounds
> drew.
> Within the compass of this pond great store of Osiers grew:
> And Sallowes lithe, and flackring Flags, and moorish Rushes
> eke,
> And lazie Reedes on little shankes, and other baggage like.
> From hence the Bore was rowzed out . . .
>   (VIII, 444–55)

All of this probably came home to the English reader as "Silua frequens trabibus . . ." did not. Indeed, the whole boar hunt is well done in Golding, whose rough-and-tumble verses often do well with scenes of hubbub and uproar, into which he throws himself with the zest of a sportscaster. (The ethical dative he is so fond of makes him the participant of many a lively scene: "And with the like celeritie he cut me Phorbas throte.") First a dog is the victim of what Golding might have called a "jolly" mistake: the spear "through his guts did gore,

25

/ And naild him to the earth." Then the fierce beast himself is hit:

> And while the Bore did play the fiend [*saevit*] and turned
>   round agast,
> And grunting flang his fome about togither mixt with blood

When Meleager, like a bullfighter, presents Atalanta with what corresponds to the ears and tail, the sons of Thestius (the "Thesties") object and demand she drop them ("Pone age . . . femina . . ."):

> "Dame, come off, and lay us downe this geare."

The rowdy little scene below shows Golding at close to his best. It begins at V, 551, with Ceres wandering the whole earth looking for her daughter Proserpina:

>   And being overwrought
> She caught a thirst: no liquor yet had come within hir
>   throte.
> By chaunce she spied nere at hand a pelting thatched Cote
> Wyth peevish doores: she knockt thereat, and out there
>   commes a trot.
> The Goddesse asked hir some drinke and she denide it not:
> But out she brought hir by and by a draught of merrie go
>   downe
> And therewithall a Hotchpotch made of steeped Barlie
>   browne
> And Flaxe and Coriander seede and other simples more
> The which she in an Earthen pot together sod before.
> While Ceres was a eating this, before hir gazing stood
> A hard-faced boy, a shrewde pert wag, that could no maners
>   good:
> He laughed at hir and in scorne did call hir "Greedie gut."
> The Goddesse being wroth therewith, did on the
>   Hotchpotch put
> The liquor ere that all was eate, and in his face it threw

The translator gets the same opportunity for macabre verve in describing the witches' brew Medea cooks up:

She put thereto the deaw that fell upon a Monday night:
And flesh and feathers of a Witch, a cursed odious wight
Which in the likenesse of an Owle abrode a nightes did flie,
And Infants in their cradels chaunge or sucke them that
they die.

(VII, 349–52)

But probably the description of Philemon and Baucis, the good-hearted old country couple in their cottage, surrounded by all of their "homely gear," gives Golding the best scope for his talents. Dryden said he could fairly see Ovid's old couple, and Golding's is no less vivid: the old lady "busie as a Bee" stirring about with her skillet and her coleworts and her hoarded bacon and her "jolly lump of Butter" to bring everything "pyping from the fyre." The final effect of the well told episode is weakened by what may be an inadvertence or what may be a rather bad joke: as Philemon and Baucis, at the end of their lives, watch each other turn into boughs and foliage, Golding says they "did take their leave" of each other. He can joke: surely he is doing so at the end of book I when Phaethon wants Clymene, his mother, to assure him that his father is really Apollo, not her husband Merops. He beseeches her

as she lovde the lyfe
Of Merops, and had kept hir selfe as undefiled wyfe

The absurdity, or the mischief, is not in Ovid.

Sometimes his realism, charmingly enough, distorts to caricature, as in the vigorous personification of Hunger in VIII and of Envy in II. Golding likes to add detail: out of a mere list of names of nymphs provided by Ovid ("Nepheleque Hyaleque Rhanisque / Et Psecas et Phiale . . ."), he makes:

Then Niphe nete and cleene
With Hiale glistring like the grass in beautie fresh and
sheene,
And Rhanis clearer of hir skin than are the rainie drops.
And little bibling Phyale, and Pseke that pretie Mops . . .

(III, 200–203)

One suspects the details were suggested by the footnotes to his Latin text: *rhanis* means "raindrop;" *phiale*, "saucer," etc. We know he incorporated such footnotes on other occasions.

What vivid and racy language this might all have been if Golding had not so often cramped or attenuated it to the meter! Even as it is, his strange, quirky, colloquial vocabulary is one of the chief delights of his translation. We notice immediately that he likes to translate a classical line into what must have had a jaunty swing in 1567. Certainly no one has translated so successfully *out* of Latin—or into so native an English. Ovid's "obscenique greges" becomes "roughts of filthie freaks"; his sleeper "alto sopore solutum" is "snorting bolt upright"; his girl "turbatis . . . capillis" becomes a "frizzle-topped wench." Ovid's dancers, which duller translators might have "leading the festal chorus" ("festas duxere choreas"), and which in Ovid have something of the dignity of processions on Wedgwood, really kick up their heels in Golding:

> Full oft
> The Woodnymphes underneath this tree did fetch theyr
>   frisks aloft.

Golding is particularly good at taking a rather noncommittal line and giving it a startling immediacy. In one long gory battle scene

> Occidit et Celadon Mendesius; occidit Astreus,
> Matre Palaestina, dubio genitore creatus

Or, as I am afraid the conventional translator might say:

> Then Celadon of Mendes fell, Astreus
> Of Palestinian mother, of dubious
> Progenitor begot . . .

Golding throws himself with vituperative gusto into the fight:

> There died also Celadon a Gipsie of the South:
> And so did bastard Astrey too, whose mother was a Jew

When a crowd in Ovid calls out for "Arma, arma," Golding's mob comes to the point and howls "Kill, kill." In a couple of passages dealing with country people, he even falls into rural dialect. Sometimes he sounds curiously modern; he says "a body would have thought" and uses "latch" in the sense of "grab," as we use "latch on to" (modern dictionaries give this as "U.S. slang").

One fond of words will probably find himself poring over the footnotes to Golding's text. He may even make out his own list of Golding-isms that ought to be revived, perhaps from among such as these:

woose: ooze
whewl: howl, whine
belk: throb
corsie: annoyance
throatboll: Adam's-apple
uppen: mention, bring up
quoath: faint
yesk: sob
awk: reversed, wrong
awkly: awkwardly
chank: chew (one chanks
   gobbets or collops)
sprink: sprinkle ("watering the
   grass" is "sprinking the
   clowers")
gnoor: snarl
toot: gaze at
parget: plaster
snudge: miser (Remark to
   gnoor at landlords: "Toot
   the parget, snudge!")

gripple: what snudges are,
   greedy
coll: embrace, hug (Latin,
   collum, neck)
queach: thicket, grove
ensue: follow ("Ensue me to
   the queach," XIV, 966)
merry-go-down: strong drink
flacker: flutter, flap
orpid: fierce
overdreep: droop over
hittymissy: hit or miss
pooke: elf, demon
bugg: monster, boogieman
frosh: frog
woodspeck: woodpecker
leechcaft: medical science

Sometimes, with Golding's weird and piquant vocabulary, we feel we are in Lewis Carroll country, in a land where corsies whewl, where orpid buggs sty awkly in the queach, where froshes yesk, and flackering pookes ensue. None of this may be quite "beautiful," but it would be hard to deny it is rich in delights of its own.

Poetry
Lost in Translation?

Poetry, thought Robert Frost, is what is lost in translation. But surely not so lost as poetry in a language we will never understand? Not quite so lost that there are no techniques of retrieval? It seems to me there are some, and that is the adventure of this volume: a treasure hunt for lost poetry.[1]

Renato Poggioli, who did an eloquent Italian version of "Le cimetière marin," has analyzed the psychological motives that lead one to translate. Perhaps the translator should not be too aware of his motives; this may be one of the pleasures frustrated by self-consciousness. I am not sure that the enjoyment I had in doing these translations is very different from that of writing "one's own" poetry.

One should translate only poems he cares very much for; poems he has been living with, more often than not, for many years. He translates partly out of dissatisfaction with the versions he has seen—not out of the certainty that he can do them better, but out of a feeling he can at least do them differently, circling in, perhaps, from yet another direction. Twenty years or more of work, off and on, with the lyrics of St. John of the Cross began when, picking up one translation in a bookstore, I saw "En una noche obscura . . ." and across from it "Upon a gloomy night . . ." Something, I felt, had to be done about this. We rarely say, in natural English, "Upon a

---

From *Sappho to Valéry: Poems in Translation* (New Brunswick: Rutgers University Press, 1971; 2d ed. Princeton: Princeton University Press, 1980).

night . . ." (It is *on* a night like this that one wouldn't send a dog out.) *Upon* here is stilted or literary; St. John's poetry is neither. I knew enough too about his passion to realize that whatever kind of darkness his *noche obscura* was, it was not what *gloomy* connotes in English.

Dissatisfaction with existing translations, when there were any, was something I felt more poignantly in the classroom. Such and such a poet, I might find myself saying, wrote sharply, colloquially; his lyrics were simple, sensuous, passionate, as in the poem on the page before us—but the class would already be looking at the page with deepening skepticism. Colloquial? simple? this unnatural word order, these expressions archaic centuries ago? And the limp rhythms? Or no rhythm at all?

Denver Lindley speaks for many of us when he says: "Communication—that is the purpose and the delight of translation. 'This is something I admire so much,' says the translator, 'something I find so profound, so beautiful, so piercing that I must make you understand and admire it too, even though you, through some inadvertence, have neglected to learn the language in which it is written. Let me show you how it goes.' "[2]

Let me show you how it goes, I imagine myself saying to the reader curious about Provençal—which he has no intention of learning. He only knows that during the twelfth century some great poetry, it is said, was written in Provence; he would be interested in knowing what it was like. Not just what it said—what it was like. Or he may have heard that Goethe is perhaps the supreme lyrical genius of Europe, and he cannot see why—he has looked at some "plain prose translations of the poetry," at some versions in arthritic verse. Both have left him puzzled: there seems no greatness here. Or he has learned, perhaps from Gerald Brenan's history, that in the fifteenth century there was a poet curiously modern, curiously like Baudelaire. But almost unknown—because he wrote in Catalan. Or that there was a woman in Galicia in the last century (her dates almost the same as Emily Dickinson's) whom some think the greatest woman poet of modern times. But almost unknown—because she wrote in Galician.

If I am to show this reader how the poem goes, I have to show him first of all a poem. The greatest infidelity is to pass off a bad poem in English as representing a good one in another language.

Poets and critics have always been fascinated by the problem of translating poetry, which, they agree, has to be translated—and yet cannot really be translated at all. In our time so much has been written, and written sensibly, about the paradox that we hardly need another discussion of this sort. There are sixteen essays and a bibliography, often with summary, of some two hundred and sixty works from 46 B.C. to 1958 in Reuben A. Brower's *On Translation* (Harvard, 1959; A Galaxy Book, 1966). There are sixteen more in the Arrowsmith-Shattuck collection. There is George Steiner's Introduction to his *Penguin Book of Modern Verse Translation* (1966); there are Jackson Mathews's studies on Valéry. There are incidental remarks by nearly all of our most distinguished poets, for those who have translated nothing are few and far between. In the essays of Harry Levin and others there are brilliant asides, and sometimes more, on the translation of poetry: a few pages of Professor Levin's comparative stylistics on how Shakespeare's untranslatability has been translated brings the whole problem into clearer focus.[3]

When we study a foreign language we work with exercises which—yes—can be translated. They used to consist of sentences like "Have you two round oranges, or is this the umbrella of your grandmother?" (I know of one girl who, coming across such a sentence, dropped her study of the language because she lost so much time trying to imagine just when she might ask *that*.) Absurd as such fancies are, they can be put into another language, probably with little loss of sense. But what is the translator to do with the second of these lines from *Hamlet?*—in which the prince, picking up the cloud imagery from the line before, plays on the words *sun* and *son*: he is sad because of something in his relationship as son.

> *King:* How is it that the clouds still hang on you?
> *Hamlet:* Not so, my lord. I am too much i' the sun.

Here the translator needs a word, one common word, that means both a male offspring and the star that is the central body in our solar system. Chances are that in no language but English does such a word exist. The Italian will look helplessly from *figlio* to *sole*, the Spaniard from *hijo* to *sol*, the German from *der Sohn* to *die Sonne*, which is closer but, especially with the problem of gender, not close enough. The simple word *sun* is untranslatable here.

Or suppose he wants to show Macbeth pondering on his bloodstained hand:

> Will all great Neptune's ocean wash this blood
> Clean from my hand? No, this my hand will rather
> The multitudinous seas incarnadine,
> Making the green, one red.

Not even the plainest of prose translators will hold that this really says the same thing as "What it's going to do is kind of redden the oceans, of which there are many and quite big ones too." Poetry is lost in translation for the same reason that it is lost in paraphrase. In Macbeth's speech the poetry is in such effects as the size and sound of *multitudinous* and the way it surges with and against the meter; in the ghost-words that haunt *incarnadine* (carnage, etc.); in the change from the sonorous Latinate words to the simple native ones in the last line.

When Macbeth says:

> Duncan is in his grave;
> After life's fitful fever he sleeps well . . .

the poetry is not so much in the idea as in the satiety of the four *f*'s, a too-muchness in the mouth as life itself has come to seem a too-muchness, and in the dreary continuity of the three long *e*'s. The problem is to carry such effects from language to language by some utensil of translation—all leaky pails indeed for such an errand.

It should be unnecessary to remind ourselves yet again that poetry is less a matter of *what* is said than of *how* it is said. The *how* of course can be so powerful that we confuse it with the *what*; it is easy to imagine, in reading Shakespeare, that we are being moved by *what* he is saying. Yet try changing the words, sometimes just a word, and even the *what* seems to vanish. Harry Levin's "The War of Words in English Poetry" (*Contexts of Criticism,* Harvard, 1957), deals specifically with those lexical auras most resistant to translation. I mean to stress below the translator's obligation to sound as well as to sense: Professor Levin has the gist of the matter in his "in practice the sense often seems to echo the sound."

In Paul Valéry's "last testament on poetics" (the reflections he wrote on his version of the *Eclogues* of Vergil), this most analytic of poets is still saying what he had been saying most of his life: "Thought is only an accessory of poetry . . . the chief thing is the *whole,* the power resulting from effects compounded of all the attributes of language . . ." (DF 306),[4] attributes which in an earlier essay he had called "the sound, the rhythm, the physical proximity of words . . . their mutual influences . . ." (DF 157). Thought is only an accessory, and an accessory which the poet may sacrifice to some advantage of the sound: "An intimate alliance of sound and sense, which is the essential characteristic of poetic expression, can be obtained only at the expense of something—that is, thought" (DF 219). If as translator I had need of an *impresa,* it might well be Valéry's "fidelity to meaning alone is a kind of betrayal" (DF 298). One thinks of Emily Dickinson's

> More genuine were Perfidy
> Than such Fidelity.

We can amplify this with a chorus of assent from those who have worked with the problem. Professor Arrowsmith puts it even more strongly: "There are times . . . when the worst possible treachery is the simple-minded faith in 'accuracy' and literal loyalty to the original" (A-S 118). Professor Carne-Ross believes that "a great deal of local distortion, of amplification and even excision, may be necessary if the translator is to follow the curve of his original faithfully" (A-S 8). And

Professor Poggioli: "After all, in every artistic pursuit beauty is the highest kind of fidelity, and ugliness is only another name for disloyalty . . ." (RB 143).[5] The kind of translation in which the poetry is lost, we might say, is the kind concerned only with meaning or message.

At times the treason of a plain prose translation serves a purpose, especially when the reader who knows something of the other language wants a guide to the thought alone, with the help of which he means to return to the poem itself and retrieve what was lost in form, in sound, in rhythm. This is not the purpose I have in mind; I am trying to show, to readers who may never look at the original, what I think they would find the poem like if they did.

At the opposite end of the spectrum from the plain prose translation is what Dryden, and in our time Robert Lowell, refer to as "imitations," in which the poet does start from an original but writes his own poem on the basis of it, with more regard for the promptings of his own talent than for the intention and tone of the foreign poet. When the talent is as powerful as Mr. Lowell's, remarkable productions may result. Although they show us a great deal of the virtue of the imitator (if one who least imitates can be called an imitator), there may be some disadvantage in the fact that they tell us little about the quality of the original: translations in which the voices of the world's great poets all speak with a single voice, translations in which Sappho and Rilke sound alike, may not satisfy all the possibilities of translation. If the translator is "himself a poet," there will always be a clash of personalities, with the personality of the translator tending to take over. Imitations—which Dryden thinks "the most advantageous way for a translator to show himself, but the greatest wrong which can be done to the memory and reputation of the dead"[6]—may be brilliant and engaging; they are not what I have in mind.

What is, again? To write poems that will show, to some degree, what certain poems in another language are *like*. One cannot translate a poem, but one can try to reconstitute it by taking the thought, the imagery, the rhythm, the sound, the qualities of diction—these and whatever else made up the original—and then attempt to rework as many as possible into a poem in English. Since no translator can manage equally all such data at the same time, with so many conflicting claims to be reconciled, what he has to do is set up a constantly shifting system of priorities: now the thought has to be flexed into a rhythm, now modulated into another key of sound, now an image has to be refocused, now some clue given to a lost allusion. There is no way—for example—to translate *nostra vita* into English so that the two simplest words for the idea, "our life," preserve the cadence of the Italian. (Unless some wag comes along with a stage Neapolitan accent and suggests "our-a life-a"—a solution probably detrimental to tone.) So something has to give: the translator's fascinating work is made up of decisions, decisions: what to give up in order to gain what? With the all-important *whole* forever in mind: a poem like the original. It may be useful, then, to say that one reconstitutes the poem. Or to think of the process as a kind of exsanguination—the medical procedure in which all blood is removed from an organism, to be replaced by new blood. In the process of translating, certainly the lifeblood of the original is drained away; the poem will survive only if the translator has living blood of his own to supply. We all know translations of poetry that are very pale corpses indeed. Again Valéry, in his essay on a French translation of St. John of the Cross, is with us: "This is really to *translate,* which is to reconstitute as nearly as possible the *effect* of a certain *cause*—here a text in Spanish—by means of *another cause,* a text in French" (DF 286). The right question to ask about a translation of poetry is not "Is it faithful?" but "Does it produce an equivalent effect?" Or perhaps, "a reasonably equivalent effect?" It seems excessive to demand of the poor translator that, since he is working with one of the greatest of lyrics, he must give us, as its equivalent, a lyric that will rank with the greatest in English—and then to condemn the translation as inadequate because it falls short of that demand.

A translation aiming at poetic equivalence has little chance of being literal, or "word for word"—although there are always readers who will compare a translation with its original so that they can "Aha!" triumphantly at any discrepancy. But linguists tell us that word-for-word translation, even at levels far below that of poetry, is often impossible. How does one translate, word for word, expressions like "How do you do" or "So long!" or "Jiminy crickets!" Or "What did you put him up to it for?"—in which hardly a word can be translated independently. Frequently indeed, as Eugene A. Nida declares, "reproducing the precise corresponding word may utterly distort the meaning" (RB 12). This has always been realized by poet-translators: Horace might have been speaking for all of them when he warned that a faithful interpreter will not translate *verbum verbo* (word for word).

To translate a poem well, as Dryden reminds us more than once, is harder than to write a new poem, in which one is always free to change direction. Although the thought of the poem may not be its main poetic constituent, the translator has a responsibility to be as faithful to it as the conflicting interests of rhythm and sound permit; certainly he is not free, except in "imitations," to follow his own will. In seeming to belittle content, I only mean that, with poetry, to translate the thought alone is not enough—indeed, is next to nothing.

If the translator is trying to show us how the poetry goes, what he writes has to be first of all a poem. The rhythm must have its élan, diction be in the right register, sound work musically or expressively. Valéry thought sound as important as sense: a poem for him was "cette hésitation prolongée entre le son et le sens" (*Rhumbs*). For Frost, the sound is "the gold in the ore." But should sound duplicate precise effects in the original? In "Le cimetière marin" there are lines composed—as even a foreigner cannot fail to notice—to mimic what they describe: the grating repetitiousness of the cicada that "scratches the dryness," for example:

L'insecte net gratte la sécheresse[7]

An "ugly" line, with the three brusque words ending in a *t* and the repeated vowel sound which is hardly mellifluous here. One would think a translator would not ignore the effect; yet it is ignored in English versions. Two of the best-known give us a plain mistranslation, as if the cicada were scratching actual earth, instead of making a scratching sound in the air. (Didn't these translators even glance at Gustave Cohen's famous *Essai d'explication*? How would anyone—though ours is a shoddy age—dare translate a poem like this without reading carefully at least fifteen or twenty of the French studies of the stylistics of Valéry's work?)

The poem has been better translated—in a way that saves the poetry—by Rainer Maria Rilke and Jorge Guillén. Both were sensitive to the harshness of the line, and both echoed it in their own, Rilke with

> Der harte Käfer ist des Trockenen Säge[8]

and Guillén with

> Nítido insecto rasca sequedades[9]

Another sound-line is about the real gnawer, the irrefutable worm of consciousness:

> Le vrai rongeur, le ver irréfutable[10]

Five *r*'s, probably the gnawingest of our speech sounds—especially when the *r* is a French one. (The translator might wonder if Valéry, from southern France, had an uvular *r* with its little rasp; he might want to listen to Valéry's own reading of the line, available on records. Just as translators of García Lorca might want to find out if the young man from Granada spoke with a Castilian or an Andalusian accent, since this would affect the sound of certain lines. This kind of information is not—*magari!*—available for all poems; where it is, it should be considered.)

The burring of Valéry's worm has not been brought over into English, as far as I know. But again the poet-translators are concerned with it. Guillén, whose language does not have the same *r*-sound as Valéry's, any more than our own has, makes a discreet but noticeable use of his more emphatic rolled *r*:

> El roedor gusano irrefutable[11]

Rilke, with a softer sound to call on than the Spanish one, tops even Valéry in his *r*-ishness:

> der Wurm, dem keiner widerspricht, der Nager[12]

But if Rilke, with his seven *r*'s, seems more expressive here, Guillén does better with the playful alliteration of persistence for the girls' fluttering fingers in

> Les derniers dons, les doigts qui les défendent[13]

This is caught exactly (partly because the languages are akin) by Guillén's

> Últimos dones, dedos defensores[14]

It is rather surprising that Rilke does nothing with the line. Could it be that, lacking Valéry's sense of fun, he thought it flamboyant?

Translations must have their own form and rhythm; but must they have the same form and rhythm as the original? We know translators who don't give a thought to the matter, or who would be scornful if they did. "I put down the words as they come," such a one might protest; "to change anything, to add or subtract syllables just to get a rhythm is dishonest!" Not to give us a rhythm may be more dishonest: the poet himself took care to put down no words the meter would not tolerate. Time after time, if the testimony of poets is to be trusted, words are suggested as much by the rhythm as by the argument. Goethe's poems seem to come directly out of lived experiences; and yet he too brooded on technique: "mysterious and great effects," he tells us, "are produced by different poetical forms." Translators indifferent to mysterious and great effects are not likely to give us a faithful translation.

More than one poet has even revealed that the form of his poem existed before the "ideas" did—that he found his mind moving in a rhythm before he knew what it was going to say. No one has put this more clearly than Valéry:

> As for the *Cimetière marin,* this intention was at first no more than a rhythmic figure, empty, or filled with meaningless syllables, which obsessed me for some time. I noticed that the figure was decasyllabic, and I pondered on the model, which is very little used in modern French poetry. . . . It suggested a stanza of six lines . . . [and other formal considerations suggested the theme of the poem]. My line had to be solid and strongly rhythmical. . . . The type of line chosen, and form adopted for the stanzas, set me conditions that favored certain "movements," permitted changes of tone, called up a certain style. . . . The *Cimetière marin* was *conceived.* A rather long period of gestation followed. (DF 148)

If there is a question of priority, it is clear that the form determined the subject and not the subject the form. I would suggest that the translator's responsibility, then, is at least as much to the form as to the ideas. Form, after all, as paced by line length and rhyme escapement, is the choreography of the poet's spirit.

We tend to think of rhyme today as mere decoration or as a mere mnemonic device. Its worldwide popularity with primitive types—savages, children, folk singers, advertising men—should indicate that something about it goes very deep in the psyche, and not the psyche alone—what is the human body but a system of rhyming parts? (Only the badly crippled move their bodies in free verse.) When there is functional rhyme in a poem, the only reason for a translator to shirk it is that it is "too hard" to make the translation rhyme—too hard to make it rhyme easily and naturally, so that the rhyming words belong as inevitably as all the other words. Slipshod rhyming is easy enough; current translations yield many examples. In my experience it may take a hundred times as long to translate into rhymed lines as it does into unrhymed—to take the constituents of a stanza of St. John of the Cross, say, and work them naturally into the *ababb* of his *lira*. But suppose it does take a hundred times as long? Time, though it is not money in these matters, may be perfection—or as close to it as one is likely to come, and for that almost no cost, in time or effort, is too great.

Yet there are limits to what can be done in transferring effects from language to language—limits in terms of what the new language will bear. When Bernart de Ventadorn carries the very same rhyming sounds of his first stanza through the seven or eight stanzas that follow, or when he composes seventy-two consecutive lines on only two rhyming sounds, the translator should face the reality of English rhyme and decide that although the trick might not be impossible in English, it could probably not be carried off without visible strain.

More important and more complicated than rhyme is the matter of rhythm. Since, even if rhythms could correspond, they would not have the same effect in two languages, is it worthwhile trying to duplicate an exotic form in English? The alexandrine, so fluent in Racine, for us "like a wounded snake, drags its slow length along." Hexameters, so natural and ebullient in Homer, so grave and sonorous in Vergil, seem to come rather pompously from our tongues. "Even if rhythms could correspond"—but the correspondence is far from perfect. Stress is heavier in some languages than in others. In the eight-syllable *romance* line used by García Lorca, the distribution of accents matters only at the end of the line; in English it makes itself felt throughout. Dante's *endecasillabo* does not have the pattern of expectations that Shakespeare's iambic pentameter does. All transfers of rhythm from language to language are likely to be approximate, analogical. But it may be better to imitate a rhythm even imperfectly than to give no notion at all of its character. Especially inasmuch as, although the rhythms have differed since Babel, their physical basis, the heartbeat and breathing of man, seem to have changed very little.

With Greek and Latin a peculiar vexation arises. These ancient rhythms were made up by patterning syllables according to their musical length—a kind of rhythm our stress-heavy language is not very sensitive to. What we generally settle for, in translating from Greek and Latin, is a transposition of long and short syllables into stressed and unstressed—which may give us as good a notion of the movement of Sappho's verse as we are ever likely to have. A notion of what her rhythm was *like*: certainly it was not like the 1920-ish free verse it is sometimes rendered as. Take a Sapphic line and try *da-dum*-ing its eleven longs and shorts:

$$\_\cup\_ \; \breve{} \; \_\cup\cup\_\cup\_ \; \breve{}$$

Is this like any rhythm we have heard in English? Yes, most of us will feel; it is like a very free iambic pentameter with the first three feet reversed or spondaic, and with an extra syllable at the end. As in John Donne's line in the "Epithalamium Made at Lincoln's Inn":

Which when next time you in these sheets will smother . . .

Or as in quite a few lines in Shakespeare's sonnets—if we make the third syllable emphatic, as we might in speech:

Hate of *my* sin, grounded on sinful loving . . .

(CXLII)

or

Bearing *thy* heart, which I will keep so chary . . .

(XXII)

But these occur in English as variations on a simple meter. An entire poem written in them might be intolerably stiff and mannered, untrue to the cadence of English. The charm and expressiveness of our metrics is that it gives a continual interplay of meter and rhythm, a continual series of variations, whereas to write Sapphics in English is to write the same metrical line over and over. This is surely why Sapphics and Alcaics sound so artifical to us—like the diversions of a learned dilettante. Hölderlin used them as effectively as possible in German; Goethe, a more spontaneous poet, was probably wise in not going beyond hexameter and elegiacs.

It seemed to me worth the trouble to give most of these translations in something like the form of the original. Yet one cannot insist that stanza forms have to be preserved. Valéry praises a French translation of St. John of the Cross that is paced quite differently from the Spanish.

If one does decide on the original rhythm, or on any rhythm, difficulties immediately crop up—difficulties which translators in a hurry will probably decide are not worth coping with. How is one to say in English "En una noche obscura . . ." in the cadence of the Spanish, yet using the simplest and most direct words, as the Spanish are the simplest and most direct for their meaning? "On a dark night" is two or three syllables too short, depending on what one decides to do about the feminine ending, which will have a different effect in English. The problem: to say "On a dark night" and yet have more syllables. "Aha! padding!" the literalist will exclaim. But not padding—unless what is added is clumsily wadded in. Why not change the metaphor to the one Keats has made famous and say the translator has a rift or two he can load with ore? The trick is to "justify" the line with materials matching so well that no one will notice the reconstruction. Any stanza of a translation starts with gaps to be filled and excesses to be planed away. This is almost the test of a translator of poetry: how deftly, how creatively does he reorganize the debris? Does he work with his materials as the original poet might have worked with his?—for in writing poetry we have the same kind of adjustments to make between what our mind would have us say and what our pulses urge us.

In rendering St. John of the Cross the translator is unusually lucky because the poet himself wrote long explications of some of his poems. The translator may have ten or twenty pages from which to pick a needed phrase or image, from materials which the poet tells us he had in mind when writing the line, and which he himself might have used if the exigencies of his form had suggested it. It is wrong to say that the translator is unfaithful in making such adjustments; there is nothing he can do except bend thought and rhythm toward each other until they touch—and there is a point beyond which the rhythm will not bend. Objections to what some may regard as intrusions, as foreign matter in the English version, generally come from those who do not understand the nature of poetry—those who read the translation and its original on facing pages, line by line, ping-pong fashion, eyes right, eyes left, triumphant when a discrepancy is found. Perhaps it would be better—many have thought so—not even to print the text of a poem together with a translation which itself is meant to be a poem. The original is an experience. The translation, different but analogous, is an experience—but the two experiences cannot well be enjoyed together.

One of the most successful poetic translations of our time is the one Rilke made of "Le cimetière marin." Rilke himself was pleased with what he felt was his success in catching the "equivalences"; yet he is often far from anything like a word-for-word correspondence. In the line about the cicada already quoted, Rilke added an image that made the insect a "saw" of the dryness; there is no saw in Valéry. The objection will come: "*Säge* is lugged in, and only to rhyme with *träge!*" In the fourth line of the poem Valéry's sea is "toujours recommencée"; Rilke adds a different notion and a different image in saying it is "ein immer neues Schenken (gift)." Aha! Habitual *aha!*-ers will find about one opportunity per line in Rilke's version, which aims primarily at showing German readers what the poem is like. (That at least is its effect; Rilke may have done the work purely for his own pleasure.) A. Grosser, in a study which translators of Valéry will have come across in *Études germaniques* (October–December, 1949), stresses Rilke's primary concern: "ce qui fait sans doute l'excellence de la traduction de Rilke: le rythme, les sonorités, en un mot la poésie. . . ." If, with all translators of poetry, I have sometimes been forced to add or omit for the sake of a higher fidelity, it is reassuring to feel behind me the shadow of Rilke. There are lovers of Goethe's "Wandrers Nachtlied" who will feel that I have profaned it by adding "to the west" in

Birds are through
That sang in their wood to the west

It is true it was added for the cadence. But it seems to me the kind of thing Goethe might have said if he had needed it for *his* cadence. It goes with the sound; it makes sense enough: birds would sing last in woods to the west, where the light would fade last; and *west* has suggestions appropriate to the poem. It seems closer to Goethe's thought than the addition which Werner Winter tells us Lermontov made in his Russian version: a line meaning "no dust rises from the road." I mention the phrase I have added to Goethe's poem; it is typical of what has happened at times in the poems translated here.

Everywhere in the translation of poetry one struggles with this problem: how to "justify"—the printer's term seems more apt than the upholsterer's—a line of so many syllables when a natural translation of the words does not yield that number. Just as everywhere one struggles with this: how can the words be changed, yet kept right and natural, when their sounds are discordant or inept in the second language? One of the most resistant lines I have come across is the opening of St. John's poem:

¿Adónde te escondiste?

Spanish readers have professed to hear, in the sonorous *dond-cond* echo, hollow reverberations of the dungeon in which the poem was written. But nothing reverberates in "Where did you hide . . . ?"

While we are thinking of equivalences, we might wonder if translations from Italian and related languages should be done in an English line shorter than the original. Many common words, which have two or three syllables in Italian, turn into our basic English monosyllables: love, death; day, night; land, sea; boy, girl; dog, cat—so that many Italian lines, translated with the simplicity they deserve, fall into shorter lines in English. What if Dante were done in eight-syllable lines, perhaps like these (which lack, however, the full drive of his rhyming)?—

> The middle of life's journey: I
>> was somehow in a somber wood,
>> off the right road to travel by.
> Not easy to describe it here,
>> that wildwood, thick and thorny! such,
>> even the memory's full of fear.
> So bitter, death is barely more

Perhaps more of Dante's crispness would come through in the shorter line? But would it be at too great a cost in dignity and amplitude?—qualities which, together with a racy vigor, come through so resonantly in the translation by John Ciardi.

I began to wonder about this years ago, during what was probably the closest and most rewarding study I ever made of a poet. Under probably the most stirring circumstances. The poet was Dante, the city Florence, with the Tuscan countryside, panoramic beyond our windows, changing from fall to winter to the spring. Here, two or three afternoons a week, before a fire on the colder days, and with wine or Campari on the table, I read through most of the *Commedia* with a young Florentine who knew English well enough to discuss the complexities of his own language. Sometimes—an additional pleasure—Robert Fitzgerald came down from Fiesole to join us. Aldo Celli would read a line, or, as the weeks went by, perhaps a dozen lines; his student would repeat them, not for the pronunciation alone, but perhaps in the hope there was some magic in the Florentine cadence. Then the questions came—searching out, line by line, the kind of information the dictionaries are chary of. They were about words mostly, about their tone, their status in the language. This word, Professor Celli would say, was still the common Tuscan word; another he had never heard, although it "sounded Florentine." One had become proverbial; another was used only as a Dante allusion. One word survived in Tuscany, but he thought not elsewhere; another sounded Sienese. One was poetic today; another suggested nineteenth-century rhetoric. One was used only by old folks in the country; another was a child's word—though he thought parents would discourage its use if they heard it. One was used in writing, but not in speech; another used only ironically, as in the funny papers or by students joking. One survived only as the name of a street in Florence.

I learned also that to an Italian ear such and such a line would sound flat, or clumsy, or overrich in music. All of this is treasure for the translator, treasure hard to come by in any other way. The translator, with poetry especially, gives us not only words but the tone of words: their tone determines the kind of English he writes. Surely among the commonest faults of translation are faults of tone: the easy and colloquial perhaps lost in the stiff and literary, or perhaps overtranslated into a slang which is born ephemeral, or into the distractingly personal idiom of an E. E. Cummings, which is not really for export.

This kind of close reading reveals other effects a foreigner would be likely to miss: what excitement, for example, there can be in displacements of emphasis, as in the second of these famous lines, in which the expected stress on the eighth syllable is shifted plangently to the seventh:

> Per me si va ne la città dolente,
> per me si va ne l'eterno dolore,
> per me si va tra la perduta gente[15]

so that *eterno* resonates with strange effect, the deepest note in the passage.

Though a modern Florentine devoted to literature may be closer to Dante than anyone alive, he is still centuries away. The reading I have described has to be supplemented by the scholarly notes of five or six editions. Achilles Fang insists that "a translator must comprehend not only his text but also its numerous glosses . . . it would be nothing short of folly to translate a passage before he is perfectly satisfied with the text and can explain every word of it." Nothing is more helpful for a translator than to be able to discuss his poem with someone who has known from childhood the language in which it is written. It seems to me there is no substitute for such discussion, when it is possible; I have been lucky enough to be able to search and research in this way most of the poems here translated. One is not likely to turn up an ancient Greek around here any more, but one can read Catalan with a native of Barcelona who speaks it in preference to Spanish; one can read Galician with someone from the northwestern corner of Spain who learned it at his mother's knee. With most languages that might concern us, help is even closer at hand. No one, even after living for years in a country, knows the language well enough to catch all the nuances of poetry: many words have for us the suggestions they have because of what they meant to us in childhood. As late learners we are always likely to blunder. I remember how pleased I was, even after two years in Spain, to find a Spanish poet referring to a round mirror as *la luna*—until an amused Spaniard informed me that this was not the poet's metaphor at all, but only the usual term for a mirror of that shape. Almost nowhere is hybris more conspicuous than in translating poetry: everyone thinks he knows more than he knows. Conceit, indolence, carelessness, haste, these are the vices of the translator; and where they thrive, the boners blossom. If these boners sometimes provide as much delight as the poetry transferred, that is probably no part of the writer's intention. There was the Spanish translator of Emily Dickinson who thought the moor she had never seen was the kind of Moor that figured in Spanish history; he had some trouble making sense of the poem. Or the translator who enlivened his text by having a lady "ride naked" through a town, when the original only meant she "rode bareback." Or the Italian who missed the idiom in "Come up and see me tonight. I've got nothing on." Boners, though they may be funny, are always a kind of ugliness, because ignorance and carelessness are ugly. Even Ezra Pound, who has given us some marvelous poems in the guise of translations, sometimes reads with too hasty an eye. When for the Provençal

> Tout m'a mo cor, e tout m'a me,
> e se mezeis e tot lo mon[16]

he gives us

> She hath all my heart from me, and she hath from me all
>   my wit
> And myself and all that is mine

it certainly looks as if he thought *tout* was like the French word and meant "all." But *tout* in Provençal is the past participle of *tolre* (the Latin *tollere*). He also seems to have confused "m'a me" and "lo mon" with other words. This is a trifle, but it rather shakes our confidence in a translator's sensitivity to, and respect for, his text. Of course one takes liberties in the interests of any poetic effect, but one should know what liberties he is taking, and with what—and above all should approach a great original with that respect and care which is a kind of humility.

Discussing the poem with a native speaker should be in addition to and not in place of some experience with the language. When the language is unknown, no amount of discussion will help very much. Recently it was my good fortune to have as my dinner companion a Japanese lady; we talked— I asking, she explaining—for perhaps an hour about Bashō's famous haiku:

> Furu ike ya
> kawazu tobikomu
> mizu no oto.

She told me it "meant":

> An old pond—
> frog jumped in:
> water's-sound.

Then she tried to show me why this is the most celebrated of all haiku. I understood every word she said, yet had almost no idea what she was getting at. "But you'd have to live in Japan!" she laughed finally. Later, consulting Professor Henderson's introduction to haiku, I was only more puzzled by his remarks on the poem, which he says Bashō thought the most important turning point in his poetic life: "Many competent critics have found in this a deep and esoteric meaning; others have considered it too darkly mysterious to understand at all." Obviously I am not ready to translate this poem, and probably never will be—although it has become the fashion for poets nowadays, sometimes encouraged by institutions, to "translate" from languages which they do not know, on the basis of literal versions, explications, and perhaps conferences with someone who does know the language. This seems to me a bit shabby. I know that others do not share my prejudice; certainly handsome poems have been produced in this secondhand fashion.

One element of poetry hardly touched on in this discussion is imagery. If a poet says something is like a compass or a glowworm golden or a red, red rose, this might seem as easy to translate as those "two brown pencils" or that "pen of my aunt." And one might feel, with Vladimir Nabokov (*New York Review of Books*, December 4, 1969), that "a poet's imagery is a sacred, unassailable thing." Yet difficulties can arise: images too are expressed in words, and words have qualities. Suppose the word for something in the source language is a long lovely word, all *l*'s and *m*'s, somehow like its meaning: Nabokov gives us an example when he says "The Russian word, with its fluffy and dreamy syllables, suits admirably this beautiful tree . . ." (RB 104). Suppose the corresponding English word is short and ugly; suppose we called the tree a scab-bark or a snotch. Images sound different in different languages; Jean Paris thinks that "sauvage vent d'ouest" is no real equivalent for "wild west wind." Or suppose the image evokes an object well known to speakers of the first language but totally unfamiliar to those of the second. Two perhaps overfamiliar examples: for the Eskimos, "lamb of God" turns to "seal of God"; and for some tribesmen of hot regions "white as snow" becomes "white as egret's feathers." Under such conditions, are lamb and snow indeed sacred and unassailable? Connotation too must be reckoned with: Sidney Monas, translating from Russian into English, changes a "mourning cuckoo" to a "mourning dove," since cuckoo has the wrong connotations in English. "The reader who takes this sort of alteration of figure to be a mistranslation," says Jackson Mathews, "has much to learn about translating poetry." Again, certain images that conveyed specific information to members of one culture may mean nothing to those of another: the sparrows, for example, that drew the chariot of Aphrodite in Sappho's poem. They sound rather silly to us. We can save the image by thinking of a cloud of sparrows, as Tiepolo might have painted them; but even so we have to know that sparrows—if that is the ornithologically correct term—were thought of as sexy birds, so sacred to Aphrodite that their flesh was used as an aphrodisiac. Maybe the translator should insert a clarifying word, just to safeguard the sanctity of the image? (Perhaps this is a step I should have taken with Valéry's "filles chatouillées." W. M. Frohock, from his wide experience with the backgrounds of French poetry, informs me that the proper way to tickle girls in southern France is with fistfuls of hay.)

Another difficulty to deal with is that frequency of image varies in different languages. Shakespeare is more concrete, invokes the senses more, than Racine: the difference is not only in individual talent but in the very languages they use. The concreteness of English is one of its glories; perhaps when a line from a less concrete language is fully translated into English it tends to settle into images "not in" the original. "The English [version]," wrote Dudley Fitts of one translation, "demands a harder, more urgent kind of particularity." All very well for Valéry to have his cicada scratching the dryness; in English we are more likely to have it scratching a dry thing, if only the air or the atmosphere. (Not, I think, the earth.) We have seen that Rilke, in translating into German, provided the insect with a saw; we might want to do something of that sort in English. Such modifications of imagery may be necessary in view of differing linguistic habits: what we want in the translation of poetry is equivalent effect, which we hardly get by writing English as if it were a foreign language. Here the translator is operating at a depth far below linguistic peculiarity, below the surface of diction and the layers of imagery,

> Auprès d'un coeur, aux sources du poème,
> Entre le vide et l'événément pur[17]

trying to discover the urgencies that expressed themselves in *these* words and *these* images in one language, but which might have surfaced differently in another. One cannot say too often that it is not correspondence of detail that matters; it is correspondence of feeling and movement and tonality. Poems have, we know, not only meaning but being; it is this very being of the poem that a translator is trying to give us.

Notes

1. *Sappho to Valéry: Poems in Translation,* 2d ed. (Princeton: Princeton University Press, 1980).
2. William Arrowsmith and Roger Shattuck, *The Craft and Content of Translation* (New York: Doubleday/Anchor, 1964), 244. All further references to this and other noted works will be in parentheses in the text.
3. "Shakespeare in Light of Comparative Literature," *Refractions* (New York: Oxford, 1962). More recent books on translation include George Steiner, *After Babel* (1975), Marilyn Gaddis Rose, ed., *Translation in the Humanities* (1977), and *World of Translation, Papers Delivered at the Conference on Literary Translation* (1970), sponsored by P.E.N. American Center.
4. Quotations from the prose of Valéry are mostly in the words of Denise Folliot (Paul Valéry, *The Art of Poetry,* Bollingen Series [Princeton: Princeton University Press, 1958], a book I would highly recommend to translators of poetry).
5. Brower, *On Translation.*
6. Preface to "Translations from Ovid's *Epistles.*"
7. "The clean insect scratches the dryness."
8. "The harsh beetle is a saw of the dryness."
9. "Clean [bright] insect scrapes drynesses."
10. "The true rodent, the irrefutable worm."
11. "The rodent worm irrefutable."
12. "The worm, that no one contradicts, the gnawer."
13. "The final gifts, the fingers that defend them."
14. "Final gifts, defending fingers."
15. "Through me one goes into the suffering city; through me one

goes into eternal sorrow; through me one goes among the lost people."

16. "[She] has taken my heart from me, and taken myself from me, and herself and all the world."

17. "Near to a heart, to the sources of the poem, between the emptiness and the pure event"—Paul Valéry, "Le cimetière marin."

St. John of the Cross
and His Poetry

I

The best account in English of the life of St. John of the Cross had been Gerald Brenan's *Horizon* article—the first of two—in May, 1947. Twenty-five years later, in the light of recent scholarship, Mr. Brenan brought his account up to date in his *St. John of the Cross: His Life and Poetry,* published with the translations of Lynda Nicholson (Cambridge University Press, 1973). The biographical account that follows is indebted to Mr. Brenan's work.

Born in 1542 in a village of Old Castile, Juan de Yepes was brought up in great poverty by a widowed mother. As a youth he worked as carpenter, tailor, painter; he had some training in art and later drew a remarkable crucifixion which Salvador Dali has made famous. He loved music, particularly the popular songs of the people. In school he probably became acquainted with the Latin poets; he would have heard all around him the Spanish *romances* or folk ballads, unrivaled in Europe.

Becoming at twenty-one a Carmelite friar, he spent four years at the University of Salamanca. Biblical studies obviously claimed a good part of his time, since "no protestant divine ever quoted Scripture more often." Just before leaving the university he met Teresa of Ávila, then past fifty, and

From *The Poems of St. John of the Cross,* 3d ed. (Chicago: University of Chicago Press, 1979).

became interested in her project for the reform of the Carmelite order: its return to a more primitive rule that would stress prayer and contemplation. In 1568, as Juan de la Cruz, he took his vows with the Reformed Carmelites. For about the next ten years his existence, in a simple country monastery and as confessor to the convent at Ávila, was outwardly uneventful.

Then in 1577 he became the key figure in a cloak-and-dagger episode. Because of the violent hostility of the unreformed Carmelites and a more far-reaching suspicion of Reformed Carmelite practices (St. John himself had been denounced to the Inquisition) he was kidnaped and dragged off to the Priory at Toledo—the large building, now destroyed, to the right of the bridge in El Greco's Plan of Toledo. There he was shut in a gloomy, ill-smelling little closet; half starved; permitted no change of his flea-ridden clothing for eight months; and beaten by his unreformed brethren at frequent intervals with such zeal that his shoulders were crippled for life.

In the midst of his sufferings, he heard one evening from the street below a popular song about unhappy love—sixteenth-century blues:

> Muérome de amores,
> Carillo, qué haré?
> —Que te mueras, alahé!
>
> (I'm dying of love;
> darling, what shall I do?
> So die then, hi-di-hey!)

Always susceptible to the charm of music and poetry, capable of hearing them *a lo divino* (as symbolizing the love between God and man), St. John, enraptured by the sadness and beauty of that worldly song, was himself inspired to expression. His greatest lyrics, the *Cántico,* the *Noche,* and some others were written in whole or in part during these months in prison, precisely *nel mezzo del cammin di nostra vita.*

His escape the following August was as melodramatic as

the kidnaping eight months earlier. With ropes twisted from strips of blanket and tunic, he let himself down from a dizzy height into the darkness. Somehow, after a stunning fall and mysterious assistance over a wall too high to climb, he found his way, through the blackness of a strange city, to the Reformed Carmelite Convent; there he was taken in "looking like an image of death," and given pears stewed with cinnamon. That he regarded his poetry as more than a pastime is shown, the very day of his escape, by his dictating some verses he had composed in prison but had been unable to write down.

The following spring was spent at a mountain hermitage, rugged and beautiful, in Andalucía. Here he completed the lyrics, and his dazzling career as poet, which had opened not many months before, was "practically finished." Then followed three years at Baeza, farther down the Guadalquivír. The charm of landscape, all the forces of nature, were an unfailing inspiration to him—what saves this oldest of clichés is that in him they actually inspired something: praise of God for the beauty of created being and for the knowledge of Him which we derive from it; this he referred to, with great affection, as *the knowledge of the evening,* distinct from the daylight knowledge of God in Himself.

In 1582 he went to Granada as prior for three quiet years; on the hillside not far from the Alhambra, "with one of the most beautiful views in the world before him," he wrote his long commentaries on the poems. In the years that followed, as Vicar General for Andalucía, he traveled widely, by burro, through southern Spain, going even as far afield as Lisbon and Madrid, sleeping, like Don Quijote, in the open air or by the brawling, overcrowded inns. In 1588, as new dangers threatened in the order, he became prior at Segovia, a post he held until May of 1591, when his insistence on chapter elections by secret ballot led to his disgrace and removal to a solitary spot in Andalucía. To destroy him once and for all, enemies within his own order set about collecting or fabricating evidence. Feeling ran so high that, rather than risk guilt by association, people with letters or papers from him thought it safer to destroy them. Only his final illness saved him from further persecution: in September of 1591 he was brought low with fever and terrible ulcers; these proving uncontrollable, on December 14 of that year he died, his voice rising from the rotted flesh in delight at the beauties of the Song of Songs. Almost immediately there were wild public demonstrations in his favor. Popularly recognized as a saint even in his own lifetime, he was canonized in 1726, proclaimed a Doctor of the Church in 1926. There are no specific references to the external events of his life in his poetry, which is surely rich, however, in such reminiscences as Brenan points out in speaking of the last lines of the *Cántico*:

> Y el cerco sosegaba,
> Y la caballería
> A vista de las aguas descendía.

(And the siege sank into quietness, and the cavalry descended at the sight of the waters.)

I do not think that in the whole of Spanish poetry there is a passage that calls up so vividly the Castilian-Andalusian scene: the line of horses or mules descending slowly to the river; the vague suggestion of frontier warfare, now over: that sense of endless repetition, of something that has been done countless times before being done again, which is the gift of Spain to the restless and progressive nations. In those last two wonderful lines with their gently reassuring fall, the horses descending within sight of the waters are lifted out of time and made the symbol of the peace of this Heracleitan land of eternal recurrence.

Nowhere in St. John's work or in what we know of his life does he indicate the slightest sense of embarrassment or self-consciousness (or pride) about his poetry, or the slightest regret when he came to write no more. Apparently he had no scruples about its being in conflict with other interests: he urged the religious under him to improvise verses *a lo divino* (in a divine sense) in their times of recreation. He left it with no grand gestures of renunciation. At times he enjoyed indulging his facility: some of his verses are mere exuberant improvisings. When moved by delight and love to express himself by way of poetry, he did so as no other ever has; when moved by delight and love to pass beyond that stage, he went gaily into *la música callada* (the silent music). One feels from his writings that no man has ever found a richer wonderland of delight or wasteland of darkness than St. John found in his own soul, often at altitudes quite beyond poetry. Probably during much of his life the intensity of his experience was too great to need or admit of expression. What Yeats has written about the poet and human love here comes to mind: had the poet been successful in love,

> who can say
> What would have shaken from the sieve?
> I might have thrown poor words away
> And been content to live.

As indeed St. John was, though "content" is too weak a word, and though his life was not the life his companions—and still less the strangers around him—were able to see.

"There are certain kinds of sanctity," said St. Teresa in one of her marvelously barbed remarks, "I do not understand." These twisted sorts of sanctity would include that of people who turn to religion and "God" out of weak blood or nightmare terrors or *mal protesi nervi* or plain hatred of the world: the feeling that if they had had the making of it, many loose ends in existence would have been tucked in with more niceness and propriety. St. John's holiness was far from being of this sort. He saw everything created as fresh and beautiful; saw, without Hopkins's torment, "the dearest freshness deep down things." The fields, the flowers, the animals, men and angels, wine, companionship, poetry, the singing voice—all were beautiful. Most rapturous of these was human love. He saw the evening world as very good, but saw beyond it something realer and more thrilling. We fall in love, we others, with our bright particular star, he with the infinite galaxies of Night.

Dámaso Alonso tells us that it is the unanimous opinion of the Spaniards who know about such matters that St. John of the Cross is the greatest Spanish poet.[1] Pedro Salinas says that his best works, with their "incomparable sensual power," are "charged with poetic potency like no other work written in this world."[2] Jorge Guillén thinks that his three best poems "form a series which is perhaps the highest culmination of Spanish poetry."[3] García Lorca too is passionate in his praise. In his essay on *duende*,[4] Lorca tells us that there are artists sponsored by an Angel that guides, endows, dazzles, shedding his grace in midair. There are those sponsored by the Muse, who comes "bearing landscapes of columns and the false taste of laurel." There is also a third type, which has *duende*: the Andalusian term for that mysterious power "that all may feel and no philosophy may explain," that all Dionysian artists at their best have, the bullfighter "who hurls his heart against the horns" or the flamenco singer "like a woman possessed, her face blasted like a medieval weeper . . . feeling the power rise from the very soles of her feet." *Duende* is

> the mystery, the roots that probe through the mire we all know of, and do not understand, but which furnishes us with whatever is sustaining in art. . . . In all Arabic music, in the dances, songs, elegies of Arabia, the coming of the *Duende* is greeted by fervent outcries of *Allah! Allah! . . .* so close to the *Olé! Olé!* of our bull rings that who is to say they are not actually the same; and in all the songs of southern Spain the appearance of the *Duende* is followed by heartfelt exclamations of *God alive!*— profound, human, tender, the cry of communion with God through the medium of the five senses . . .

St. John of the Cross belongs not with the Angel, as we might suspect, nor with the Muse: taking him with two of the greatest names in Spanish poetry Lorca acclaims him thus: "The Muse of Góngora and the Angel of Garcilaso must yield up the laurel wreath when the *Duende* of St. John of the Cross passes by. . . ."

And is it just accidental, the remarkable similarity between the tone and imagery of St. John's greatest poems and Lorca's brilliant account of the poet at work?[5]

> The poet who embarks on the creation of the poem (as I know by experience), begins with the aimless sensation of a hunter about to embark on a night hunt through the remotest of forests. Unaccountable dread stirs in his heart. . . . Then the poet is off on the chase. Delicate breezes chill the lenses of his eyes. The moon, curved like a horn of soft metal, calls in the silence of the topmost branches. White stags appear in the clearing between the tree trunks. Absolute night withdraws in a curtain of whispers. Water flickers in the reeds, quiet and deep . . .

My present concern is with St. John as poet, not as mystic. Mysticism itself cannot write poetry; it can only stammer about the ineffable. Probably no abnormal state, no kind of "inspiration," can give us a work of art. We have to be awake to describe a dream, says Valéry—who reminds us also that one does not have to be going sixty miles an hour at the time he is designing a locomotive. García Lorca believes that no great artist has ever worked in a state of fever.

Hundreds of anecdotes about the masters show that they were canny craftsmen more often than mysterious winged creatures. St. John of the Cross, certainly, was a technician as well as a visionary. When asked by a nun if his poems were the result of inspiration or of his own hard work, he answered, as any good poet would: of both. "Daughter, some of them God gave me and some I looked for myself."

The poet, García Lorca reminds us, is a professor of the five bodily senses. It may be amazing to some that whereas St. John's mystical quest drove him into a dark night where the senses had to be abandoned, in the world of his poetry he never left them. "We are immediately fascinated," says Guillén, "by these forms that do not break with the laws of our world." To describe the love and love-longing between God and man, St. John, in his greatest poem, never uses the word *God* at all, but looks for a metaphor that will not break with the laws of our world. He finds it in what he considers the best thing we know here on earth: our human love. God is *el amado*, the loved one, the one we might affectionately call our "love" or "lover." Or He is *aquel que yo más quiero*, "the one I love the most," or *mis amores*, "my love," or *vida mia*, "my life," or even *carillo*, "darling"—and what puritan could address His Grandeur that way? St. John's metaphor has a precedent in the most loving and lovable part of the often dire Old Testament, the Song of Songs, which was his favorite part of the Bible and, it seems, his favorite poem. Its amorous imagery is everywhere in his *Cántico*, whose narrative is based on the pursuit of courtship, the promise of betrothal, the fruition of marriage. Even in his own time the theme must have drawn raised eyebrows and embarrassed giggles. St. Teresa tells of a sermon on the same theme broken by ignorant chortles from the congregation. She tells too of nuns who were scandalized by the Song of Songs:

> You may think that in these Canticles there are some things which could have been said otherwise. Our dullness being what it is, I should not be surprised if you did: I have heard some people say that they actually tried not to listen to them. O God, how miserable is our condition! We are like poisonous things that make poison of all they eat . . . !

But the puritan penumbra had not fallen on St. John of the Cross—it seems never to have occurred to him that the language of human passion might be an improper metaphor for divine love. Nor is he fevered by it; critics have never ceased to wonder at the freshness, sweetness, and delicacy with which he has handled the theme.

Always metaphor-conscious, he explains that he is using this or that as a figure of speech, or that he is using such and such a figure so as not to mix the metaphor. He does not blur levels of reality; in his great poems there are no obtrusive signposts pointing skyward. Once we look at the poetry with a workman's eye, perhaps what we notice first is what Guillén calls coherence of metaphor. But St. John is careful too about lesser things. Once he writes out for us a technical description of a stanza form, complete with number of syllables and rhyme scheme. In his best work he keeps to a tight pattern, generally with lines of seven and eleven syllables.

"The sound," said Robert Frost, "is the gold in the ore." St. John, who loved music and folk song, was sensitive also to the analogous music of speech, and to the way sound can dramatize meaning as well as state it. In his famous showpiece line—not the kind of trick any poet would want to do often—he tells us that the things of this world afford only a kind of vague and stammering communion with God. The line, in natural Spanish, stammers too:

> Un no sé qué que quedan balbuciendo.
>
> (An I-don't-know-what that they keep stammering.)

That he was taken by the expressiveness of the repeated k's is shown by what is apparently a first attempt at the effect:

> que me quedé balbuciendo.
>
> (That I kept stammering.)

Dámaso Alonso, in a study that does not discount the mysticism, provides some discerning analyses of expressive sound effects, and Emilio Orozco has written several pages on sounds in the last stanzas of "The Spiritual Canticle" that "humanize" and "materialize" speech by the very sensation of physical adherence in the lip movements that produce them.[6]

All of this suggests that when St. John was writing his poems his attention was not on his "thought" alone. The relation between thought and sound has been described by Paul Valéry, the one who has perhaps gone deepest into the poetic process:[7]

> If he is a true poet, he will nearly always sacrifice to form (which, after all, is the end and act itself, with its organic necessities) any thought that cannot be dissolved into the poem because it requires him to use words or phrases foreign to the poetic tone. An intimate alliance of sound and sense, which is the essential characteristic of poetic expression, can be obtained only at the expense of something—that is, thought.

Conversely, all thought which has to define and justify itself to the extreme limit dissociates and frees itself from rhythm, numbers, and resonance—in a word, from all pursuit of the sensuous qualities of speech. A proof does not sing. . . .

In his poems St. John was not proving; he was singing. His mystical experiences, he insists, cannot logically be described at all, "for it would be ignorance to think that sayings of love understood mystically, such as those of the present stanzas, can be fairly explained by words of any kind"—and this because the human mind is not programmed to process data of a nature beyond its own. St. John explains why he preferred poetry:[8]

Who can express that which He makes them desire? None certainly; not even the very souls through which He passes. It is for this reason that by means of figures, comparisons and similitudes, they let something of that which they feel overflow and utter secret mysteries from the abundance of the Spirit, rather than rationally explain these things. These similitudes, unless they are read with the simplicity of the spirit of love and understanding they embody, seem to be nonsense rather than reasonable expression, as may be seen in the divine Songs of Solomon and other books of the Divine Scripture, in which the Holy Spirit, since he cannot express the fullness of his meaning in common language, utters mysteries in strange figures and similitudes . . .

But since he had been asked—as what poet is not?—what his lines meant, he did undertake to elucidate the three great poems—with the caution, however, that his readers remember that poetry can say better than prose what there is to be said. What resulted is probably the most detailed self-explication ever written. There are about one hundred pages on his twenty-four-line "The Living Flame of Love," and then a revised explication about fifteen pages longer. Both the "Ascent of Mount Carmel" and "The Dark Night," nearly five hundred pages in all, start out as explications of a short lyric about the dark night—and never get beyond line 10 of the poem.

One example should make clear what his method is. In stanzas 29 and 30 of "The Spiritual Canticle" we have:

> Wings flickering here and there,
> lion and gamboling antler, shy gazelle,
> peak, precipice, and shore,
> flame, air, and flooding well,
> night-watchman terror, with no good to tell,
>
> by many a pleasant lyre
> and song of sirens I command you, so:

The prose exposition is as follows:[9]

1. The Spouse continues, and in these two stanzas describes how, by means of the pleasant lyres, which stand for the sweetness habitually enjoyed in this condition, and also by the sirens' song, which stands for the delight that He always has in the soul, He has just brought to conclusion all the operations and passions of the soul which before were a certain impediment to quiet pleasure and sweetness. These things, He now says, are the digressions of the imagination, and He commands them to cease. Furthermore, he brings under control the two natural faculties, which somewhat afflicted the soul before, and which are wrath and concupiscence. And also, by means of these lyres and this song, He shows how in this condition, as far as possible in this life, the three faculties of the soul—understanding, will, and memory—are brought to perfection and put in working order. It is also described here how the four passions of the soul—grief, hope, joy, and fear—are tempered and controlled by means of the satisfaction which the soul possesses, signified by the pleasant lyres and the sirens' song, as we shall now explain. All these impediments God now wishes to cease, so that the soul, at her own will and without interruption, may have full enjoyment of the delight, peace, and sweetness of this union.

> Wings flickering here and there,

2. He calls the digressions of the imagination "wings flickering" since they are light and swift in their flight first to one place and then another. When the will is quietly enjoying delightful communications from the Beloved, they are likely to

annoy it and by their swift flights to disturb its joy. These the Beloved says that he commands by the "pleasant lyre." This means that since the sweetness and delight of the soul are now so rich and frequent and strong that they could not hinder it as they used to do, when it had not reached so high a condition, they are to cease their restless flights, their impetuous dartings and extravagances. This is to be taken in the same way as other parts of the stanza which we have to explicate, such as:

lion and gamboling antler, shy gazelle,

3. By the "lion" is understood the acrimonies and impetuosities of the irascible faculty, which is as bold and brave in its acts as lions are. By the "antler" and "gazelle" is meant the other faculty of the soul, which is the concupiscible, the power of desiring, which has two effects: one of cowardice and one of boldness. It produces the effects of cowardice when it finds that things are unpleasant, for then it withdraws into itself and is timid, and in this it is like a gazelle, for even as these animals possess the concupiscible faculty to a greater degree than other animals, so too they are very timid and shy. It produces the effect of boldness when it finds that things are pleasant, for then it no longer retreats nor is timid, but boldly advances to lust after and accept them with its passions. In regard to boldness this faculty is compared to the "gamboling antler" of animals which have such concupiscence toward that which they desire that they not only run toward it but leap after it, for which reason they are called "gamboling."

4. So that, in commanding the lion, the Spouse restrains impetuous and extravagant wrath, and in commanding the gazelle He strengthens the concupiscible faculty with respect to the cowardice and timidity of spirit which caused it to shrink before; and in commanding the gamboling antler, He satisfies and quiets the desires and appetites which roamed restlessly about before, gamboling like antlered beasts from one thing to another, in order to satisfy the concupiscence which is now satisfied by the pleasant lyre, whose sweetness it enjoys, and by the song of sirens, upon whose delight it feeds. It is to be noted that it is not wrath and concupiscence which the Spouse commands here, for these faculties are never absent from the soul, but their troublesome and tumultuous acts, which are denoted by the lion, the shy gazelle, and the gamboling antler; it is necessary that in this condition they should cease.

peak, precipice, and shore,

By these three words are denoted the vicious and disorderly acts of the three faculties of the soul—memory, understanding, and will—which are vicious and disorderly when they are carried to a high extreme, and also when they are at a low or deficient extreme, or even when they are not at either extreme, but tend toward one or the other; and so the peaks, which are very high, stand for acts which are extreme in being overviolent. By the precipices, which go down low . . .

A comparison between the stanzas and their explication illustrates as well as anything I know the difference between poetry and prose.[10] In the poem, meanings are suggested by imagery and music; in the prose, they are rather drearily spelled out and overelaborated. St. John does not mix the two modes: the lion of the poem is a lion, as real as Rilke's: *Zähne zeigt und Zunge* (it shows teeth and tongue). It is not "the lion of acrimony," or anything so hybrid, for the poet, like Ezra Pound much later, believed that the natural object is always the adequate symbol. His poems are, as Guillén observed, "almost completely uncontaminated by allegory."

"But if you meant 'the acrimonies and impetuosities of the irascible faculty,'" a literal reader might have objected, "why talk about a lion? Aren't you being unfaithful to your own thought?" The poet might have replied that he was not trying to express a thought; he was looking for an image. The prose makes it clear that there were many things he might have said for everything he did say in the poems: from the great welter of the nonverbalizable he selected an image that condensed as much as possible and did not make nonsense of the image next to it. What he selected was influenced too by a cadence, or by his need for a certain number of syllables or, every few words, by his need for a rhyme.

III

All of these remarks are relevant to the problem of translating poetry: there are still readers who insist on the "thought," which seems more important to them than it ever did to the poet. Even experts may forget: one critic objected to earlier versions of these translations because the translator had not remembered, he said, that every word of St. John was to be "taken literally." Yet time and again in his prose St. John insists that nothing is to be taken literally; he does not even take himself literally, and on one occasion declares that although he is explaining his poem in a certain way, "there is no reason why anyone should be limited to this explanation."

Although the prose is inferior to the poetry in expressiveness—in imagery, drama, music, passion—it has claims of its own, as throwing light on the poetry. Yet there have been translators of the poetry who have not consulted it. Critics too have shown a general unawareness: one reproved these translations for making the rivers too noisy and the islands too remote and strange, in stanza 13 of the "Canticle." The poet was merely thinking, the critic assured us, of the little Tajo with its clumps of mud and willows. He was not: the prose tells us that these rivers "assail and submerge all they meet . . . their sound is such as to drown out and take the place of all other sounds . . ." and it tells us that "the strange islands are surrounded by the ocean and are far away over the sea. . . ." It is true that obligations of rhyme and rhythm and the difference in length between corresponding expressions in Spanish and English have sometimes led me to add this or that, but generally what I have added (to the great poems) is something the poet tells us he had in mind—and might just as well have said in place of what he did say had the demands of his rhyme and rhythm persuaded it.

All I have said above implies a theory of the translation of poetry: the translator has an obligation to form as well as to content, and if rhythm meant as much to the poet as "thought" did, or if he felt a sound effect worth achieving, the translator should at least be aware of that effect and work toward it, if he can. He will frequently fail; it is a commonplace that poetry cannot be translated. But perhaps it can sometimes be re-created, as Rilke re-created Valéry, or as Valéry re-created Vergil. Without being Rilke or Valéry, one can try to work as they did, and not merely be content to give the thought of a poet who was not primarily concerned with thought. How many drab little translations one sees commended for their "fidelity"—a fidelity, alas, as unimpressive as that of a wife whose homeliness is the surest protection of her virtue.

In Mallarmé's famous summary, poetry is not made out of ideas, but out of words. Perhaps the same may be said for its translation. It is surprising how many translators have not known, or not tried to find out, what kind of words St. John used. Experts who do know—such as Dámaso Alonso—tell us that the poet liked simple everyday expressions, popular, colloquial words that occur in folk song and that the country people would be likely to use. Rarely a literary word. But in the translations one comes across diction like "Whither hast vanishèd, Belovèd?" or "Oh who my grief can mend?" or "O hapless-happy plight!" Is this even good English, let alone colloquial English?

These translations, most of them, have been much revised. Some readers feel that revision, which plows and plods, is the enemy of inspiration, which strikes like lightning. Not true: revision is the desire to have a long love affair with inspiration and not just an evening's fling. The Spanish text, even seen through hours of drudgery and over heaps of worksheets, has never lost its freshness; the poems seem miraculous as ever. It is easy to see why so many Spanish poets, poets utterly unlike San Juan de la Cruz (the name they knew him by) have acclaimed him as the greatest poet of their language. In his far briefer flight, he touches on intensities which I think Dante himself has not ventured near.

At times the extraterrestrial flights of his poetry have reminded me of the imagery of science fiction; at other times of the dreamy sorcery of the surrealists. But recently, since Arno Penzias and Robert Wilson have been given a Nobel Prize for their discovery of the lingering warmth of the explosion with which our universe began, another set of images suggests itself. For the poetry of San Juan is about what preceded the Big Bang, about how—to use only an unscientific image where we have no scientific fact—a great hand opened in the timeless nowhere to release its rocketry of Time and Space and History, its expanding pyrotechnic display that, eighteen billion years later, is proliferating into new forms with undiminished versatility and brilliance. The great hand opened, San Juan would have said, out of the love and splendor that it wished to share, and delight and ecstasy were what it had to offer, at least to anyone courageous enough to survive the Dark Night that is the dragon of this story. The human mind is uneasy when it finds itself outside the pigeonholes of space and time—finds itself where words like *when, outside,* and *where* have lost all relevance. Perhaps only a poet like this one can use our own five senses to propel us beyond all *when* and *where*.

Notes

1. *La Poesía de San Juan de la Cruz,* 3d ed. (Madrid: Ediciones de Aguilar, S.A., 1958).
2. *Reality and the Poet in Spanish Poetry* (Baltimore: Johns Hopkins University Press, 1966).
3. *Language and Poetry* (Cambridge: Harvard University Press, 1961).
4. "The Duende: Theory and Divertissement" in *Poet in New York,* trans. Ben Belitt (New York: Grove Press, 1955), 154–66.
5. "The Poetic Image in Don Luis de Góngora" in *Poet in New York,* 175.
6. *Poesía y Mística, Introducción a la Lírica de San Juan de la Cruz* (Madrid: Guadarrama, 1959).
7. *The Art of Poetry,* trans. Denise Folliot (New York: Random House/Vintage, 1961), 291–92.
8. Translated from the *Prólogo* to the *Cántico Espiritual* in *Obras de San Juan de la Cruz,* vol. 3, ed. P. Silverio de Santa Teresa, O.C.D. (Burgos: El Monte Carmelo, 1930), 3–4.
9. Ibid., 139–40.
10. Cf. Sister Rose Maria Icaza, *The Stylistic Relationship Between Poetry and Prose in the Cántico Espiritual of San Juan de la Cruz* (Washington, D.C.: Catholic University of America Press, 1957).

Dante and His Eidola
Regions beyond Philosophy

I

One of Wallace Stevens's "Adagia," no doubt written out of a mischievous hope of stirring up the stodgier among us, holds that "perhaps it is of more value to infuriate the philosophers than to go along with them." Though my title may seem invidious, I have no wish to infuriate. I would only suggest that, because of the very limitations the philosopher chooses for himself, there are regions in which the poet moves about more easily.

For Dante, there is no name that endures longer or confers more honor than that of poet. In his realm of art and music, the *Purgatorio,* he has Statius admit to having borne that name when alive:

> col nome che più dura e più onora
> era io di là . . .[1]

Earlier in the *Purgatorio,* when events themselves offered testimony to the power of art, Dante probably had poetry in mind as well as song. In the second canto, Dante, meeting the soul of Casella, a musician he had known, begs him to sing something, if he still can, that will make Dante forget the dreary journey through Hell. When Casella obliges with a song, not only Dante but even Vergil and the souls on their way to the vision of God are so enthralled by its sweetness that they forget themselves and their goal—until Cato, the custodian of the place, bursts scandalized upon them to break the trance. Dante, in the Earthly Paradise itself, goes so far as to attribute to poets a mysterious and inspired sort of knowledge: in their visions of the Golden Age they had some dreaming intuition of the Garden of Eden and of man's life before the Fall. This surprising suggestion is put in the mouth not of a poet, but of Matelda, who, as representing not the contemplative but the active life, might be supposed to have some bias against the dreamy poets.

In the *Purgatorio*, Dante gives an account of his own way of writing:

> I' mi son un che, quando
> Amor mi spira, noto, e a quel modo
> ch'e' ditta dentro vo significando.[2]

His source, he says, is emotional. Poetry is not directly a kind of knowledge, though the experiences it affords may vivify what knowledge we have into fuller realizations. Knowledge is a union between our mind and what is known; poetry is a union that involves us more completely: it engages, besides our mind, not only our passions and our imagination, but also our senses and the very physiology of our being. To exist in the mind alone is to exist unnaturally; we are not completely happy there—not fulfilled, as we say now—any more than the separated soul in its temporary unnatural state after death is completely happy. The philosophers Dante knew would have agreed. "Homo non [potest] esse beatus," said Aquinas, "nisi anima corpori vere uniatur" (A human being cannot be happy unless the soul is really united to the body). Dante shows us the souls in heaven waiting for their refurbished bodies.

Since poetry is not a kind of knowledge, it is not immediately concerned with meanings. "A poem," another of Stevens's "Adagia" has it, "need not have a meaning and like most things in nature often does not have." We cannot say what the "meaning" of a flower is—yet which of us would say it is meaningless? The most serious of voices told us to consid-

71

er the lilies of the field, how they grow. Presumably we are to find significance in that consideration. Yet we cannot say that the meaning of lilies is that we should not be solicitous about how we dress. This is what Stevens is telling us about poetry: it can have significance without having a meaning we can pinpoint. In one of his Mellon Lectures at the National Gallery of Art, Jacques Maritain had something similar in mind when he wrote:

> When it comes to poetry . . . we are confronted with an intuition of emotive origin, and we enter the nocturnal empire of a primeval activity of the intellect which, far beyond concepts and logic, exercises itself in vital connection with imagination and emotion. We have quit logical reason. . . .[3]

And again:

> Our intelligence is aware of the existence of a signification, but the signified remains unknown. And it is enough for the poem to have radiance, as a black diamond has, and for the intellect to receive a delight. . . .[4]

Poetry then is not a matter of the *logos*: reason and its expression. But it is not a matter of the *eikon* either: the sense-image standing for something more than itself. We could do with another term here; I wonder if it would be helpful to take over a third Greek word and say that poetry, which is neither *logos* nor *eikon*, might be seen as a kind of *eidolon*?

Homer uses the word εἴδωλον in a couple of ways. In book IV of the *Odyssey*, when Athena wants to get a message to the despondent Penelope, she makes what Homer calls an *eidolon*. It is in the shape of a woman, a particular woman Penelope knows. It is not an *eikon*, for it has some principle of life within itself; it can move, enter rooms, stand by doors and at the heads of sleeping people, speak and answer and persuade. In book XI the souls of the dead are called ψυχαί or εἴδωλα. More physical than the *umbre* of Dante's afterlife, they have life within and retain their human powers, although weakened until they drink the good red blood from this world and are reinvigorated.

In the *Helen* of Euripides we meet another famous *eidolon,* that of Helen of Troy, who in the Prologue tells us that she never went to Troy at all, but lived comfortably in Egypt all through the war. Hera had given Paris a phantom; it was for a phantom that the Greek and Trojan fought so long. Helen calls that phantom an εἴδωλον ἔμπνουν—no artificial *eikon* but a *breathing image.*

The creations of the poet are, we might think, like *eidola.* Made by magic, they not only give the illusion of reality but in their way are real. They begin to stir with a life breathed into them by the poet. And then, wonderfully, they live with the life we breathe into them as we read, as the *eidola* of Homer live on the warm blood they drink. It is with our psychic energy that the creations of the poet exist for us: the poet has embodied in them the potentialities that we can animate, as if we had another self, another body in which our minds can live and explore regions they would not otherwise dare enter. Dante tells how the developing body of man receives the soul when that body is ready; so the poem receives the breath of life when the elements are properly disposed. The philosophers can give us a sort of skeleton ("Aristotle is a skeleton," said Stevens of one of the best of them), a set of X-rays less real than the wildest portraits of Picasso. Only the artist can give us *eidola.*

II

We see how the ways of the philosopher differ from those of the poet if we compare passages in which Aquinas, the philosopher, and Dante, the poet, are dealing with similar material: the role of appetite or instinct as a motive force. First the philosopher:

> cum omnia procedant ex voluntate divina, omnia suo modo per appetitum inclinantur in bonum, sed diversimodo. Quaedam enim inclinantur in bonum per solam naturalem habitudinem, absque cognitione, sicut plantae et corpora inanimata; et talis inclinatio ad bonum vocatur appetitus *naturalis.* Quaedam vero

ad bonum inclinantur cum aliqua cognitione; non quidem sic quod cognoscant ipsam rationem boni, sed cognoscunt aliquod bonum particulare; sicut sensus cognoscit dulce et album, et aliquid hujusmodi. Inclinatio autem hanc cognitionem sequens dicitur appetitus *sensitivus*. Quaedam vero inclinantur ad bonum cum cognitione qua cognoscunt ipsam boni rationem, quod est proprium intellectus. Et haec perfectissime inclinantur in bonum; non quidem quasi ab alio solummodo directa in bonum, sicut ea quae cognitione carent; neque in bonum particulare tantum, sicut ea in quibus est sola sensitiva cognitio, sed quasi inclinata in ipsum universale bonum; et haec inclinatio dicitur *voluntas* . . .[5]

And then the poet:

> Ond' ella, appresso d'un pïo sospiro,
>   li occhi drizzò ver' me con quel sembiante
>   che madre fa sovra figlio deliro,
> e cominciò: "Le cose tutte quante
>   hanno ordine tra loro, e questo è forma
>   che l'universo a Dio fa simigliante.
> Qui veggion l'alte creature l'orma
>   de l'etterno valore, il qual è fine
>   al quale è fatta la toccata norma.
> Ne l'ordine ch'io dico sono accline
>   tutte nature, per diverse sorti,
>   più al principio loro e men vicine;
> onde si muovono a diversi porti
>   per lo gran mar de l'essere, e ciascuna
>   con istinto a lei dato che la porti.
> Questi ne porta il foco inver' la luna;
>   questi ne' cor mortali è permotore;
>   questi la terra in sé stringe e aduna;
> né pur le creature che son fore
>   d'intelligenza quest' arco saetta,
>   ma quelle c'hanno intelletto e amore.
> La provedenza, che cotanto assetta,
>   del suo lume fa 'l ciel sempre quïeto
>   nel qual si volge quel c'ha maggior fretta;
> e ora lì, come a sito decreto,
>   cen porta la virtù di quella corda
>   che ciò che scocca drizza in segno lieto.

Vero è che, come forma non s'accorda
  molte f ïate a l'intenzion de l'arte,
  perch' a risponder la materia è sorda,
così da questo corso si diparte
  talor la creatura, c'ha podere
  di piegar, così pinta, in altra parte;
e sì come veder si può cadere
  foco di nube, sì l'impeto primo
  l'atterra torto da falso piacere.
Non dei più ammirar, se bene stimo,
  lo tuo salir, se non come d'un rivo
  se d'alto monte scende giuso ad imo.
Maraviglia sarebbe in te se, privo
  d'impedimento, giù ti fossi assiso,
  com' a terra quïete in foco vivo."
Quinci rivolse inver' lo cielo il viso.[6]

The difference is not only in the expressive power of
Dante's prosody, although it is true that the rhythm has the
palpitation, sometimes quickened, of living things; the rhyme
takes us forward at a steady and confident pace. Every fourth
or fifth word has to rhyme with two others, and yet there is
never the suspicion that a word is there only because it
chimes. If we feel its presence, we feel it as a strength, as we
do with *sorda* in line 30, or as we do in the conclusive vigor of
the third rhymes that fall on a now sensitized and expectant
area of our awareness. Lines like Dante's make us realize how
right Baudelaire was in saying "prosodies are not arbitrarily
invented tyrannies, but a collection of rules demanded by the
very organization of the spiritual being, and never have pros-
odies and rhetorics kept originality from fully manifesting
itself. The contrary, . . . that they have aided the flowering of
originality, would be infinitely more true."

Dante's presentation differs from that of the philosopher
in being given a dramatic setting. The discussion is colored by
the human emotions and needs of the participants. Dante
asks for an explanation because he is troubled; Beatrice, as
her behavior shows, answers with pity and affection. It occurs
as part of the most engrossing, hair-raising, heart-rending,
ecstatic narrative ever told—Odysseus is an armchair trav-

eller in comparison. We have been through the black and scarlet horrors of hell and seen human grandeur indomitable there; we have awakened, just before dawn, on the serene but mysterious shore of a surrealist mountain, the highest in the world, soaring at an angle of more than forty-five degrees into the clouds; we have made our way up this, painfully, crag by crag, delighted by music, terrified by living fire; at the end we have found ourselves in the most enchanting forest ever described by a poet, where brooks flow with an inner luminousness of their own beneath the blowing and musical trees; and as we stand on the very top, so high that air moves only with the movement of the world, and stare into the sun itself, we are suddenly caught up off the earth and drawn into the exhilarations of outer space. As we are whisked upward, faster than the speed of light, Dante asks the question that is answered in the text given above. What worlds of experience, passion, and urgency lie behind it!

In comparison the words of Aquinas are spoken in a vacuum. There is no dramatic background. His voice is disembodied; if he feels excitement there is nothing in the tone to reveal it. Not a word is shaken by emotion out of its conventional place; the few images are of something vaguely sweet, something vaguely white—we never know what. This is pure mind speaking, with no feeling that shows itself, no reference to the ruin-haunted jungle of the imagination, and with only the most grudging references to the senses. No breath comes and goes; no blood throbs anywhere. None of this is said in disparagement; Aquinas is speaking as a philosopher must: out of the reasoning mind alone.

Dante gives us a person talking, not just a mind at work. The talk is physicalized by images from a world we live in: being is a *great sea,* our goals are *ports;* instinct is like a *bow* that points us somewhere, like *arrows*—and when the bow and arrow are introduced, our goal is then seen as a *target.* There are other images from the physical world: the moon, lightning, a mountain river, leaping flames. The very sound becomes expressive in the driving repetitions of "ne' cor mortale è permotore," in the rough-textured energy of "quella corda che ciò che scocca drizza," in the stubbornly pulsing *p*'s of the "c'ha podere di piegar, così pinta, in altra parte."

Almost every time there is such a discussion in Dante, it is motivated by the urgency of a human situation. In canto XI of the *Inferno*, for example, we are ready for, and need, an account of the categories of the damned. Dante, passing at nightfall through the doorway with its terrifying inscription, had been taken by a ghostly figure into hell. He had heard the thunder of lamentation and imprecation in every language man ever used, had seen furious Charon, with his eyes like pinwheels of fire, beating the desperate sinners into his boat with an oar, had gazed on the majestic sadness of the great pagans, who would never see God's face, had heard the story of Paola and Francesco, so heart-breaking it had left him in a faint. He had seen souls slugging and biting at each other in the black mud, seen a rabble of snaky demons on the battlements threatening to turn him into stone (Vergil took the threat seriously). He had stood in awe before the figure of Farinata, whose indomitable humanity not even hell could break; finally, in a place of red-hot tombs—tombs so hot that no blacksmith, no foundry on earth needs hotter metal—he had come to a great cliff and been driven back, gasping, by the stench of deeper hell. It is there, as he takes shelter in the lee of a fiery tomb, that Vergil tells him how this place of terror is divided. This is no mere theoretical discussion: every term Vergil uses is achingly alive to him, and to us. We have seen malice, seen hate, seen violence and all the rest of it. No sooner is the explaining over than we all find ourselves in a landscape that seems the fiercest of Alpine regions after some great cataclysm, and barring the way in a moronic fury is a monster half bull and half man. The analysis of evil is set among scenes of evil embodied.

Circumstances also vitalize the discussion of the nature of love, set, most meaningfully, halfway through the *Purgatorio*, at the very middle of the *Commedia*. Love, which Dante said inspired his poetry, is the root of all action, subhuman, human, and divine; it is right the discussion of it should be central. Here too Dante and Vergil have seen wonder after wonder on the amazing pinnacle of rock, far in the South Pacific where no man was known to sail and live. They have come, after many vicissitudes, to the top of one of the many stairways cut in the rock, they see the last rays of the sun on the peak high above them, the stars begin to appear on every side, and with the coming of the dark their powers of motion mysteriously leave them. It is there, on the lonely terrace, in response to a question of Dante's, that Vergil explains, most movingly and humanly, the nature of love. He finishes about midnight as the moon is rising. Dante begins to nod and drowse, but is shaken awake by a great rout of runners, sprinting headlong on the narrow ledge in the darkness, and shouting as they run. This is no classroom for philosophers. All of the discussions in the poem—about lunar physics, about systems of government, about the history of Rome, about theories of embryology—all are motivated by a human situation; they take us into what we might call the regions beyond philosophy.

Urgent as these discussions are, we are always made to feel that the drama of event comes first. In the fourth canto of the *Inferno*, Dante writes "Non lasciavam l'andar perch' ei dicessi . . ."—We did not stop walking just because he was speaking. On other occasions too he mentions that such talk did not delay their advance in the least; there is no pausing anywhere for academic lectures. When topics are proposed and elucidated, it is because someone wants to know, but unless there is an obstacle they go on walking. Often the drama is complex, as in the interplay of emotions while Francesca is telling her story. Paolo stands beside her lamenting; Dante questions and then after standing silent with sorrow and pity, cannot hold out against his grief and collapses; Vergil, with his superior knowledge, is a presence of silent commiseration and understanding—and above them all, but not intruding in the poem, is Dante the writer, whose level of awareness is well above that of Dante the pilgrim. Dante the writer knows the answers to all the questions Dante the pilgrim can ask. Though no one in the poem says that Paolo and

Francesca did wrong, the situation, the setting, and the events would seem to say so in a way we cannot easily mistake.

Dante never admits that his vision is something he is making up; he insists with the utmost earnestness that what he is showing us is reality. These are experiences to *live*, he keeps suggesting, and not merely to contemplate. If we are sensitive enough we do live them, though it may take time to learn how: T. S. Eliot says there are parts of the *Paradiso* we can hope to realize only toward the close of our lives. Dante, as character in the poem, is shown these things to give him, says Vergil, "esperïenza piena"—full experience—of the realities of sin, death, and the afterlife: in the poem he is even made to do certain things because without the actual experience he would not believe. The reality of events is vouched for by occasional glimpses of what we know is the real world. All the bustle of the Venetian shipyard, for example, is described at more length than the context might seem to demand: all the rowdy, furious, tar-daubed activity to remind us that this is the world in which the truths of the poem have their meaning. When the monster Geryon comes swimming up out of the gulf of blackness, a great dragonlike figure with the face of a just man (as fraud often has), Dante goes so far as to swear he really saw it; he documents his oath by the photographic quality of the images. The monster is said to come swimming up like a sailor who has dived down to loosen the anchor; when it rests its paws on the brink it sways there like a great scow drawn half up out of the water. The reactions of Dante the pilgrim to the world of his vision are vibrant and genuine; he is surprised himself by things that happen; at times he hardly believes what he sees (and in saying so he makes us believe in them all the more). Often he is alarmed and terrified; the flames are once so real that he refuses to enter them even at the bidding of Vergil, the reality so mordant that he turns his eyes away, presses his palms to his ears, is blinded and deafened by excessive sensation, faints when it becomes unbearable. Once he is rebuked by Vergil for his lively interest in a vulgarly attractive incident. The reality is so complete that it overflows the framework of the poem: several times Dante tells us that there are matters he has to skip because there is too much to describe, or something too overwhelming to describe. This reality extends to the inner world of the pilgrim, rich in psychological images, rich in a range of emotions often at fever heat. There is a memorable example in the speech on Italy in canto VI of the *Purgatorio*: grief-stricken, indignant, sarcastic, gentle, acrimonious, pitying, reproachful, savage, melancholy, vindictive, horror-stricken, wheedling, ironic, snide, sardonic, bemused, ferocious, commiserating—all this in the space of seventy-five lines!

We are not told how Athena and Hera made their *eidola*. Poetry too may seem to be made by a kind of magic, but we can isolate elements in its construction—elements which no poetry can exist without, though pure *logos*, as such, can get along quite well without them, as the passage from Aquinas has shown us. Poetry, like other kinds of human communication, is built on armatures of thought and feeling; these are present, and vigorously present, everywhere in Dante. I would like to turn, however, to three of the more magical elements—image, sound, and rhythm—and offer a little gallery of the sort of contribution each can make.

III

First of all, the image. "Nihil est in intellectu," say the philosophers, "quin prius fuerat in sensu" (Nothing is in the intellect without having been previously in [one of] the sense[s]). But for the poet there is no mere *prius*—no *before*; realities that move him remain in the senses or exalt the senses with them as they move into higher realms. Jacques Maritain has described art as the divination of the spiritual in the things of sense, and its expression in the things of sense. No poet has ever felt the necessity of this kind of expression more strongly than Dante, who says anything and everything in terms the senses can grasp. It is only through things of this world that we can understand the sublime truths: the Word itself had to be made flesh in order to reveal its nature to humanity. In canto IV of the *Paradiso,* Beatrice explains the language of accommodation to Dante: because it is only through sense perception that the intellect receives its data, abstract matters must be put for us in terms of the senses: so scripture shows the angels in human form and speaks of God as raising his hand against his enemy, or setting his foot on evil, or smiling on the good. Image then is no mere decoration, but a necessity of our very being. At the beginning of the *Inferno,* Dante is told he will be taken where he will hear and see certain things; he appeals to his memory to show its proper perfection by recalling what he saw.

Everything in his poem—from the very first sentence with its roadway and dark forest—is in terms of an image. We are shown Dante's whole universe so clearly that we can draw it; the journey itself, the narrative, is all concrete imagery. Every discussion, as we have seen, has its setting, and Dante is so precise about the physical appearance of his world that we, as readers, have no doubt he is reporting what he saw. Nothing happens in a void; we are told where the sun is, which way the shadows fall, whether the pilgrim swings around on his left or right foot. Dante uses the circumstantial method as cleverly as Defoe ever did, with a thousand little touches as convincing as the one that caught Allen Tate's attention: the centaur, before he begins to speak, lifts an arrow to comb the beard back from his lips. To describe the sudden deflating and collapse of a demon swollen with arrogance, what better image than of billowing sails that collapse in a tangle when the mast snaps suddenly? To show how the steadfast will tends always toward its goal, what better (and simpler) image than that of a flame, which strives always upward unless external force is brought to bear on it? To show the passionate appetite of the intellect for truth, and the peace it finds in attaining it, what better (and simpler) image than to say it rests in the truth like a wild beast in its den? One could easily find a hundred such examples of some abstract truth—the kind philosophy leaves as bare abstraction—put simply and vividly in terms of the commonest objects of sensation. Nothing is too common for Dante to dare to make use of: the real trick is to find an image which is down-to-earth but still surprising, not a farfetched image whose application we puzzle over.

Each part of the poem has its characteristic imagery. Hell is a series of lurid murky landscapes as full of diabolical life as a Hieronymus Bosch: a river of crimson blood, in one scene, washes through the glum twisted wood of the suicides, its undergrowth shattered by the fury of black dogs running toward stretches of sallow sand on which rains a yellow fire from above. From such scenes there is the sudden change to the predawn serenity on unearthly shores beneath the mountain of Purgatory; then the alternations of day and night in the clear air as we ascend; the Botticellian richness of the earthly paradise; and finally the ascent into the dazzling brilliance of heaven, where the imagery is all light and music and the dance.

The very punishments are images of the sins they punish. The fortune-teller wishes to look further ahead than God wills? Very well: his head is twisted backwards in a kind of terrible arthritis, so that the tears run down the gutter of his spine. The simonist wishes to invert values and put dishonest money in his purse? Very well: he is himself plunged head down in a wallet of rock, with flames playing on the soles of his feet in ghastly parody of the sacred tongues of fire.

In describing the sculptural friezes of the *Purgatorio*, Dante tells how they set up a quarrel between our senses. The clouds of incense are so real that our eye says *Yes* but our nose says *No*; the singers are so realistic that the eye says *Yes* to their singing, but the ear again refuses. Poetry does not have this limitation; the poet is free to use all senses, and we say *Yes* to all. Images of sight, hearing, smell, taste, touch, muscular sensation are all invoked: stones stir under the climbing feet; Charon's skiff, loaded with the dead, sinks deeper in the water; the sun is felt on the bridge of the nose or the left shoulder; as we look at a falling star, it swings our eyes around across the heavens. Even our muscles come alive and take part in the totality of the experience. Often we are involved physically without being aware of it; there are sensations of warmth and chill, of snugness and exposure in an image (from the *Paradiso*) that seems purely visual:

Come l'augello, intra l'amate fronde,
   posato al nido de' suoi dolci nati
   la notte che le cose ci nasconde,
che, per veder li aspetti dïsiati
   e per trovar lo cibo onde li pasca,
   in che gravi labor li sono aggrati,
previene il tempo in su aperta frasca,
   e con ardente affetto il sole aspetta,
   fiso guardando pur che l'alba nasca.[7]

IV

The second of what we have called the magical elements in
poetry is the sound of the words, an element whose utility has
rarely had much appeal for the philosophers, and which is
lost in translation. In contrasting the passages by Aquinas and
Dante we pointed out some lines in which sound alone con-
tributed to meaning by reinforcing it. It is not fanciful to
suppose that sound can make meaning more vivid by miming
or dramatizing it. For physiological reasons alone, based on
the muscular ease or effort with which they are produced,
sounds can suggest ease or difficulty, speed or slowness, light-
ness or weight, and a limited number of other physical
qualities; these suggestions can carry over, by analogy, be-
yond the physical, to such qualities as languor or agitation,
alacrity or lethargy, triviality or importance. It has always
been admitted that certain words—not all words—are phys-
ically akin to what they mean. Plato, sometimes more poet
than philosopher, devotes much of his *Cratylus* to this ques-
tion of word-sounds appropriate for certain effects: the
vibrating tongue that gives the rolled *r* of many languages, for
instance, is appropriate for words of movement, since "the
tongue was most agitated and least at rest in the pronuncia-
tion of this letter"; the *n* is sounded from within, and there-
fore goes with the notion of inwardness. Sir Herbert Read, in
his *English Prose Style,* thinks this kind of "vocal appropri-
ateness" the most important aspect of the problem of style.
The great writer, he believes, uses a high percentage of vo-
cally appropriate words. By these Read means not just the

obvious onomatopoetic words, like *hiss, whirr, cluck, bubble,* or even words whose lip and mouth movements are mimetic, like *blare, flare, brittle, creep, puddle, sling, globe,* but also those words that for less definable associations seem to charade their meaning, words like *glitter, swoon, mood, sheen, horror, smudge.*

Dante, who had classified words according to their sound, was sensitive to the connection between sound and meaning. In the *Inferno* he wishes he had

> le rime aspre e chiocce,
> come si converrebbe al tristo buco[8]

and time after time he does find the expressive sounds. When the lion appears to him in the first canto of the *Inferno,* its appearance is so terrifying that he says the very air seemed affrighted:

> sì che parea che l'aere ne temesse[9]

The tense accented *ae* in *aere* and the sibilants in *temesse* are like a thrilling hiss of terror in the air. When he describes how he falls to the ground after hearing the story of Paolo and Francesca, sounds dramatize the heavy thud:

> e caddi come corpo morto cade[10]

The lugubrious long *oo* sound of his *u*'s bring home to us the gloomy mood and ululations of the second circle of hell:

> Io venni in loco d'ogne luce muto,
> che mugghia come fa mar per tempesta[11]

Erich Auerbach in *Mimesis* has noted the "dark o-sounds" with which Farinata, to Dante's terror, suddenly speaks as he towers up from the tomb:

> "O Tosco che per la città del foco
> vivo ten vai così parlando onesto,
> piacciati di restare in questo loco"[12]

Sound can be emphatic, as in these lines from the *Purgatorio*, in which the *d . . . d . . . mor . . . d . . . mor . . .* and the *enti . . . enti . . .* bite in like the very teeth they tell of:

> pargoli innocenti
> dai denti morsi de la morte[13]

Dante seems to have remembered these repetitions when he varied them in the *Paradiso*:

> con quanti denti questo amor ti morde[14]

The sound can be harsh when the thought calls for it, as it does at the bottom of hell, where Ugolino gnaws like a dog on the skull of the hated archbishop:

> riprese 'l teschio misero co' denti,
> che furo a l'osso, come d'un can, forti[15]

A marvellously imitative example of expressive sound, one of the best in literature, is in the tenth canto of the *Purgatorio*, when Dante is describing how the proud move laboriously, doubled over under the weights they carry, and barely able to breathe:

> e qual più pazïenza avea ne li atti,
> piangendo parea dicer: "Più non posso."[16]

We pronounce *p* with a little puff of breath; here the six puffing *p*'s and the sighing sibilance of *posso* embody in the very sound the agony of the burdened sinner. An equally spectacular example of expressive sound is in the lines in which Buonconte da Montefeltro tells how he came to his death. He lost his life where a little river (by flowing into the Arno) loses its name; he had come there with his throat pierced in battle, fleeing on foot, no doubt weighted with armor, and staining the plain with his blood.

> Là've 'l vocabol suo diventa vano,
> arriva' io forato ne la gola,
> fuggendo a piede e 'nsanguinando il piano[17]

In the first line the name of the river vanishes in a mist of breathy *v*-sounds. But it is the last line that is unforgettable: how heavily the gouts of blood splash to the ground in those thick repeated nasals: *en, e'n, an, inan, an*! Dante uses sound as a painter uses pigment, applying whatever tints or hues the material would seem to ask for. The examples above have been harsh or gripping; they stand out perhaps because we expect poetry to be "musical" and are surprised—as we are meant to be—by expressive dissonance. Dante can be musical too when he has reason to be—perhaps no poet more so. For years I cherished, as a musical line, the one which describes Paolo and Francesca floating toward Dante like affectionate doves:

> Volan per l'aër dal voler portate[18]

Much chiming sound: *volan, voler; per, aër, voler; per, por.* So the line appears in the editions by Torraca, Provenzal, and others. Too bad that most editions prefer "vegnon per l'aere"!

There are many such passages as the allegro of these following lines from the *Paradiso,* with their quick and easy vowels, smooth *n*'s and *l*'s:

> Quale ne' plenilunïi sereni
> Trivïa ride tra le ninfe etterne[19]

or which have the musicality of the famous passage about the wayfarer at evening, lost in thoughts of home:

> Era già l'ora che volge il disio
> ai navicanti e 'ntenerisce il core
> lo dì c'han detto ai dolci amici addio[20]

V

The third of what we have called the magical elements of poetry—though the magic is perfectly natural—is rhythm. Rhythm has been thought of as the soul of poetry; it is the principle by which the *eidolon* becomes *empnoos*: draws breath, comes alive as it begins to pulsate. Like sound itself, it is lost in translation.

In talking about Dante's rhythm we could easily become entangled in technicalities. What follows is much simplified. Dante's lines are *endecasillabi*: hendecasyllabics, or eleven-syllable lines, which he considered richer in possibilities than other line-lengths then in use. But the syllables are not counted as written: when two vowels come together, even in different words, the first generally drops out of the count. It is said to be elided, rather as we might slur "the evil" into something like "th'evil." So *selva oscura* in the passage below counts as four syllables, not five; *via era* as three, not four. Lines that on the page may seem to have thirteen or more syllables are, by this way of counting, eleven-syllable lines. Dante is precise in keeping to this number—with one rare exception to be mentioned below.

He is not, however, writing syllabic lines, as Marianne Moore and W. H. Auden understood them. Dante's lines have a pattern of accents too; it is these that give the vigor and variety to his versification. There are two basic patterns. In the first, accents must fall on the sixth and tenth syllables, as in the first and third lines of the poem:

<blockquote>
Nel mezzo del cam̅min di nostra vi̅ta
mi ritrova̅i per u̅na selva oscu̅ra,
che la diritta vi̅a era smarri̅ta[21]
</blockquote>

In the second basic pattern, the accents must fall on the fourth, eighth, and tenth syllables, as in the second of the lines above. Most of the lines in the poem are cadenced in one of these two ways.

It is clear that the spoken lines have other accents besides these pivotal ones: on the first syllable of *mezzo* and *nostra* in line 1, for example. As readers with a background of poetry in English, we may be inclined to read the lines as if they were iambic pentameter with an extra syllable at the end, as in

To be or not to be, that is the question.

Many lines can be read that way; they tend to have an iambic drive. But Dante was not thinking 2-4-6-8-10; he was thinking 6-10 or 4-8-10. That left him a good deal of freedom with the rest of the line, and he made the most of it.

One liberty he takes with even the basic forms is to stress not 4-8-10 but 4-7-10. Hitting the unexpected seventh syllable comes as a thrill of surprise to the reader sensitized to the expectations of 4-8-10; it gives that syllable an importance it would not otherwise have. The poet can also get powerful results by stressing a syllable the meter does not normally give prominence to. Most of the expressive effects rhythm can achieve lie rather in deviations than in compliances. Deviations are possible only when there is a firm base to deviate from.

Dante, like all good poets, makes of his meter a system of dynamics that can reinforce meaning. One of the pleasures of reading him is in noticing what a variety of rhythmical resources he has. A few examples follow.

The 4-8-10 pattern shapes the line more firmly than the 6-10 one does. As more certain, it is more reassuring, and therefore appropriate for the serene and confident majesty with which Beatrice addresses Vergil in the second canto of the *Inferno*:

> I' son Beatrice che ti faccio andare;
> vegno del loco ove tornar disio;
> amor mi mosse, che mi fa parlare[22]

A shift of accent to the seventh syllable, however, touches a sensitive nerve in our awareness, as in the second line of the words inscribed over the entrance to hell:

> Per me si va ne la città dolente.
> per me si va ne l'etterno dolore,
> per me si va tra la perduta gente[23]

Lines 1 and 3 are firmly stressed 4-8-10 lines. Trying to read the second line in that way, we find ourselves wanting to say *etterNO*. But the word is not accented *etterNO;* it is *etTERno;* it is only by doing some violence to our expectations that we pronounce it correctly, by doing sort of a double take that focuses our attention, for a minisecond, on it. The eternity of *etterno*—and of hell—is made to vibrate in the very rhythm.

An abrupt and unexpected accent on the first syllable makes more startling the thunder clap that arouses Dante in the fourth canto:

> x
> Ruppemi l'alto sonno ne la testa
> un greve truono . . .[24]

The omission of the eleventh syllable, which Dante rarely allows himself, can give a sense of curtailment or loss. It is almost with a sob that Vergil cuts short the line in which he tells why he has lost the chance of going to heaven:

> e per null' altro rio
> lo ciel perdei che per non aver fé[25]

Putting strong accents in parts of the line that do not normally have weight can call attention to the accented word, as in Dante's dream of an eagle that descended like a thunderbolt:

> x
> terribil come folgor discendesse[26]

or in the line about the green-winged angels cleaving the air to attack such a serpent as tempted Eve:

> x   x
> Sentendo fender l'aere a le verdi ali[27]

Here the rhythm is strengthened by the vibrant repetition of *en . . . en . . . en.* Such rhythmical effects cannot be separated from sound effects. We saw another example of such synergy in the line about Ugolino's doglike gnawing on the skull of his enemy. The horror of the scene leads Dante to treat his meter with unusual brutality; it is hard to be sure what rhythm is intended in the savage

che furo a l'osso, come d'un can, forti[28]

VI

With such elements as image, sound, and rhythm the poet restores the flesh and blood of life to the shapely skeleton the philosopher discloses. We might also have spoken of his modes of diction and their modulation, the dynamics of his syntax and sentencing, the architectonic grandeurs and symmetries of part and whole.

Such apparently adventitious features seem trivial when compared to such inner ones as intelligence, inspiration, insight, vision. Axiologically perhaps they are, as particles of carbon or nitrogen seem trivial when weighed against the human spirit. But without such particles, even that spirit would cease to exist in any way the world could know it. Poetry, no matter how grand its thought or how burning its passion, cannot survive unless both find their incarnation.

It was for what Dante added to philosophy, for his *style*, that in his very first canto he expresses his grateful indebtedness to Vergil:

"O de li altri poeti onore e lume,
vagliami 'l lungo studio e 'l grande amore
che m'ha fatto cercar lo tuo volume"[29]

Mastery of the factors of style did not come easily, but only after " 'l lungo studio e 'l grande amore." For Dante, the poet is a *fabbro,* a blacksmith, a worker in stubborn materials. Toward the close of the *Paradiso* he says that thanks to the labor of many exhausting years he was able to write his poem—and then only because all heaven and earth had lent a hand. Earlier, in the *Purgatorio,* he had begged the favor of the Muses, reminding them of how he had suffered hunger, cold, and sleepless nights in their service. Through such efforts he was able to take us into the regions where his *eidola* wander, often larger than life, regions closed to philosophy, as his Paradise was closed to the noblest of the pagans—even to Aristotle himself, whom we might regard as the perfection of human reason.

Notes

1. ". . . with the name that most endures and most honors I was [famous] there" *Purg.* XXI, 85–86.
2. ". . . I am one who, when love inspires me, pay attention, and as he dictates within, so I go putting it into words" *Purg.* XXIV, 52–54.
3. *Creative Intuition in Art and Poetry* (New York: Pantheon Books, 1953; Meridian reprint, 1955), 55.
4. Ibid., 198.
5. ". . . since all things proceed from the divine will, all in their own way are inclined by appetite toward the good, but in different ways. For some are inclined toward the good by a natural disposition alone, without knowledge, as plants and inanimate bodies are; and such an inclination toward the good is called *natural* appetite. Others however are inclined toward the good with a kind of knowledge; not indeed so that they know the very nature of good, but they know some particular good, as the sense knows sweetness or whiteness or something of that sort. An inclination that follows this kind of knowledge is called *sensitive* appetite. Still others are inclined toward the good with the knowledge by which they know the very nature of the good, and that is a property of the intellect. And these are inclined toward the good in the most perfect way; not indeed as directed toward the good only by another, as those things which lack knowledge are; nor as directed toward a particular good only, as those that have only sense knowledge; but as inclined toward universal good itself; and this inclination is called *will*. . . ." *Summa Theologica,* Pars 1ᵃ, Quaest. LIX, Art. 1.
6. "Then she [Beatrice], after a sigh of pity, turned her eyes toward me with the look that a mother turns on her delirious child, and began: 'All things have an order among themselves, and this is the form that makes the universe like God. Here the

higher creatures see the sign of the eternal worth, which is the goal for which the ordinance touched on is made. In the order I'm speaking of, all natures are inclined, by different destinies, more or less near their principle; whence they move toward different ports over the great sea of being, each with an instinct given it which carries it on. This is what lifts the flame up toward the moon; this is the motive power in mortal hearts; this presses together and compacts the earth; nor does this bow impel only the creatures that have no intelligence, but also those that possess intellect and [the ability to] love. Providence, which sets all of this in order, with its light makes that heaven [the Empyrean, outside of space] always quiet in which the speediest sphere [the Primum Mobile] revolves, and that is where, as to a destined site, the power of that bowstring, which aims everything that it shoots toward a happy target, now impels us. It is true that, just as the form [which results] many times is not in accordance with what the art intended [to produce], because the material [it works with] is deaf [and doesn't] respond, so sometimes the creature, which has the power [through free will] to swerve elsewhere [even when] thus impelled, does depart from this course; and as one can see fire [lightning] fall from the cloud, so the original impulse, turned by false pleasure, falls to earth. You should not wonder, if I am correct, any more at your rising than at a river falling from a high mountain all the way down. It would really be something to wonder at if, with nothing to stop you, you had remained below—as wonderful as if, on earth, there were no motion at all in a living flame.' And then she turned her gaze back on the heaven" *Par.* I, 99–142.

7. "As the bird, among the leaves it loves, settled on the nest of its dear brood through the night that conceals things from us, who, so that she can see the look of them she longs to see, and so that she can find the food to feed them on—in which even hard work is pleasant to her—anticipates the time on an open branch, and with warm affection waits for the sun, gaze fixed for the dawn to break" *Par.* XXIII, 1–9.

8. ". . . rhymes rough and harsh, such as would be right for this dismal hole" *Inf.* XXXII, 1–2.

9. ". . . so that it seemed that the air was in fear of it" *Inf.* I, 48. Charles Singleton, who substantially follows Giorgio Petrocchi's critical edition done for the Società Dantesca Italiana, 1966–68, has "tremesse" (trembled) instead of "temesse." I prefer the

"temesse" of such older editions as those of Torraca, Momigliano, Provenzal, Sapegno, Grabher, and others, as poetically superior: more daring, less conventional.

10. ". . . and I fell as a dead body falls." *Inf.* V, 142.

11. ". . . I came into a place mute [devoid] of all light, that bellows as the sea does in a storm" *Inf.* V, 28—29.

12. "O Tuscan, who through the city of fire proceeds alive, speaking so decently, may it please you to stop in this place" *Inf.* X, 22—24.

13. ". . . the little innocent ones, bitten by the teeth of death" *Purg.* VII, 31—32.

14. ". . . with how many teeth this love fastens on you" *Par.* XXVI, 51.

15. ". . . he again seized the miserable skull with his teeth, which were tough, like a dog's, on the bone" *Inf.* XXXIII, 77—78.

16. ". . . and the one who showed the most suffering by his appearance, seemed to say, weeping, 'I can't bear any more' [Literally, 'More I am not able']" *Purg.* X, 138—39.

17. ". . . there where its name disappears, I came with my throat pierced, fleeing on foot and staining the plain with blood . . ." *Purg.* V, 97—99. Singleton has "sanguinando"; most editors prefer the bloodier " 'nsanguinando."

18. ". . . fly through the air, carried by their desire" *Inf.* V, 84.

19. ". . . as on the quiet nights of the full moon Trivia [Diana, the moon] laughs among the eternal nymphs [the stars]" *Par.* XXIII, 25—26.

20. "It was now the hour that turns backward the desire of those who sail away, and softens their heart, the day when they have said farewell to their dear friends" *Purg.* VIII, 1—3.

21. "In the middle of the journey of our life I came to myself in a dark wood, for the straight way was lost" *Inf.* I, 1—3.

22. "I am Beatrice who send you; I come from a place I long to return to; love moved me, which makes me speak" *Inf.* II, 70—72.

23. "Through me one goes into the suffering city; through me one goes into eternal sorrow; through me one goes among the lost people" *Inf.* III, 1—3.

24. "A heavy roll of thunder broke the deep sleep in my head" *Inf.* IV, 1—2.

25. ". . . and for no other fault did I lose heaven than for not having faith" *Purg.* VII, 7—8.

26. ". . . terrible as lightning it descended" *Purg.* IX, 29.

27. ". . . hearing the air split by the green wings" *Purg.* VIII, 106.

28. See n. 15.
29. "O honor and light of the other poets, may the long study and great love that made me search through your volume avail me" *Inf.* I, 82–84.

On Making an Anthology

Why do so at all?

Because why not? An anthology is a collection of poems. Collecting things needs little defense; we recognize it as something childish but very natural. Like the pack rat and the crow, people, from childhood on, are by nature collectors. Of almost everything, in a world so largely made up of collectibles: pieces of rock, old bottle glass, cast-iron toys, dead butterflies. As a boy, I collected cigar bands, scuffing the Chicago curbs, head down, an eye out for those crinkled bits of gold and crimson, with their foreign mottoes and tiny portraits of exotic señoritas. Sometimes crouching, almost underfoot, on a busy sidewalk in the December winds to chip a rare specimen out of the frozen gutter, its ice marbled with the ocher veinings of those who preferred to chaw and spurt their tobacco rather than light up.

Even earlier, almost without knowing it, I had begun to collect poems. I must have been only four or so when I heard my father, in a melancholy surf-booming voice, intone: "Break, break, break, On thy cold gray stones, O sea. . . ." Probably my first poem. Others came too in the same offhand fashion. They were not neatly classified and coddled in notebooks, as the colorful *La Violeta* and *Belle of Monterey* were; mostly they were left to shift for themselves in any old corner of the memory, turning up at intervals when I was looking for something else.

From *The Harper Anthology of Poetry* (New York: Harper and Row, 1981).

There are anthologists, I am told, content to ply the shears and slather paste. I found it urgent to establish something like physical contact with the poems; to know them as they first came into the world. Easy enough with contemporary poems—those of Eliot, or Stevens, or Auden—which I saw in the pages of magazines or in books come freshly off the press in smart new jackets. But making contact with books that came out in 1855 or 1798 or 1633 or 1557 took more doing. Even so, not satisfied with what some editor told me the poem was, I felt I had to make sure of it before I could count it as a catch. It mattered to handle the books, to turn their pages, to see and *feel* them as the poet's contemporaries had done. This compulsion took me to the rare book rooms of famous libraries, especially of the Houghton and Widener at Harvard and the Newberry in Chicago. For years this was a pleasant pastime—cleaner too than chipping at the mottled ice.

This dusty industry had its pleasures. It is a satisfaction to be able to say: "I have known this poem from its birth" and not merely "I have taken this poem on faith from an accredited editor." How different the poems look, there on their old stamping grounds, from the computerized uniformity they assume in the columns of modern reprints.

Can anyone pick up John Donne's packed and huddled little *Poems* of 1633 without feeling something like an electrical tingle? Or George Herbert's *The Temple,* of the same year—a humble three by five inches in small type, a book hardly larger than the palm you hold it in? Very different, half a century later, the generous volume of Andrew Marvell's *Miscellaneous Poems,* complete with portrait—but then Marvell was a "Late Member of the Honorable House of Commons." (Not one of these great names had a single book—not even the slimmest of chapbooks—published during the writer's lifetime.)

Skipping to a later century, what a luxury to open the 1819 edition of Cantos I and II of Byron's *Don Juan* and to find, on a page larger than this one, two leisurely stanzas, instead of the four to seven per page we are likely to get in a busy modern edition. Or to pick up a copy of the *Lyrical Ballads* of 1798, in which Wordsworth and Coleridge redirected the course of poetry, and to find written in it the name of an early owner: "A. Tennyson. Christmas day, 1838." Or to leaf through the copy of Herman Melville's *Battle-Pieces* that belonged to Mrs. Melville and to find a handwritten revision that gives a better reading than the printed one.

Literary trivia, some of this, but trivia high in human interest. What would have been mere literary texts, had I been willing to snip and paste, had now become Memorable Experiences.

With a few poets I had the richer excitement of handling their very manuscripts. At Yale, the little handwritten book of poems that Edward Taylor left in 1729 with instructions to his heirs that it was not to be printed, its four hundred pages of cramped and thorny script denser and smaller than single-spaced typing. Almost without readers for two hundred years. At Harvard, the manuscripts of Jones Very's poems, some scrawled off in pencil, apparently as they came to him, with abbreviations and without punctuation, some written with deliberate care for the printer's eye. At Harvard also, the manuscript book in which Frederick Goddard Tuckerman wrote out, on lined paper, his grief-stricken sonnets, with afterthoughts and revisions written between the lines. Most moving of all, at Harvard and Amherst the very packets that Emily Dickinson left threaded together in her bureau drawer: hard to believe those were my fingers on the page where hers had lingered.

This turning over of faded pages was done for my own reassurance and pleasure; I had no thought of passing on to today's readers the spellings of yesterday, in which the words seem to come not from the poet's living throat but from Ye Olde Antique Shoppe.

All poets were modern poets when they wrote; their readers were contemporary readers. They would have seen, in 1609, nothing unusual in the look of Shakespeare's Sonnet 73, which begins:

That time of yeeare thou maiſt in me behold,
When yellow leaues, or none, or few doe hange
Vpon thoſe boughes which ſhake againſt the could,
Bare rn'wd quiers, where late the ſweet birds ſang

For most of us, this presentation impedes the passionate immediacy of the poem; no matter how ſweetly the birds ſing, they will never quite be real. All easy enough for scholars, but one should not have to become a scholar to read, without these inky tics and twitches, great poems of the past. We can give our readers Elizabethan spelling; we cannot give them Elizabethan eyes.

What came from the poet's pen was clear and fresh and *modern;* I would like it, as far as possible, to look that way today. Having once made sure what the poet wrote, I felt free to update spelling and punctuation (which the poet, or the printer, did not use consistently) toward what the poet might have used if writing now. A wish to present the poems in their immediacy has led me also to reduce the capital letters of which writers and printers made profuse but inconsistent use during the seventeenth century and later, as in Marvell's "On a Drop of Dew":

> See how the Orient Dew
> Shed from the Bosom of the Morn,
> Into the blowing Roses

This begins to look too much like a swanky ad, perhaps for a perfume labelled Orient Dew.

And by what authority, no doubt some readers wonder, are *you* telling *us* what the best poems are? Not *telling,* quite. What I am doing is offering. Anthology: ἀνθολογία—a gathering of flowers. An anthology is a bouquet. One may of course quarrel with a bouquet, find it in good taste or in bad. But I have not made these choices wholly on my own. Though this is an anthology of poetry in English, my taste and expectations have been formed on a broader base: on human nature as it expressed itself also in other languages and over centuries more remote than any covered here. I have had my long-time advisers; let me introduce them.

For many years I have been hearing voices. Mostly they came to me in English, sometimes as fresh and crisp as today's headlines, sometimes broad or drawled or in a brogue, as if from a far country across the sea, or from a century long gone, when shadowy figures danced around the Maypole. They came in other languages too; sometimes in ancient Greek or its island dialects, or in the resonant Latin that echoed off the marble of the Colosseum or the pillars of a Sabine farm. Sometimes they came, with music, in the language of the troubadours near Fonqualquier or Ventadorn, or of those who wandered south across the Pyrenees, or on into Andalucía. At times they came in indignant Tuscan with its dusky aspirates. Or they came in French, the *bon bec* Villon loved. They came from tough Castile or soft Galicia. Some later came from Weimar.

The voices I heard were those of poems talking. Telling me the human secrets we all share. Telling me about themselves, and what they were. These voices have been my advisers over many years. I still turn to them with a question when I hear a new voice and wonder if it is genuine or only one of the many phantoms that come like mayflies with the season. From whatever century, in whatever language, what they said was much the same. They told me it is not true that humanity evolved from some lower form toward the end of the 1950s. Proofs of humanity, they told me, go back many centuries before that time; voices vibrantly human can be heard from the time of Sappho, of Catullus, of the Archpriest, of the Anglo-Saxon minstrels who wrote "The Seafarer" and "The Wanderer," of the anonymous medieval poets who in the Harley Lyrics sang the joy and pain of lovers in the spring.

The voices told me that humankind changes little as the centuries pass and that the same scenes are played over and over again. They told me that we have eyes that make the empty air prismatic; that we have ears that make the dumbest sound waves speak. That we have other sensors too—for warmth, for smell, for texture and the contours of the world.

Through these, part by part, the universe takes shape within our heads. So consciousness awakes and with it passion, enough to singe or freeze the very flesh. Such abundance of conscious life that skull and breast cannot contain it, any more than a volcano can its lava.

They said that with a poet all this inner seething converts to words—to shapes of breath that leave the body to report on the glowing gulfs within. It is breath not blown away, as most breath is; it is breath trying to create for itself, out of words that have color and weight and reek and gusto, a body like the body it just left. We are none of us, the poems mocked, mere disembodied spirits. We must have, as your English poet said, a local habitation and a name. Must have imagery, as you yourselves have retina and eardrum and fine fingertips for feeling. Must speak in throat- and lip-shaped phrases, must move in rhythms as your heart does, on tides for which your breathing sets the tempo. Must have a skeleton of healthy sense, a skin in touch with textures of the world. We are made, they told me, in *your* image; we have no other archetype but you.

They taught me that poems are good to the degree that—while existing as voice alone—they can beam the intensities of our nature into the world of words. When I ask them what quality they think essential, they answer: *life!* They repeat *vitality, intensity.* Inertness, dullness, they warn, are the qualities most alien to their nature. Poems have the kind of life we have when most alive, the kind that sets the eye aglow and cheek aflush, that makes the fists clench or the fingertips caress. The poet's knack is to transfuse that vitality into words, to make words so resonant, so vibrant with the *poet's* feeling that they take on a life and behavior of their own, begin to interact in strange ways—loving and cantankerous—with one another, doing with their shape and heft and sound and rhythm what our bodies do with changing pressure in the arteries, electric currents through the galaxies of nerve. A poem is a success to the degree that it transfuses the passionate complexity of our being—our body-and-soul being, not dry mind alone—into a body-and-soul made all of words as palpable as things are. Men and women must have written such poems almost from the dawn of consciousness on earth, though none remain to us as old as their ice-age animals in caves are. Of those that do, the many myriads, this anthology can give only a selection from poems written in one language over a small part of human history.

For me, then, poetry has been defined by poems themselves, and not by a passel of critics waving butterfly nets with labels like *provenance* and *genre*. What poems have told me has to do with the essence of poetry and not with its changing shapes. I have not bothered them merely with frivolous questions like "Is this a proper sonnet?" or "Is this an accepted form of heroic couplet?" The breath of poetry, like everything else in the universe, does indeed come forth in shape and rhythm, but in no prescribed ones. Often it finds its own, as nature does. In this it is far freer than the heart, that fuddy-duddies on in old iambic; far freer than the breath, still timed to pulses metered in pentameter.

We like to collect things. And we like to show our collections to others—that too is childish but very natural. But we show them only if we feel there is something special about them— one unique piece of rock, one bottle of oddly vivid green. I have become fond of my collection of poems, even take pride in it. This seems an allowable pride; none of these poems is of my writing; the pride I take is in the work of others. When I read them I feel like the old woman in William Carlos Williams's poem, munching the plums from her paper bag:

> They taste good to her
> They taste good
> to her. They taste
> good to her

These poems taste good to me—I have included nothing only because urged by someone else to do so, least of all because urged by a computerization of modern preferences or by the constituency of some currently influential poet.

Many anthologies have a solemn air; we might go so far as to say, a prune-faced look. As if the garden of poetry, which should be a Garden of Earthly Delights, had a sign over the gate proclaiming ENJOYMENT STRICTLY FORBIDDEN. As great a poet as Robert Frost often used the word *fun* in speaking of poetry. Too many anthologies do not see it that way. NO LAUGHTER ON THE PREMISES. Though poetry expresses the full range of our human nature, it is not so with them: our sense of humor and our sense of nonsense have been exiled from this garden. And yet it was the sensible Horace who said, "Dulce est desipere in loco," which we might English as "There are times when it's fun to act silly." This too is a well-authenticated part of our nature, and quite possibly a safety valve against our darker energies.

A second fault is that too many anthologies favor the star system. To shift our figure to a more worldly field, they favor great corporations over small businesses; they like Big Names, prefer cartels, monopolies, conglomerates to the friendly corner wordsmith. If we look over the whole range of poetry in English, we find that many of the most charming, poignant, and memorable poems have come from bit-part poets who never achieved superstar status, from poets like Dyer, Tichborne, Greene, Southwell, Greville, Dekker, Godolphin, Cartwright, Cowley, Rochester, Barnes, Beddoes, Emily Brontë, Clough. Not one of these is given a cameo role, or even the time of day, in too many anthologies.

A good poem is always in some way surprising; so is an anthology that is really alive. Too many anthologies have few surprises; they tend to stay in well-worn ruts and take no chances. If we stick to the middle of the road, however, we will know very little about the countryside, especially about its dewiest and greenest coverts. Why not fling over the reins now and then and do something simply for the wild fun of it, as poets themselves have been known to do?

Too many anthologies will surprise us, though not pleasantly, in their downgrading of American poets. Possibly we could do without Freneau—possibly. Much more puzzling is the omission of Jones Very and Frederick Goddard Tuckerman, who wrote some of the best poems of their century. Sometimes not even such important American pioneers as Masters, Sandburg, Lindsay are to be found. It is embarrassing to mention what vogue poets of a later decade are there in place of them, possibly because, with contemporary poets, too many anthologies jettison their exclusivist policy for the use of the scattergun. Unable to make up their mind which ones belong, they include a little of everybody whose name has flashed, however wanly and fitfully, across the contemporary skies.

Of the way anthologists fumble when dealing with their contemporaries we have no lack of horrible examples from the past. One might think that Sir Arthur Quiller-Couch, after weighing the best poems of many centuries for *The Oxford Book of English Verse,* could have dealt judiciously with the poets of his own time. And yet he puts, ranked with the mighty dead, such names as Henry Cust, the Honorable Emily Lawless, Norman Gale, John Swinnerton Phillimore, and Wilfred Thorley. In an authoritative anthology of *The Younger American Poets* published in 1904, we find such names as Frederick Lawrence Knowles, Alice Brown, Arthur Upson; the editor regrets the absence of Holman F. Day, Virginia Cloud, Josephine Dodge Daskam. And who are among the missing? Robinson, then age thirty-five. Robert Frost, then age thirty.

Such examples should be a warning, but they never are. Whenever we pick up an anthology with such a title as *The Hundred Best Contemporary Poets,* we can be sure it will contain a very high proportion of Thorleys, Phillimores, and Daskams. And quite possibly no Robinsons or Frosts. It is stirring to think that somewhere there is a brilliant young poet, belaurelled with Guggenheims and darling of many an arts council, o'er whose shoulders even now the benevolent Muse inclines and, beaming on that brow that might be the young Apollo's, vows with maternal pride, "He will be the Holman F. Day of his era!"

Our nearsightedness with our contemporaries tends to magnify mediocrities. On the other hand, as the biographies have shown, many of the best poets throughout the centuries have been invisible in their own time. Many have written their letter to the world only to have it lie in the dead-letter offices of posterity for decades, or even centuries. The odds are not impossible that the young man or woman who will one day be recognized as the greatest poet of our time has—like Donne, Herbert, and Marvell—not published a single chapbook all life long.

When his work, so often belittled, is completed, the anthologist is left with this reflection to console him: his drudgery has done what little it could do to make amends for some of the omissions and injustices of the past, and perhaps, just here and there, it has brought light to some small corners of the darkness.

English Poetry

The First Three Centuries

Nowadays we would think it rather backward of anyone to look down on the art of the Middle Ages. For finally, though it took some centuries to do so, we have learned to look at it, learned to see the beauty that was always there in those honey-colored ivory plaques and book covers of the twelfth century, in the goggling fantastic capitals of St. Trophime, in the kaleidoscopic jewel-studded enamelling on copper, in the almost musical folds of the drapery of the polychromed madonnas and angels of the thirteenth century, in the silver gilt and rock-crystal of many an altar vessel, in the ceiling-high tapestries with their gaudy young folk courting in fields of a thousand flowers, in the whimsical detail of drawings on the margins of Gothic manuscripts, or in all those Books of Hours, the Belles Heures, or the Très Riches Heures, or in the miniature Hours of Jeanne d'Evreux—beauty of detail and ensemble, from the little boxwood triptychs with fifty animated figures carved in four square inches, to the great cathedrals more than a century high.

The charm of medieval music too has finally reached us. But what of the poetry?—those lyrics as well turned as ivory, as bright with detail as any cloisonné, as craftily planned as the triptychs or the most cunning Book of Hours? Of these we still use the words that some centuries ago were used of the art: how Gothic, how ungainly, how ill-proportioned, how didactic they seem to many. But only because they are something we have not yet learned to see, not yet learned to hear. And this may be because poetry, unfamiliar poetry, does not come to us with the immediate sensuous delight of art or music. The language looks strange, as the proportions of the art once did. But it is not nearly as strange as it looks—these are difficulties we can overcome almost in minutes, instead of the months we are willing to give to a foreign language. Suppose we try, though. Suppose we work a little at those sculptured locks until the strange doors swing for us. What we are likely to find, though seen freshly and in new perspective, is ourselves.

If Shakespeare, in 1600, perhaps helped by Prospero, had been able to look forward to the poetry of our time, and then had been able to look backward to the earliest poems in English, the distance behind him would have been greater than the distance before. What is probably the earliest complete English lyric to survive was found, in our own century, on the margin of a cathedral manuscript, scrawled there by some unhappy lover nearly eight hundred years ago:

> Theh thet hi can wittes fule-wis
> of worldles blisse nabbe ic nout

The language does look strange to us. Put into modern English in a way that would hint how it sounded as a poem, it might read:

> Though I've a clever head, I know,
>   Joy in this world have I none,
> And all for a lady—of those who go
>   In hall and chamber, the fairest one!
> When first she became another's, though,
>   Locked in a castle wall of stone,
> I was a ruined man, struck low:
>   All skin and bone.
>   No one now can encourage me
>   To live, be happy. I'd rather be
>   Down with the dead tomorrow.
>   I can well say this of me:
>   Heavy hangs my sorrow.

Written down about 1200, this would probably have been composed in the reign of Richard the Lion-Hearted, who had been king for the ten years before, though he had spent only a few months of that time in England and made no effort to learn the language. Richard spoke Provençal and no doubt French. Several of the English kings who followed him would have had trouble even getting along in English, for French had been the language of the court since William the Conqueror came over in 1066 with his Normans and whatever other Frenchmen he had rounded up—not enough of them to overrun the country, but enough to impose their language on official circles. For about three centuries English was a depressed vernacular in the trilingual country, with the court speaking the kind of French that went its own way as Anglo-Norman after the loss of Normandy in 1204, and with the clergy and the learned professions working in Latin. Even poems in English were written along French lines and under French influence: Chaucer himself has been called a French poet writing in English. It must have taken some independence for him to do so; there is no clear evidence that his king, Edward III, could himself speak English with any ease.

We may be surprised that one of our earliest lyrics has so elaborate a rhyme-scheme—so much more formal, more canny, than one sees in the magazines today. But Richard was Provençal; his century was the century of the great troubadours. The king himself was one of them; many others he knew. His mother, who survived him, was the famous Eleanor of Aquitaine, whom Bernart de Ventadorn, the greatest of the troubadours, had been in love with—it was said—and followed to England for a while when she married Henry II. The early English poem is very like a Provençal lyric in its richness of rhyme; whoever wrote it *could* have met Bernart, could certainly have known his poems or the work of other Provençal troubadours. At times the Provençal influence was strong at court, and, because of the Bordeaux wine trade, in commercial circles—so strong that it aroused protests from the French and English, who felt discriminated against in favor of the foreigners. The writer could have known this poetry, the earliest and probably the best love poetry in the European tradition—but the chances are that its influence reached him at second hand, through the Provençalizing poets of northern France.

Our little blues song from about 1200 comes also out of the foreign cult of courtly love: the longtime and from-afar-off worship of an unavailable and unnamed lady, without whose mercy the disconsolate lover foresees his death. Englishmen did not die for love as often as the more susceptible southerners threatened to; their attitude has more often been that of Shakespeare's scornful Rosalind: "Men have died from time to time, and worms have eaten them, but not for love." But the poem also comes from the realities of medieval marriage: the lady, apparently of the aristocracy, may have been an important heiress who was married off—if not indeed carried off—by force. She is now locked in a castle, and a secure one of improved construction: the early Norman castles had been built of wood on a mound of earth.

The poem is unusual in being an indoor poem. Most of the early lyrics, like "Mirie it is," find all outdoors in sympathy, or not in sympathy, with the lover. One common type, the *chanson d'aventure,* has the poet riding out on a spring day—and a romantic thing happens to him on his way somewhere. The spring poem, or *reverdie* (poem of regreening) was by no means just a literary convention. Only in our discouraged era has April, for some of us, become the cruellest month. But if one had spent the long weeks of winter in a medieval castle—not to speak of the humbler possibilities—with unglazed windows, with only an open fire for central heating, sometimes right in the middle of the hall (for chimneys were an innovation early in our period) with nothing to eat but salted or smoked meat from scraggly animals slaughtered months before, some dried beans or peas or shrivelled apples on the side—if one spent a medieval winter like this, with no place to go, no place to be alone with a special friend—then spring was really a time of release and exuberance. To be able to get out into the woods again, to be able to sing "Sumer is icumen in," must have been as exciting a change as a trip to Fort Lauderdale or Bora Bora today.

Much early English poetry, then, was a kind of import.

Some also showed Latin influence: it tried to be like either the rhymed and accentual hymns of the church, known even in Anglo-Saxon days, or like the earthier lyrics of the wandering scholars and their like—the *Carmina Burana,* for example— lyrics which tended to be in the same meters as the hymns and sometimes burlesqued them, the way "As I went on Yol day" is a kind of burlesque of the liturgy.

With so varied a linguistic background, it is not surprising that a poem might be a cloisonné of two or three languages; the sprightly "Of one that is so fayr and bright" slips easily back and forth from English to Latin, like a poem only half translated. Or when poems were completely translated, per- haps for the enlightenment of the humbler churchgoers, they might keep the original rhythm and the original rhyming, so that Latin patterns went into the shaping of English verse.

But was all poetry of the time, we might wonder, Latinized or Frenchified? What had happened to the native lyrics— those of the long Anglo-Saxon tradition—those rawboned rhythms sinewy with alliteration, indifferent to rhyme and syllable-count? Such lyrics there must have been, even though the extant manuscripts show nothing but some rather long and lugubrious elegies. After 1066 the whole tradition disap- pears for about three centuries, to surface spectacularly dur- ing the lifetime of Chaucer with the social indignation of *Piers Plowman,* the witty elegance of *Sir Gawain and the Green Knight.* Poems that Chaucer himself might not have liked, might have thought not his kind of poetry, might indeed have found outlandish and obscure: there were English poems written then that he would have found about as difficult as we do today. But the native poetry, even while submerged, let itself be felt in the melancholy of such poems as "Foweles in the frith" and the later "Lollai, lollai, litel child," which seems more pagan than Christian in its gloomy view of existence. Technically the native strain encouraged that fondness for alliteration that runs through so much medieval poetry (ex- cept for that of Chaucer and his followers). And the mo- mentum of its strongly emphasized accents probably affected even the way in which the French syllabic line was taken over.

At that time English poetry had its chance at the purely syllabic system that has come into vogue in our own century—had its chance and turned it down because the old rhythms were running too strongly in the blood, turned it down in favor of the emphatic accents that pulse through all the Germanic languages, Anglo-Saxon and modern English among them. Some writers never did convert successfully to the newer measures: when trying the Chaucerian lines they would let rugged traces of the older system crop out, giving us a strange broken-backed rhythm that was neither the one thing nor the other.

Some of the best poems in the continental manner—some really fine poems—were found in the British Museum manuscript known as Harley 2253: one of the few manuscript collections that have come down to us. It seems to have been made, perhaps around 1320, in a religious house, by a monk who wanted a collection of pieces he had heard recited or sung by entertainers or wandering scholars or just anyone who happened along with a poem. Poems did get around. Highways were crowded in the Middle Ages: houses were so uncomfortable one might as well be roughing it on the road. In the Harley lyrics we find what have continued to be the characteristic English rhythms: stressed and unstressed syllables alternating, not mechanically but with a lilt, on the whole freely iambic (iambic is *lub-dúbb,* like the heartbeat), in lines of from two to seven stresses, including—before Chaucer found it—some of the five-stress lines that have been a staple of our rhythm ever since. The rhyme schemes are as elaborate as in our rather plain little poem of 1200. But the poems are far warmer, more varied, more musical, have far more sense of the world around: of landscape and weather and dress and the color of a girl's eyes. Though the stanza contour may have been foreign, the accent and the vigor of the rhythm are English—and so is the feeling for the realities of life and love. There is little abstract pining here. A few of the poems— "Alysoun," "Lenten is come with love to toune"—are as good as anything of the sort ever written. The typical Elizabethan pastoral, with its happy babble of "Hey, nonny nonny," can be a poor thing in comparison. Some of the religious poems are impressive too: "I syke when I singe" has a stark dignity like that of Masaccio's crucifixion—as the later "I have laborede sore" recalls the athletic hero of Piero della Francesca's Resurrection at San Sepulcro.

The Harley lyrics are a more precious inheritance than the lyrics of Chaucer, whose genius for narrative hardly shows to advantage in his little poems, which seem a bit thin, a bit literary—"the note," he says of "Now welcom, somer," "ymaked was in France." Chaucer may have written with more emotion in the "many a song and many a lecherous lay" which he says were his, and for which he asks forgiveness in the retraction at the end of the *Canterbury Tales*. But these have been lost. In the extant lyrics, he falls into a kind of lovely artificiality with his ballades and roundels and rhyme-royal stanzas; there is nothing to compare with the lyric sweep of his own *Troilus and Criseyde*. In the next century, in which Chaucer's influence proved largely a curse, the English poems of Charles d'Orléans are an exception: less polished than the Chaucer of the lyrics but more colloquial, more immediate. It is strange that, of the two, Chaucer seems the more French. Charles has long had an illustrious name as a French poet; only in our time has he been recognized as a poet in English too. Captured at the battle of Agincourt in 1415, he spent the next twenty-five years in England as a well-treated but well-guarded prisoner. It is hardly surprising that at the end of that time he was released "speaking better Englishe than Frenche," as the chronicler Hall tells us—for by the fifteenth century English was the language one heard in England. The English diction of Charles is somewhat quaint and clumsy, somewhat overidiomatic, as if he were trying to compensate for his foreignness. But what he gives us is the sense of a real human voice dealing with the realities of his existence. Even the later French poems, written on his return to France, seem to have been humanized by his English experience: he might have reversed Chaucer's credit line and said that the note was made in England.

The fifteenth century, overshadowed by Chaucer's academic imitators, is one of the poorer patches in English poetry, except for the beginnings of the ballad, and except for the carol, which, native as it quickly became, was itself of French origin. Though we have some earlier examples, it is in the fifteenth century that carols really come into their own. The *carole* was originally, most researchers agree, the ring dance of the folk: a four-line stanza—the commonest form—would be sung by a ring leader while the dancers paused to listen (*stanza*, which means "room" in modern Italian, meant "a place for stopping"); the fourth line, by its rhyme, would cue them into the refrain, which all would sing as they danced, circling to the left. (Only witches danced counterclockwise.) Early carols were not Christmas carols; had, in fact, associations of paganism and revelry disturbing to the clergy. It seems with reason: in 1574 in Aberdeen, fourteen women were charged with "playing, dancing, or singing of filthy carols on Yule day." There are carols too of social indignation— protest carols—such as "Peny is a hardy knyght," which complains about the power money has to subvert law and justice. Carols were for times of festivity; since there was more occasion for festivity during the twelve days of Christmas than on other holidays, more carols were sung then. By and by they came to be associated with Christmas, and took on a Christmas coloring. One sensible critic has pointed out that there were few Easter carols because Easter, after the winter, was in a season of depleted larders—there would have been little to celebrate with. At any rate, as early as 1520 sheets of "Kesmes corals" were sold in England; in time they were thought of as just songs rather than as songs for dancing, and today none but the scholars care whether the French word *carole* comes from the Greek *choraules*, "a flute player," or from the Latin *corolla*, "a little wreath or garland."

Most of the poems we have been talking about were influenced by poetry written abroad. As for the native influence, perhaps no poem gives a better idea of the pre-1066 manner than the hot-tempered "Swarte smekyd smethes" of about 1450, another lyric of protest or indignation, storming at the moonlighting blacksmiths who keep people awake with their clangor. Here is the old verse line with a pause in the middle, and with two of the syllables in each half-line heavily whanged by both alliteration and the natural accent of the words. The effect, brawny and boisterous, is determined by beat alone. Unemphatic syllables are disregarded in the count and fall where they may, so that there is something abrupt and rugged about the movement of the line—an effect certainly appropriate for this irascible poem about the decibel level. More often when the old-fashioned four-beat line turns up, it is softened by varying the alliteration and by regularizing—giving a lilt to—the rhythm by rationing the unstressed syllables so that never more than two come between the beats. Maybe two, maybe one, maybe none—but almost never the three or four we find in "Swarte smekyd smethes." The newer music of the four-beat line is seen in one of the most spirited of the *Ubi sunt* (*Where are . . . ?*) poems:

> Whére beth théy   bifóren us wéren,
> Hoúndes ládden   and hávekes béren?

and it is the typical carol rhythm:

> Hónnd by hónnd we schúlle us táke
> And jóye and blísse schúlle we máke

We might think of this line, common in English poetry ever since, as a fusion between the drive and energy of the Anglo-Saxon line and the cadence and measure of the French-inspired one. It has endured, sometimes as the sprung rhythm of Gerard Manley Hopkins and Mother Goose, sometimes as the "loose iambic" of Robert Frost. E. E. Cummings, like many others, was fond of it.

No doubt there were other influences besides the Latin and French: Irish, Welsh, Scandinavian. Touches of a far-off Celtic strangeness have been sensed in "Maiden in the mor lay," one of the worldly, perhaps even pagan, poems that the Bishop of Ossory, before 1360, tried to Christianize in his famous Red Book by writing edifying new words for the familiar music. This brings home to us as well as anything the fact that the lyric poetry of the Middle Ages is generally classified as religious or secular. Far more religious poems survive than nonreligious; it was the monks who had the quills and ink and parchment, and who wrote down most of what was written down. No doubt they knew, probably they composed, worldly poems, but they must have been hesitant about using expensive vellum to preserve them in the monastery library, what with a religious superior probably breathing down their necks now and then as they worked.

Even so, the two kinds of poetry did not repel each other; mutual influences were many. Love poems sometimes refer to the loved one with religious fervor; they swear a devotion in terms that seem more appropriate to the Virgin. More surprisingly, religious poems use the language of earthly love: the Virgin is described as a glamorous young girl, perhaps even as the devotee's sweetheart. In such Christian poems as "I synge of a mayden" or "Ther is no rose of swych vertu" there may be ancient pagan inklings of a nature queen, some goddess of trees and blossoms and the spring. No English poet, however, went so far as a French artist did: there is no better example of the way heaven could be brought down to earth in the fifteenth century, or of what Huizinga calls the "dangerous association of religious with amatory sentiments," than Jehan Foucquet's painting of his half-topless madonna, undressed in the height of fashion. Tradition, which may be only gossip sanctified by time, says she was modeled, in all of her "blasphemous boldness," on the king's mistress.

In 1224 the Franciscan friars, true *ioculatores Domini,* had come to England, full of their founder's spirit of joy and love. They had a good deal to do with the development of the religious carol; a fervor like theirs helped kindle those passionate poems of mystical love-longing that Richard Rolle and his followers are credited with in the fourteenth century. The fervor is expressed with less extravagance in the better poems of a generation or two later: poems like "Quia amore langueo" and "Christ makith to man a fair present," which keeps under musical control its hymn to the violent and mysterious irrationality of love. The fervor is probably expressed best of all, because most simply, in two early fifteenth-century poems, which E. K. Chambers thinks "reach the highest level of which medieval poetry was capable": "I synge of a mayden" and "Adam lay ibowndyn." Both have the freshness of folk song—but one would guess they were written by a literary artist of tact and resourcefulness: generally it takes self-conscious processes of some complexity to produce anything so charmingly simple. How charming the simplicity is comes clear if we recall the work that other self-conscious literary artists were producing for the deluxe illuminated manuscripts that correspond to our coffee-table art books—those collections of "aureate" poetry that sang of their maiden rather differently:

> O Maria by denominacioun,
> Fulgent as the beame celestyne,
> Called unto hir coronacioun.
> Phebus persplendent made his abdominacioun,
> Devoidyng all in tenebrosite

Far more religious poems survive than secular ones. Who knows how many lovely songs, to how many an Annot or an Alison, to how many a Mannerly Margery Milk and Ale, were lost because no clerk found an opportune blank page or a wide margin?

For that matter, why were any medieval poems written down? Only a few were printed in their own time. For nearly three hundred years after our broken-hearted lover scrawled in that margin his thirteen lines about the lost lady, England had to wait for printing—had to wait until Caxton set up his press in 1476. Even reading was not what it is today: there was nothing like efficiency speed-reading; many who could read probably did so with much lip movement and mumbling, finger working slowly under the words. Chaucer's Clerk of Oxenford, though he spent all he had on books and learning, had only twenty volumes at his bedside—or perhaps not that many: Chaucer only says he would rather have had twenty books than fancy clothes or musical instruments. Today we take most poems from the page—so that some poets, like Cummings or the more recent "concrete" poets, make even typography meaningful. But, for medieval man, contemporary poems were ear-poems, not eye-poems, and they were kept, not on bookshelves, but in the memory of those who liked them. If they were written down, it was so they could be played off again, like a record. Often they were written as prose, to save space; the rhymes, after all, showed where the lines ended. This explains why spelling as a science did not exist; there was no right way to spell even one's own name. Spelling was just a way of indicating sound; if a scribe wanted to write "Mine eye" he might feel that "My nigh" served very nicely.

Middle English, as Ker reminds us, was not a language; it was many languages. Caxton complained as he went into the printing business that the dialect of one part of England could not be understood in another part. An Englishman leaving his native village might be taken for a foreigner before he had gone so very far. An author, then, had no nation-wide readership; he wrote for his neighbors.

But even within one dialectal region, even within one poem, or one line of one poem, the same word might be spelled differently. Whoever wrote down "My deth I love, my lyf ich hate" indicates the first person singular by "I" or "Y" or "ich" indifferently. This is a problem for the editors: should one be faithful to spelling that the author had no notion of fidelity about? Some editors have gone so far as to normalize old spelling. But this too gives a false impression: however the poem looked, it was never that tidy. Some characters once used are used no longer: the y-shaped th sound in Ye Olde Antique Shoppe, for example. That ye was pronounced the. As for Shoppe, or Schoppe—should the final e be sounded? About the best we can say is—sometimes. In the Harley lyrics, of around 1300, it seems that it generally was pronounced, unless elided before a following vowel. For a generation or so after Chaucer it seems that it was pronounced—here and there. We do not know exactly when it faded away altogether. It matters, though, in the cadence of poetry. Not so much, if at all, in alliterative verse of the strong-stress type, since unstressed syllables do not figure in the rhythm. But it matters with Chaucer's kind of verse. Everything becomes simple enough if we read Chaucer in the cadence of iambic pentameter, in the swing, say, of "I hate to see that ev'nin' sun go down." Sound the *e*'s if needed for the rhythm. Our English ear is often the best guide to the sound of medieval poems, which look thornier than they are. Richard Rolle wrote only a generation or so before Chaucer, but he came from Yorkshire, and his dialect is less familiar than Chaucer's:

> Luf es a lyght byrthen, lufe gladdes yong and alde,
> Lufe es with-owten pyne, als lofers hase me talde

Hardly a word is "spelled right" here, and yet when heard the lines are clear enough, made up as they are of everyday words we still recognize.

But poems were written down—we might wonder how and where, and in what way they got to us. By luck, most of them. They were scribbled on margins, or on the backs of official documents. Written on flyleaves, or on any white space left between more solemn matters—perhaps so faintly they have to be recovered by ultraviolet light. In Latin sermon notes, or in a student's workbook. In a commonplace book, rather like a modern scrapbook, in which the owner kept anything that might catch his fancy: lists of mayors, recipes, odd bits of information, favorite poems. Sometimes they are found with music, since lyrics of the thirteenth century especially were meant for singing. Some are preserved in what may have been a minstrel's songbook—three such are extant—about pocket-size, so perhaps meant to be carried about. The famous Harley 2253 is a religious house miscellany: a parchment folio of 141 leaves, about the size of typing paper today. It contains 48 pages of Anglo-Norman religious pieces, and then, written in a different hand, religious pieces in Latin, saints' lives—and many of the best medieval lyrics. The works of certain famous or popular writers exist in manuscripts that are really collected editions: Chaucer, for example, and his plodding followers. Charles d'Orléans seems to have had his own personal manuscript. The popularity of Richard Rolle and his revivalist fervor is shown by the fact that there are more manuscripts of his work than of any other medieval writer.

Lyric poetry, involved less with contemporary events than with eternal ones—love, death, all that happens most intimately to the person—is less dependent on historical background than other kinds of poetry. If one is in love, it doesn't much matter whether the girl is wearing a millefleur kirtle or a denim miniskirt. One has to be pretty much a worshipper of the past to feel that boiling oil on the flesh is somehow nicer than napalm, or that a shaft of splintered oak through the visor, carrying scraps of metal and cheekbone into the brain, is more romantic than an exploding grenade. The essentials hardly change: after the first death there is no other—though in a different sense than Dylan Thomas used the words. But this is why, to the surprise of one critic, lyric poets of the time seem so indifferent to the events of fifteenth-century life, to its social tensions, its War of the Roses, its breakdown of law and order. This is why, to another critic's surprise, "very little of the poetry dealing with contemporary political events has survived." There is a practical consideration here: poems about contemporary figures, contemporary events, can be hazardous to the health of the writer. But there is a deeper consideration: the "now" subjects, the ones on everyone's tongue, in everyone's ear at any given time, the subjects that turn into the morning headlines, are not often the stuff of which lyric poetry is made. Poems for today are soon poems for yesterday; what is most topical soon attracts only the pedants.

No single state document, a historian tells us, has had such influence on the course of history as the Magna Charta of 1215. Yet if anyone wrote an Ode to the Magna Charta nobody bothered to save it. A black-eyed blonde named Alison, a girl with a slender waist one noticed when she laughed, was more interesting to the poet. There are no poems on the Model Parliament of 1295, nor on the Merciless Parliament of 1288. Though the census of 1085 aroused widespread indignation, there are no poems about it. Around 1250 many were wondering if the royal prohibition against tournaments ought to be more strongly enforced. No poems. In the early fourteenth century, the annual wool export was 35,000 sacks; by the mid-fifteenth it had dropped to less than 8,000 sacks—a source of concern to many, of tragedy to some. "WOOL DROPS 5,000 SACKS!" might have been a headline, if the Middle Ages had had that plague too, but probably not a lyric poem. And so with the other burning questions of a long-gone day: all the talk about open-field farming versus enclosure for sheep runs; or whether or not villeins (serfs) should be given their freedom and let run at large, instead of being bred like cattle; or whether certain minority groups could be admitted to guild membership; or whether 43 percent was too high an interest rate on a loan.

Then what were the poems about? Love happy or unhappy. Love for man, love for woman, love for God's mother— or, as in Foucquet's painting, a heady confusion of the two. Or if not love, death (". . . *is* there more? More than Love and Death? Then tell me its name!" wrote Emily Dickinson, herself a lyric poet, two or three years before she died). Death must have come with special poignancy in these centuries of war and plague: the Dance of Death moves gruesomely through the fourteenth century, trailing worms and ravelled flesh; less gruesomely through the fifteenth, which gives us the gravity of "Farewell this world," the best of all those poems in which the dead come back with plangent words for the living.

Or the lyrics may be about lesser things which matter only to the individual: about someone's pride in being a brunette, when the ideal of beauty was the blonde with grey eyes far apart. Or even about having a bad headache, maybe a hangover—as in Dunbar's poem "My heid did yak yesternicht." A trifle—and yet Dunbar, though not for this poem, is the greatest lyric poet of the period—greater, certainly, than the better known Skelton, with his saucy but ramshackle effusions. To call Dunbar greatest of the period is to limit his achievement. J. W. Baxter, in his *William Dunbar* (1952) holds that "Burns was a great song-writer rather than a great poet, and if this distinction is upheld there can be no question that Dunbar is the greatest of Scots poets." Hugh MacDiarmid, in starting the twentieth-century Scottish literary revival, gave as his war cry: "Not Burns—Dunbar!" whom he found singularly modern.

There were topical poems in the time: the Agincourt carol, the verses about the Barons' War. But they are not among the best poems. Among the topical poems are "God be wyth trewthe" and "Peny is a hardy knyght," the first about the general lack of integrity in lords, in ladies, in lawyers, in the church; the second about the power of money to subvert justice and win a high place for the wealthy. And yet these are hardly poems of that age alone, as a glance at any newspaper will show us. What we cannot know is how often a drop in the wool market or a rise in interest rates prompted a poet to write, *de contemptu mundi*, a lyric on mortality or death; or how often one of the endless dreary wasteful wars might have made him cry out, in words like Browning's:

> Shut them in,
> With their triumphs and their glories and the rest.
> Love is best!

But what were the times like? In a series of poems known as the Vernon lyrics—a strange, tense, protracted group of moralizing poems on themes that verse handled in the fourteenth century only because prose was not mature enough to, a series that in its rather forbidding charm is almost a test of whether or not one can like much medieval poetry—in the Vernon lyrics there is a stanza, here somewhat modernized in spelling, that tells us what one contemporary thought of his times:

> Now harlotry for mirth is hold,   *held*
>   And virtues tornen into vice,
> And simony hath churches sold,
>   And law is waxen covetise;

Our faith is frail to fleche and fold: *waver and sag*
    For truth is put to little price;
Our God is gluttony and gold,
    Drunkenness, lechery, and dice

Is this 1370? Or 1970? Medieval London? Or modern Las Vegas?

If we could have found ourselves in that England of centuries ago, we would have found it in many ways disturbingly familiar. There was almost always war. The Hundred Years War began in 1338, and somewhat outran its name; the civil War of the Roses began when that ended, and continued, off and on, until Henry VII won his crown on the battlefield in 1485. The first was a series of imperialist adventures abroad; it raised taxes, ruined businesses (unless one had a lance and armor factory), cut down the population, released troops of unpensioned ex-soldiers that prowled around the country like outlaws, practicing the only trade they knew. If human butchery had ever been glamorous, it was fast ceasing to be so. What was a knight to do against the elusive bowmen drawn up out of reach, shooting with practiced accuracy their long arrows ten a minute, until the very sunlight flickered, as under a light cloud cover? Arrows would not pierce the most expensive armor, perhaps—but how many had that? A battle under the circumstances must have been rather like a chain-reaction pileup on the freeway—except that as one lay tangled in wreckage the Welsh knifemen could run up, loosen a helmet, and slit one's throat. There was often trouble at home, strife between the barons and the king, which seemed to sanction violence on all lower levels and made it difficult for the weak central government to act on the appeals for law and order. There were uprisings of the peasants, armed with crude but effective scythelike implements. There were demonstrations, riots, sit-down strikes. An agricultural boom in the thirteenth century, a bad depression in the fourteenth. There were not only oppressed minorities, there was a vast oppressed majority: all the poor. There were repeated visitations of the Black Death, borne by hordes of rats—almost as devastating and continuous a threat as the atom bomb today, and perhaps more terrifying, because the causes were not known. No use even protesting: Ban the Plague! More than a third of the population was wiped out in 1348–49. In its wake there were problems of wages and the labor supply. There were even, or so men thought, problems of ecology: as early as the fourteenth century many complained that the Thames was "stopped up by divers filth and dung thrown therein by persons who have houses along the said course, to the great nuisance and damage of all the city." There were complaints too that forest and farmland were being destroyed by the land-hungry sheepmen. There was always the generation gap: oppressive old kings would die and the young take over, in turn to become old and oppressive. Through it all the seasons changed, and the life of the ordinary man went on. Through it all there was a time to be born, a time to die, a time to mourn, and a time to dance—a time to every purpose under the heaven. And, about each of these, there was a time for poems.

Poetry in the Time of Henry VIII

The story of English poetry in the first half of the sixteenth century is largely the story of poetry at court, the story of the "new company of courtly makers, of whom Sir Thomas Wyat th' elder and Henry Earle of Surrey were the chieftaines," as the Elizabethan critic Puttenham wrote toward the end of the century. Poetry at court, everything at court, happened under the gigantic shadow of Henry VIII. Before we look at the poetry, suppose we look for a moment at the figure of Henry.

After the reign of his penny-pinching, multimillionaire businessman father, the new Henry, then only seventeen, came to the throne in 1509 as a kind of golden boy—physically and intellectually perhaps as impressive as any young man who had ever come to the English throne. In an age when men were shorter than now, Henry was over six feet tall, probably the equivalent of six feet four today, and weighing close to two hundred and fifty pounds. The build of a professional football player—and Henry was fond of flaunting it; he liked to hunt all morning, joust all afternoon, dance all night. He had abilities too not common among athletes; he wrote, in Latin, a book on theology that was a sensation at the time and long afterwards; produced a few graceful poems; in music, both as composer and performer on several instruments, was excelled by no one at court except the few professionals who are now minor names in the history of music. Almost a marvel, Henry: the chronicler Edward Hall describes him as "exercisyng hym selfe daily in shooting, singing, daunsyng, wrastelyng, casting of the barre, plaiyng at the recorders, flute, virginals, and in settyng of songes, making of ballettes, & he did set two goodly masses, every one of them five partes."

His queen, in her early twenties, was as popular as he was—at times indeed more popular. Everybody agreed that she was very pretty, in her Spanish dignity; it is said that she spoke Latin more fluently than Henry himself. For some years the young king was much taken with her; was even uxurious. It seems that this unreliable lover never again found a woman he was so in love with, admired so much, or relied on so heavily as Catherine of Aragon. For some years it was a happy, spectacular, extravagant court; Henry, repressed during his childhood, now threw money to the winds on tournaments, banquets, masked dances—the "pleasant guise"s Wyatt mentions?—on clothes woven with gold, on jewels, on music. Poetry was written as naturally as pavanes were played or galliards danced, and for some of the same reasons: it was all part of the game of love that courtiers had been adept at for some centuries. Much of Sir Thomas Wyatt's earlier verse seems this sort of game-poetry, part of the witty social ritual, like our cocktail-party small talk, aimed at impressing this or that lady or simply at displaying the courtier as a man of charm and accomplishment. Though a strong, handsome, and attractive figure, the best poet of his time, Wyatt seems to have been unlucky in love; the most typical note, in what are probably his earliest poems, is that of complaint about the fickleness or "new-fangleness" of the ladies. Sometimes he may have been teasing, or posing as the melancholy cynic vocalizing "La donna è mobile"; sometimes his feelings must have been only too real. Experts are not completely sure whether these early Tudor "balets"—rather light, swingy, conventional lyrics—were meant to be sung or not. Music and poetry had been united in the earlier Middle Ages, but in the fourteenth century each had tended to go its own way. We know that some poems were sung. The music of "Westron Wynde" and other songs has been preserved with the words. Perhaps some poems were meant to go with current popular tunes, as in *A Handful of Pleasant Delights,* an anthology of half a century later, in which the poems were advertised as "Newly devised to the newest tunes." The composer and rhymer Thomas Whythorne tells us in his autobiography how "in thes daies I yuzed [used] to sing my songs and sonets sumtym to the liut and sumtyms the virginals." There is no evidence that Wyatt himself was a musician, as his king was; the lute he addresses, the lute he says one lady threatened to break, was most likely only a metaphor. Probably those balets of his were breathed into a fair lady's leaning ear, or recited to a courtly group by candlelight on a festive evening, or more often probably meant to be handed around in manuscript from friend to friend. Reading was then more of a social recreation than the solitary pastime it is now. These poems, most of them rather same and tame *vers de société,* are not as much admired as they were in the nineteenth century, when Tennyson's recommendation got Wyatt included in *The Golden Treasury;* they at best continue, gracefully but rather dully, a medieval convention. We do not feel much urgency here; John Stevens, in his *Music and Poetry in the Early Tudor Court,* plays with a hyphen to effect when he says that the poets (of these poems) were "courtly-love makers" rather than "courtly love-makers." Yet it is hard to tell when conventions become the vehicle for genuine passion: some of Whythorne's stereotyped lyrics arose out of intense emotional excitement.

Wyatt wrote a great many balets. A poem like "Blame Not My Lute" represents the genre at about its best. They were part of the revelry and spectacle that Henry encouraged, though it cannot be said that he encouraged poetry to the extent that he encouraged music. Perhaps he thought it more dangerous. What Henry wanted above all was to turn the clock back—or reverse the hourglass—to the days of chivalry, with himself as a combination King Arthur–Sir Lancelot. He fancied the allegorical shows and pageants of earlier days, and, dreaming of Crécy and Agincourt, was forever hatching some "notable enterprise" against the French. Unfortunately his wars, one after another, turned into operation rathole—a few unimportant cities won and lost in France, at vast expense that finally exhausted his father's fortune and were a source of irritation and concern to his money-conscious councillors, the "foul churls," as haughty young Surrey later called them, who thought more of balancing the budget than of winning hard-to-hold laurels abroad. England was not then in a position to conquer much of anything: Scotland itself was a problem. Henry was far less powerful than the spectacular devil-may-care young French king, with his well-organized state of fifteen million subjects, as compared with Henry's rather loosely organized state of three million. It is hardly surprising that the competitive Henry was jealous of Francis I; when the latter tripped him up in an impromptu wrestling match at the Field of Cloth of Gold in 1520 it was almost an international incident. Henry was far less powerful too than Catherine's uncle, the Emperor Charles V, who controlled Spain, the Netherlands, the kingdom of Naples, much of Germany, and had possessions in North Africa and the New World. France and the Empire were the giants; during most of Henry's reign his foreign policy consisted of trying to sow discord between them, trying to sustain England's role as the *tertius gaudens,* the lucky third party that can sway the balance between two far more powerful antagonists.

The carefree days of Henry's youth did not last more than a decade or so; during Wyatt's first years at court the skies were already darkening. The atmosphere was troubled, even the international situation embroiled when Anne Boleyn returned to court after a year or two in France. By then the king had already been unfaithful to Catherine—with Anne Boleyn's elder sister among others—and his roving eye soon fell on the new girl at court. About 1525 Wyatt, who had somehow been involved with her, was sternly warned off; probably at that time he expressed his frustration by adapting a sonnet of Petrarch's in his "Who so list to hunt, I knowe where is an hynde."

On her father's side, Anne belonged to the new aristocracy of "foul churls" descended from tradesmen; on her mother's side she was a Howard, the Duke of Norfolk's niece and a cousin of our poet Surrey, then just a child. There was no family more powerful, except the king's. Holbein's drawing shows Anne as quite a pretty young girl—but then Holbein made all the girls look pretty; he was not the most dependable artist for Henry to send later all over Europe doing portraits of prospective fiancées. Wolsey, the first of Henry's two powerful ministers, called Anne the night-crow; others had worse names for her. Obviously she had some kind of attraction for men, although she was not outstanding for beauty, intelligence, wit, or virtue. Her appeal for Henry seems to have been chiefly that Anne, profiting from her discarded sister's example, refused to settle down as the king's mistress. For several years she had the nerve and skill to keep him at arm's length. The king was still without a male heir; Catherine had had several miscarriages, had borne several children dead or soon to die—and a mere girl, the Princess Mary. With his knowledge of theology, Henry began to wonder, it may be sincerely, if his marriage was not under a curse: his once loved bride had been, after all, his dead brother's wife. For several years, by threat, persuasion, and bribery, he tried to get the pope to annul the marriage. But since Italy was largely controlled by Catherine's uncle, whose unruly troops had half ruined Rome in the very year Henry began to talk about a divorce, the pope, even apart from the merits of the case, was reluctant to act. Henry then began to wonder, it may be sincerely, if he, Henry, was not after all head of the church in England, and therefore in a position to arrange his own divorce. This is what he did when Anne, with perfect timing, became pregnant in 1533. Her child, alas, was a girl, useless from Henry's dynastic point of view: although, could he have known, even Henry might have admitted that his daughter Elizabeth would not do badly on the throne. Anne lasted longer as a resistant sex symbol than as a rather petulant wife; when in 1536 she had a son born dead Henry had her put to death on probably trumped-up charges of incest and adultery. On the very day of her execution he married Jane Seymour, a pleasant girl who was lucky enough to die, probably of Tudor medical procedures, soon after she had given him the male heir he wanted.

Executed at about the same time as Anne were five men

accused of misconduct with her. Among them was her brother, George Boleyn, Viscount Rochford, who had some name as a poet himself, and is thought to have written while in prison the stanzas beginning so much better than they end:

> O death, rock me asleep,
>   Bring me to quiet rest,
> Let pass my weary guiltless ghost
>   Out of my careful breast.
> Toll on, thou passing bell;
> Ring out my doleful knell;
> Let thy sound my death tell.
>   Death doth draw nigh;
>   There is no remedy

Probably the five were guilty of no more than "pastime in the queen's chamber," as a courtier described it: social evenings of singing and dancing and poetry and jest, flirtation only to the extent that these can be flirtation. Wyatt too was arrested; it was rumored that he too would die.

With this background in mind, we understand better some of the recurrent themes of his poetry: the longing for steadfastness and secrecy in love, the complaints about infidelity, new-fangleness, and desertion; a worried awareness of the instability of fortune. Most of what he translated from the Latin was about how to achieve peace of mind amid the flux of vicissitude.

The tension in the air may even help to account for the famous arrhythmia of his meters in some of the translations and sonnets. Or that may have come from his noting the purely syllabic meters of French poetry, or the not purely iambic swing of Italian; or because he was trying to impose pentameter on the "broken-backed" four-stress line of medieval verse. His irregularity is sometimes made too much of. There are very few lines in his best poems that cannot be read by the living voice, with its natural stresses and hesitations, as variants of the basic rhythm. In his best poem—best even though it is a famous anthology piece—even a line like can be cadenced by a voice moving in iambic pentameter, lingering here, compensating there, in a way that does no violence to the metronome ticking at the back of our minds. If the occasionally fitful rhythm, the "pausing" or broken-backed line, does express Wyatt's trepidation, we might expect to find it nowhere more marked than in the sonnet he wrote on the fall of Thomas Cromwell, Henry's efficiency expert in church reform, in 1540. Kenneth Muir (*Life and Letters of Sir Thomas Wyatt*) gives two quotations from the chronicler Hall that show how terrifyingly sudden that fall was:

> The 18th day of April, at Westminster, was Lord Thomas Cromwell created Earl of Essex, and made Great Chamberlain of England . . .

> The 19th day of July [of that same year] Thomas Lord Cromwell, late made Earl of Essex . . . being in the Council Chamber, was suddenly apprehended and committed to the Tower of London . . . And the 28th day of July was brought to the scaffold on Tower Hill. . . .

A spectator tells us that Wyatt was so moved at the execution of one who had been a friend and patron that when Cromwell cried out to him in the crowd, "Wyatt could not answer, so many were the tears he shed." And yet the sonnet he adapted from Petrarch to express his grief is perhaps the most regular he ever wrote; there is no pausing or hovering at all in

> The piller pearisht is whearto I lent,
> the strongest staye of myne unquyet mynde

Man has never been the most loyal of the animals, but rarely has lack of faith been so flaunted as in the world Wyatt knew. Breaking treaties was standard practice: two kings would combine against a third; once one of the two partners was too deeply involved to extricate himself without loss he might find that the other had blandly made a separate peace—or perhaps even joined in with the enemy. Catherine's own father, Ferdinand the Catholic, (as Garrett Mattingly tells the story in *Catherine of Aragon*) was once accused of twice deceiving another ruler. " 'He lies, the sot,' cackled Ferdinand in high good humor, 'I have deceived him five times.' " It was not unusual for a nobleman to swear friendship one day, share his friend's secrets, and use them to send him to prison the next. Trials for treason were often so much window dressing for legalized murder: once brought to that bar of justice, few escaped. When Norfolk, Surrey's father, was accused of treason the key witnesses against him included his wife and daughter—a betrayal he had earned by many betrayals of his own. Later Norfolk turned against his own son when Surrey became a political liability. Henry's behavior with those he had loved— with Catherine, with Thomas More, with so many who had served him best—was not reassuring. "Indignatio regis mors est," the courtiers would remind themselves; "The king's anger is death." And one was never sure when Henry would be angry; when his anger might just explode in a great roar of backslapping laughter, or turn to the maniacal rage from which no one—not even the woman he had loved last night— was safe. Wyatt, brave and cool as he was, may well have been a little shaken at times, and the agitation may have shown in his rhythms.

> They fle from me that sometyme did me seke
> with naked fote stalking in my chambre

is poignant enough if we think of it as about his old girl friends and about one in particular. It is more poignant if we think of the world he lived in.

So what seem the stock attitudes of courtly love, the adjurings to be faithful, to be steadfast, to keep silence, were anything but literary themes in Henrician England; though shallow poems might be written about them, they were the grimmest of realities. This is movingly shown by a little manuscript book of poems that is the chief source for many of the

Wyatt pieces we have today. The Devonshire MS—as British Museum MS Additional 17492 it sounds like another dull bibliographical item—is a kind of album in which a group of friends wrote verses, like a modern scrapbook for souvenirs or snapshots or autographs. It was apparently owned by several young people at the court of Henry VIII, young people who passed it, confidentially, from hand to hand, adding poems or comments as they were moved to—poems they knew, or poems they wrote themselves. It has been referred to as a kind of ladies' album of parlor verse; considering what might be at stake, the term seems unfair. Many of those who handled it came to tragic ends: Anne Boleyn, her brother, her four friends were among them. One of the owners seems to have been Mary Howard, Surrey's sister, the young bride of Henry Fitzroy, the king's illegitimate son, whose death Surrey grieves for in one of his best poems. Another was Margaret Douglas, who as niece of the king was valuable marriage material in the body-swapping of international diplomacy. When, without the king's knowledge or permission, she married Thomas Howard, Surrey's young uncle, both were thrown into prison. Margaret was released because of illness, but Thomas died there the following year: prison reform was not among Henry's interests. The Devonshire "ladies' album" has poems—not very good poems—in which the young couple profess their lasting love for each other, cost what it may. The very first poem, which seems to be signed with Wyatt's initials, sets the tone of the book:

> Take hede betyme leste ye be spyede;
> your lovyng eye yee canne not hide;
> at last the trowthe will sure be tryde,
>   therefore take hede!
>
> For Som there be of craftie kynde
> thowe yow shew no part of your mynde,
> surely there eyes ye cannot blynde,
>   therefore take hede!

This sounds like any of the artificial refrain-poems about a long outdated tenet of courtly love. To the young people who kept the album it was something more than that. Whythorne, under safer circumstances, tells, in his curious spelling, how he wrote in a deliberately ambiguous way—"sumwhat dark & dowtfull of sens bekawz I knew not serteinly how shee wold tak it, nor to whoz handz it miht cumen after that she had read it. . . ."

Probably Wyatt wrote most of his smoothly metered song-like poems lightly enough in his early years at court, before "pastime in the queen's chamber" became a matter of life and death. Few of his poems can be positively dated. It does seem that after 1536 a change came over him—the year in which he saw, from the barred window of the prison he was not sure he would leave except for his own death, the execution of a former sweetheart, and, at least in his mind's eye, the death of their friends on Tower Hill. He says he was a changed man:

> These blodye dayes have brokyn my hart;
> My lust, my youth dyd then departe
> And blynd desyer of astate
> . . . .
> The bell towre showed me suche syght
> That in my hed stekys day and nyght

He sounds much aged; at the time he was thirty-three, with six years of life remaining. In those years he fell in love, more happily than in the past, with Elizabeth Darrell, who had been one of Catherine's maids of honor; he lived with her when he could at Allington Castle in Kent. He was away for two years as Henry's ambassador to the Emperor in Spain. How important a position that was, what tact and vigilance it required, we can appreciate if we remember the diplomatic situation. Both Catherine and Anne Boleyn were dead by then, but the Emperor had not forgotten that Henry had renounced his aunt and declared her daughter illegitimate. Wyatt's chief mission was to keep Charles as well disposed to Henry as possible, and to make what trouble he could between Charles and the king of France, lest they combine against England in what they might publicize as a holy war against heretics. On Wyatt's return from Spain he was arrested on the usual charge of treason—a rival's bright idea for getting rid of him. His spirited and witty defense, which would not have availed if Henry had been dead set against him, soon won his freedom, it seems partly at the urging of Surrey's cousin, the young queen Catherine Howard, a poor sexy "juvenile delinquent," as her biographer calls her, who a few months later died a natural enough death for the times: she was beheaded.

During his last years Wyatt probably worked at his satires and translations of the Penitential Psalms. The "translations" are among his best work, in part because they are not really translations at all. A few decades later Sir Philip Sidney was to describe how, in looking for a theme or technique, he was

> Oft turning other's leaves, to see if thence would flow
> Some fresh and fruitfull showers upon my sunne-burnd
>   braine

Under Henry, when it was not always prudent to say directly what one had in mind, one could turn others' leaves to see if Seneca or Petrarch or another had already said something like it, and then express one's own anger or despair in the guise of another's. We have seen how Wyatt did this to show what he felt about Anne Boleyn and about Cromwell; similarly, when he wanted to attack the hypocrisy and danger of life at court he did an English rendering—with appropriate changes—of a satire of his contemporary Italian Alamanni on that same theme. There can be more passion, more urgency in the translations than in the sometimes pleasant, sometimes lugubrious lyrics in which he continued the medieval commonplaces—lyrics less "his own" than the translations were. Surrey, though he sometimes translated straight, or as if doing literary exercises, also used Wyatt's technique, as in his biblical paraphrase. He did something more daring—if it had fallen into the wrong hands—in adapting a passage from Lydgate so that it might express, some think, what he felt about the king who had recently ordered the execution of two of his cousins:

> Th' Assirian king in peace, with foule desire,
> And filthy lustes . . .

Wyatt's death in 1542 of a sudden fever seems to have deeply moved the young Earl of Surrey, who wrote one of his best poems on the older poet's death.

Henry Howard, given the courtesy title of Earl of Surrey, was younger by what was then almost a generation. Probably they had never seen much of each other; Surrey was more a personal friend of Wyatt's son, who was to be executed in 1554 for leading a Protestant rebellion against Queen Mary. Surrey, son of the Machiavellian Duke of Norfolk, was of far higher birth than Wyatt; his family had some claim to the throne itself, a circumstance which the arrogant young man did not play down, and which had much to do with his execution at the age of twenty-nine. Uneasy lay the head that wore a crown, perhaps; even uneasier lay the head that had some right to wear one.

Surrey wrote few poems like Wyatt's short-line Devonshire balets, which belonged to the carefree 1520s, and were probably out of date when Surrey came to court a decade later. He was still under twenty years old when his cousin Anne Boleyn and her friends met their abrupt deaths. These moved him less, at any rate, than the death that same year of young Richmond, Henry's illegitimate son, with whom he had spent the two happiest years of his boyhood, and who had married Surrey's sister. He was disturbed too by the king's marrying into the inferior Seymour family; Queen Jane's brother, Hertford, was to become Surrey's chief rival for position and prestige. On one occasion Surrey so far forgot himself as to strike Hertford at court—an offense for which the penalty would normally have been the loss of his right arm, amid much gruesome ritual. But the king was fond of his dead son's impulsive friend: Surrey was imprisoned for a while at Windsor, where the scenes of his childhood moved him to another of the best of his poems. Fellow poets and friends as they apparently were, Wyatt and Surrey would have been at odds both politically and religiously. When Cromwell, the coldly efficient minister who had followed Wolsey as Henry's factotum, was executed in 1540 (at least in part because, hoping to find allies among the Lutheran princes of Germany, he had helped arrange Henry's farcical marriage with the dull German nonbeauty Anne of Cleves) Wyatt was moved to tears. Surrey would have been jubilant: he lived in a dreamworld of vanished chivalry, in which Cromwell and his like represented only the baseborn new men who more and more seemed to be taking over control of the government. And yet Surrey's admiration for Wyatt as man and poet enabled him to overlook divergencies of view he would not have tolerated in another. Surrey himself was hopelessly behind the times: out of step with political developments, even out of step, though war was one of his great loves, with what was latest in military technique, so that when he was finally given the command in France he had long been chafing for, the tactics he used and the dispatches he wrote seemed straight out of the *Morte d'Arthur* of an earlier age. About his fearlessness there was never any question; but about his common sense there was a great deal. He insisted, for instance, on holding the captured city of Boulogne—a city of little use to the English except as a symbol of imperialistic hopes, and a severe drain of English blood and money. Even Henry's natural sympathy for young Surrey was put to the test when Surrey wasted the lives of officers and technicians expensive to train and to replace. Henry's hardheaded money-conscious council was more hostile. In March of 1546 Surrey was recalled to England; by the following January he had been arrested and executed on charges of high treason and conspiracy to commit murder. The court was able to use Surrey's own words and actions against him: the proud and embittered young man, in so many ways like Henry himself, though without Henry's resilience when resilience was needed, had hinted that after the king's death—and it was close enough to treason to suggest that the king could die—his own family might take over provisional control, and that would have meant by the usual Tudor purge of potential rivals.

Surrey was a far more restless and turbulent spirit than Wyatt, though not much of this turbulence shows in the poetry. Knowing little of discipline himself and rarely well behaved for long (except with his wife, whom he loved), quite unable to smoothe out the difficulties of his own life, he has to be given credit for establishing that well-behaved form, the English sonnet, and for smoothing out English versification till it had lost all traces of the older roughness—and some of its vitality as well. Since in their own time poets are often rated as much by the figure they cut as by the excellence of their work, and since Surrey was the more sensational figure and of higher rank, he was thought a finer poet than Wyatt almost until our own century. His career was more flamboyant; his poetry more tame. One could not call either a dedicated poet; both concentrated on the discipline of poetry in their youthful years, before the life of action had begun; both returned to it as a distraction, a pastime, or occasionally as a vent for feelings they could not otherwise express.

It was all right for a lowborn pen pusher and job-scrambler like Skelton to publish his little books with their top-heavy titles; noblemen, however, avoided the stigma of print. It would have been highly insulting to ask a gentleman, "What have you published?" When Anne Boleyn was crowned queen of England, the official providers of "verses and ditties" were Nicholas Udall and John Leland, hardly in Wyatt's class as poets. Wyatt's own function was to serve as Chief Ewer: he poured scented water over the hands of the queen at the banquet. One likes to imagine what sparks may have flown when their glances met.

The ban on professionalism in letters lasted long into the reign of Elizabeth, and indeed beyond—perhaps it was like our own preference for original works of art over mechanically reproduced copies. As late as 1614, Professor Rollins reminds us, there were those who despised all printed books; it was said of such that they "esteeme of verses upon which the vulgar in a Stationers Shop hath once breathed, as of a piece of infection; in whose fine fingers no papers are wholesome, but such as pass by private manuscription."

Yet Wyatt—could it have been because of his contact with men of letters abroad?—may have had a more modern attitude. The best source of his poems is his own Egerton manuscript, much of it carefully written out by a secretary of some kind, yet with entries and revisions in his own hand, just as if he were preparing it for the press. Some believe he had possible publication in mind when he wrote—if indeed it was he—in the Devonshire manuscript:

> And patientelye, o Redre, I the praye
> take in good parte this worke as yt ys mente,
> and greve the not with ought that I shall saye,
> sins with good will this boke abrode ys sent

Credit for offering the poems of Wyatt and Surrey to the world has to be given to the printer and publisher Richard Tottel, whose *Songes and Sonettes* came out, years after the death of both poets, in 1557, in the reign of Queen Mary. Tottel feels he has to make some apology for violating the taboo; his note from "The Printer to the Reader" pleads that "it resteth nowe (gentle reder) that thou thinke it not evill doon, to publish, to the honor of the Englishe tong, and for the profit of the studious of Englishe eloquence, those workes which the ungentle horders up of such treasure have heretofore envied thee." The distinguished modern editor of this *Miscellany*, as it began to be called in the nineteenth century, believes it to be "the first printed anthology . . . the beginning of modern English verse. . . ."

It was not the first, however. Some twenty years before, about the time Anne Boleyn and her friends were put to death, a Tudor printer was bringing out the first printing of a ninety-page anthology called *The Court of Venus*, or, in a later printing, *A Boke of Balettes*. No complete copy exists today, but we have enough pages from three copies of three separate editions to know that it contained poems of Wyatt—perhaps a substantial selection, if the proportions in the twenty-five or so surviving pages are representative. We have no way of knowing whether or not Wyatt authorized the publication; the printer may have come into possession of the poems surreptitiously. The little book, with its worldly love poems, seems to have given offense at the time; later on, it was savagely attacked by the more straitlaced of the reformers, and especially by John Hall, whose *The Court of Virtue* (1565) converts, by moralistic parody, some of its poems into religious verses, after declaring that

> A booke also of songes they have,
> And Venus court they do it name.
> No fylthy mynde a song can crave,
> But therein he may finde the same

Since Hall also mentions "other bokes of lecherous Ballades," it may well be that there were more collections of poems published in Wyatt's time than we had suspected—*The Court of Venus* suggests that there were. It would not be surprising if such editions—probably regarded as throwaways, as we regarded the early comic books—were lost without a trace: only one copy of the first edition of Tottel's own anthology, after all, escaped destruction.

But if not quite the first of its kind, *Songes and Sonettes* is one of the most important and influential books in English literature—the collection that passed on to the Elizabethans the world of Tudor court poetry. Tottel himself was probably surprised at the success of his modestly produced anthology; a reprint was called for the following month and at least seven other editions before the end of the century. Only Surrey's name appears on the title page, probably because of his rank and glamor; possibly too because the name "Sir Thomas Wyatt" was suspect at the time: Wyatt's son, of the same name, had recently been put to death for leading a rebellion against the queen. When Wyatt is mentioned in the book, it is specified that he is "the elder." The title page led many to think of it as Surrey's book, and of Surrey as superior to Wyatt; yet Wyatt, though in second place, had nearly one hundred contributions to Surrey's forty. Nicholas Grimald also contributed forty pieces; the ninety-odd remaining were by "uncertain auctours."

The poems obviously were not all new at the time; some had been written nearly forty years before. Tottel, or whoever prepared the MS for him, had tried, not unreasonably according to his lights, to bring what seemed old-fashioned up to date. With Wyatt's work this meant smoothing away some of the irregularities that we now think part of his charm—it meant changing some of the "pausing" or "hovering" lines into regular pentameters. John Stevens finds the shift from the more irregular early rhythms to an insistent iambic a mysterious and unaccountable change of taste—he suggests it may be due in part to a Protestant reform that was trying to make everything plain and systematic—as if the same spirit that shattered the stained glass and statues of the monasteries and chapels also reduced the occasional waywardness of Wyatt's lines to a kind of dogtrot. Today we certainly prefer the expressiveness of what Wyatt wrote in such lines as

> It was no dreme: I lay brode waking.
> But all is torned thorough my gentilnes
> into a straunge fasshion of forsaking

to the tamer thing Tottel's anthology made of them:

> It was no dreme: for I lay broade awakyng.
> But all is turnde now through my gentleness
> Into a bitter fashion of forsakyng

—and which we find even today in some anthologies. In Wyatt's lines, the voice, to sustain his rhythm, hovers wonderingly on the "no dreme," "brode waking," and "straunge"; in Tottel, it moves mechanically ahead, as if not quite conscious of what it is saying.

Tottel's *Miscellany* is hardly a book many of us today would choose to have with us as our one book on a desert island. There are bright moments in the Wyatt and the Surrey sections, but once we get into the "uncertain auctours" a certain dreary monotony settles in. The *Miscellany* is not really very miscellaneous. The "lover" who is featured in so many of the titles does little but complain about his "wofull state"; he complains that he is misunderstood, rebuked, disdained, forsaken, enslaved, or "delayed with doutfull cold answers"; when for any reason his "harty love" is not requited, "he declareth his paines to excede far the paines of hell." Some complaints seem not without basis; that, for example, "of a woman rav-ished, and also mortally wounded." Occasionally a hopeful note is struck:

> But open thou thy manly mouth, and say that thou wilt
> come.

There are no religious poems, but—what may be worse—much lugubrious moralizing on "the wretchedness of this world" or about how "when adversitie is once fallen it is to late to beware." A favorite if depressing thought is that "they of the meane estate are happiest," or that "the pore estate is to be holden for best."

Nor is the style exhilarating. Sometimes we are battered with alliteration:

> The lyfe is long, that lothsumly doth last:
> The dolefull dayes draw slowly to theyr date:
> The present panges, & paynfull plages forepast
> Yelde griefe aye grene to stablish this estate.

And we are continually dulled by two of the dreariest rhythms in English: the fourteener (seven iambic feet) and its deformed relative, poulter's measure (alternate lines of six and seven iambic feet—of twelve and fourteen syllables—so called be-cause poultrymen were said to give twelve eggs for the first dozen and fourteen eggs for the second). Wyatt seems to have invented this monstrosity, but had the discretion to use it only a couple of times. Surrey took it up more enthusiastically, and then for a while everybody was doing it; it soon became the "in" thing, the only way to write for people really up to date. Few good poems were written in it; one of those few is "Girt in my giltless gown," an answer to Surrey's aggrieved "Wrapt in my careless cloak." The unknown poet, one hopes really a woman, wields the looping lines very smartly indeed to tongue-lash a complaining lover and deflate masculine pretensions.

"The grave of early Tudor poetry"—so one critic calls Tot-tel's *Miscellany*. Yet, perhaps because there was nothing bet-ter, it held the field through edition after edition; with it we are on our way to the Elizabethan anthologies with their lavishly scrolled titles: *A Paradise of Dainty Devices, A Gorgeous Gallery of Gallant Inventions*. When the famous anthology had been out about seven years, William Shakespeare was born at Stratford.

So far we have been discussing poetry written by a very few people, the "new company of courtly makers." And the other three million Englishmen—what were they writing or quoting or singing or dancing to, during this half century? The poetry of the court is preserved in MS books, in songbooks, in the *Miscellany*. But the poetry of the people, our rude forefathers—where was it preserved except in the skulls that tumbled one by one into the country churchyards? Yet somehow, in strange ways, much of it endured; a ballad sung in Henry's England, a ballad perhaps never written down, might still turn up, still be recognizable across seas and centuries, in the mountains of Kentucky today.

The favorite dance-song of the folk in earlier centuries, the carol, was still being written in Wyatt's time. But the late carols, without their music, are not very good: less spontaneous, more directed to organized socializing, than the earlier ones. Less often religious. One of the most noticeable differences between the poetry of the sixteenth century and that of earlier times is that after the reign of Henry VII there is almost no religious poetry being written. Perhaps because prose was being used more and more for devotional purposes; perhaps because the new humanistic spirit directed attention to this world; perhaps because the Reformation, after about the first third of the century, discouraged many of the old themes as superstition. "The Cherry-Tree Carol"—not technically a carol at all—is charming; rather typically, though, it is based on an apocryphal gospel. "A Lyke-Wake Dirge" is hardly written in terms of Christian symbolism. "A God and Yet a Man" might be called a theological lyric rather than a religious one.

Yet the eerie "Lyke-Wake Dirge" is a voice from another world of poetry than that of the courtly makers. So is the mysteriously graphic "Lully, Lulley," the only ballad-like poem known to exist both in an early manuscript and in the repertoire of folk singers in our own time. So are folk songs like "Waly, Waly." All three of these poems are occasionally classified as ballads. Probably it is to the ballad that we have to turn to get an idea of what was best in the popular poetry of the sixteenth century.

We tend to think of the ballad as impersonal, objective, concerned with story; of the lyric as personal, subjective, concerned with feelings. In form the ballad is lyrical—written in lyric measures and actually meant to be sung. And if the ballads tend to point us to external objects and situations, they point passionately to what is passionate; dialogue tends to be a stichomythia of lyrical cries. As ballads evolve, they often evolve toward the lyric; what is purely factual (Jane Reynolds of Plymouth and her seaman husband, James Harris) drops out; what is emotionally gripping (the demon lover) remains. If anyone ever knew exactly when and where Sir Patrick Spens made his ill-fated voyage, or what his important mission was, they long ago ceased to care—they have left even the historians hardly a clue. But they have never forgotten the lyric detail:

> O lang, lang may the ladies stand,
>   Wi' thair gold kems in their hair,
> Waiting for thair ain deir lords,
>   For they'll see thame na mair.

It seems fair to say that all ballads aspire to the condition of lyric. We might go even further and agree with W. P. Ker, who in *Medieval English Literature* declares that "all ballads are lyrical."

Some belong in any anthology of the lyric—but where are we to put them? Ballads are notoriously hard to place in time: their real age has little to do with the date of their first recorded appearance. "A ballad taken down from folk-singers in the twentieth century," says M. J. C. Hodgart (*The Ballads*) "may have a more ancient history than one found in a fifteenth-century manuscript." Ballads of today and of long ago tend to talk in the same manner, tend to be independent of all current fashions in poetic diction.

We think of the ballads, with their sex, violence, and abrupt meetings with the dead—though some of these are with us today—as going back to more primitive times. And yet practically all of the great ballads made their first official appearance in the polite world of the eighteenth century. Alexander Pope had published "The Rape of the Lock" fifty years before the ballads that are now so familiar became known to the world of letters. The first important collection was Bishop Percy's *Reliques of Ancient English Poetry,* in 1765, which came as a revelation to much of Europe. Within another half-century, nearly all of the ballads we think of as great had come to light. There were exceptions, and presumably still might be. "The Unquiet Grave," which Sir Edmund Chambers thinks is possibly as early as the sixteenth century, was first printed in 1878—the words taken down from the lips of a girl in Sussex as she sang them. When we see it now:

> The wind doth blow today, my love,
> And a few small drops of rain

it is hard to believe that Sir Thomas Wyatt might have heard it from some minstrel as he sat in a cushioned corner with Anne Boleyn. But the spelling of ballads is that of the time in which they are written down (as the dialect, so often Scottish, is that of whoever happens to be singing the songs, or collecting them). Suppose we faked our little Sussex song like this:

> The wynde doth blowe to daye my love
> & a fewe smale droppes of rayne.

Can we hear that any better as coming from long ago?

It has been suspected, in fact, that correspondents who sent ballads to the famous collectors, to Percy, to Robert Burns, to Sir Walter Scott, sometimes did take it upon themselves to antique the spelling. This may have happened with *Edward, Edward.* It is known too that such poets as Burns and Scott improved the versions that passed through their talented hands—how could they resist? More than likely there are stanzas or lines in the "ancient ballads" that are the contribution of an eighteenth- or nineteenth-century Muse.

But how many of these ballads that appeared in the eighteenth century might have been heard in the England of Henry VIII? There is no certainty about this; it seems likely enough that most of them had already been drifting around, perhaps for a century, though not in the exact form they were to have after being processed by a Percy or a Burns or a Scott. We know there were ballads around as early as the fifteenth century. Indeed even earlier: R. M. Wilson in his *Early Middle English Literature* quotes from the record of a law suit of 1280 a stanza which has the rhythm and what he calls the "authentic note of ballad":

> Wel, who shal their hornes blow,
>   Holy Rood the day?
> Now is he dead and lies low
>   Was wont to blow them ay.

A great many ballads must have been circulating in England before the possibility of cheap printing, in the sixteenth century, made a different kind of circulation possible. And a different kind of ballad, the journalistic one-page or one-fold broadside ballad, often concerned with recent news stories or sensational crimes, no longer necessarily anonymous, and rarely as memorable as the old folk ballads. But few things in literature are as memorable as the best of them.

Yeats and the Careless Muse

I

The careless muse: the poets, more often than not, have had a kind word for disheveled beauty. When Herrick admitted that sweet disorder, distraction, things erring, neglectful, confused, tempestuous, careless, wild, more bewitched him than when art was too precise in every part, he was repeating a theme of Ben Jonson's in the little song from *Epicoene:*

> Robes loosely flowing, hair as free:
> Such sweet neglect more taketh me
> Than all th' adulteries of art

With Jonson we are on our way back to the classics, to such passages as that of Ovid in the *Amores,* where the poet admires as *neglecta decens* (becomingly unkempt) a girl still disheveled in the morning. Venus first appears to Aeneas with tresses windblown: *dederatque comam diffundere ventis.* It is not easy, in fact, to find the poet who prefers a girl soignée. Better to clip the locks off entirely, so one can contemplate a bracelet of bright hair about the bone, or calm hair meandering in pellucid gold. Or so one can write a mock-heroic poem. But until the glittering forfex snips the tresses, the poet tends to ad-

---

Delivered as the Twenty-first Peters Rushton Seminar Lecture at the University of Virginia (1961) and published in *Learners and Discerners,* edited by Robert Scholes (Charlottesville: University Press of Virginia, 1964).

mire them, with Keats, half lifted by the winnowing wind, or he cries with Browning

> Dear dead women, with such hair, too—what's become
> of all the gold
> Used to hang and brush their bosoms? . . .

or sings with Rossetti

> The hair that lay along her back
> Was yellow as ripe corn

or with Hopkins: "loose locks, long locks, lovelocks. . . ." Even Milton, in his brief Prufrockian dream of a *fête champêtre*, sees himself sporting with the "tangles" of Neaera's hair, and his later Eve

> Her unadorned gold'n tresses wore
> Dissheveld . . .

So with the moderns. Wallace Stevens contrasts elaborate Oriental and English coiffeurs with the morning dishevelment of a girl *neglecta decens:*

> Alas! have all the barbers lived in vain
> That not one curl in nature has survived?
> Why, without pity on these studious ghosts
> Do you come dripping in your hair from sleep?

Robert Frost, who himself associates with a cunningly offhand muse, sees one of his loveliest if most disturbing visions of girlhood

> standing to the waist
> In goldenrod and brake,
> Her shining hair displaced

Even Eliot grows lyrical here:

> Blown hair is sweet, brown hair over the mouth
> blown,
> Lilacs and brown hair

The one exception I think of is Ezra Pound, always fussy about hair arrangement. He likes it elegant, with formalized hairdos "cut straight across [the] forehead," or piled up "on the left side of her headpiece . . . ," or "done in small ringlets" or "strait" or "a basketwork of braids." Even when he translates εὐπλόκαμος he does up the hair and covers it: the girl that Homer said had nice curls now appears "trim-coifed." But the poets almost unanimously are for unbound tresses. None more than Yeats; in nearly half of the poems in *The Wind Among the Reeds* he mentions long hair loosened.

But we dawdle too long outside the beauty parlors of Parnassus. Which way, one may wonder, is poetry from here? We can return via Cicero; a passage in the *Orator* might be paraphrased as follows: A speaker [and surely a poet] should not seem too fastidious in putting words togther; there is a *non ingrata neglegentia,* a certain carelessness not unattractive because it makes him seem first a human being and only then a man of eloquence, a kind of carelessness to be achieved only with great care. "Quaedam neglegentia est diligens" (A certain [kind of] carelessness is painstaking). Just as certain women are loveliest without jewels or elaborate curls, so this easy way of speaking pleases most when it seems that little or nothing has been done to improve it. *Neglegentia* is Cicero's word: Ben Jonson's "sweet neglect."

Why have the poets and their critics found this delight in disorder? Is it because disorder is more winning than composure? Horace still charms with graceful negligence, Pope reminds us: and by means of "brave disorder" we snatch a grace beyond the reach of art. Or is it because the poet, his mind on greater things, is above minutiae, realizing (again with Pope) that not to know some trifles is a praise? Or is it because disorder is closer to the spirit of nature, that "rerum concordia discors" (a dissonant harmony in things)? Ben Jonson, in his setting for *The Masque of Blackness*, seems to feel so: his machine-made waves imitate "that orderly disorder, which is common in nature." Or, finally, is it because disorder is a mark of emotion? Longinus says so—if indeed we need an authority to validate what we see around us. Placidity, he says, expresses itself in neat arrangement; emotion, however, in disorder: ἐν ἀταξίᾳ δὲ τὸ πάθος.

Here then are four suggestions as to why carelessness is dear to the poets: it is pleasing in itself, it is magnanimous, it is true to nature, and it is characteristic of passion. Particularly the last three account, though not completely, for the long alliance between Yeats and the careless muse.

II

My title is from "Among School Children." Yeats is saying that even the greatest men at the time of their fame have become scarecrows: old coats upon old sticks to scare a bird. Plato, Aristotle, and

> World-famous golden-thighed Pythagoras
> Fingered upon a fiddle-stick or strings
> What a star sang and careless Muses heard[1]

Careless muses—the adjective is curious. According to an older etymology the word *muse* grew from a root meaning *mind*. The derivation, even if discredited, suggests a popular interpretation: the muses are the mindful ones, the personification "of the highest intellectual and artistic aspirations"—anything, it would seem, but careless. For Chaucer, the muse was "mighty"; for Spenser, "lofty," "tender," or, especially, "mournful." In *Henry V* Shakespeare cries "O for a Muse of fire!" The poets disparage her too, as in a lovers' quarrel: for Donne she is "undiscerning"; for Milton "thankless"; for Wordsworth "niggardly" and "unchary," as in his case she sometimes was. But whatever her faults, she tends to be a hardworking lady; she "labors" with Iago in the throes of composition, as indeed she labors with the poets. There are few handouts from the muse.

Tennyson wrote of the "placid marble muses, looking peace." But Yeats found them quite different. "The Muses," he wrote in *A Vision*, "resemble women who creep out at night and give themselves to unknown sailors and return to talk of

Chinese porcelain . . . or the Ninth Symphony. . . ." His own muse, he was persuaded, grew younger as he grew older and more rheumatic; but she came to have not the innocence of youth so much as its exuberance and its wildness, the latter a quality Yeats thought inherent in the creative personality. When criticized for not rising for the national anthem, he wrote "There are only three classes I respect, the aristocracy who are above fear; the poor who are beneath it, and the artists whom God has made reckless." The artist resembled the human types that Yeats most admired: the horseman with his aristocratic nonchalance, the fisherman with his indifference to the workaday world and its interests, the beggar with his happy-go-lucky unconcern. The casual manner, in fact, became the very touchstone of integrity:

> And call those works extravagance of breath
> That are not suited for such men as come
> Proud, open-eyed, and laughing to the tomb.

Of course literature has always had its great disdainers: Dante's Farinata, up to his waist in the fire he scorns, is possibly the most memorable. Many an Elizabethan, on and off the stage, died like the Thane of Cawdor:

> As one that had been studied in his death,
> To throw away the dearest thing he owed,
> As 'twere a careless trifle.

If the heroes of Yeats seem less studied than impulsive, it may be because their creator professed to disdain the way of logic. His *Autobiography* tells how he hated (though he admired) the "logical straightness" of Shaw: it was not the crooked way of life. Presently he had "a nightmare that [he] was haunted by a sewing machine, that clicked and shone. . . ." For Yeats, there was more insight in fervor than in logic:

> A passion-driven exultant man sings out
> Sentences that he has never thought

Thought in the mind, that is, for there was also a thinking of the whole body, a thinking in a marrowbone. The mere brain-thinker is a half man; his partial mind has to be completed by passions of the flesh and blood. This is probably best put in "Michael Robartes and the Dancer," which lectures a young girl on the unimportance of mind compared with physical beauty:

> But bear in mind your lover's wage
> Is what your looking glass can show.

When she protests, she is told that women can be happy, and make men happy, only on condition that they

> banish every thought, unless
> The lineaments that please their view
> When the long looking glass is full
> Even from the footsole think it too.

To which the puzzled girl can only reply: "They say such different things at school." The muse too should seem not to take thought, thought which only "increases unreality."

> Thought is a garment and the soul's a bride
> That cannot in that trash and tinsel hide.

Whatever may be obscure in the cones and gyres and wheels and spheres of *A Vision* (that true Coney Island of the mind), certain things are clear. Of the twenty-eight incarnations or phases of the moon, Phase 15, that of the full moon, is the phase of complete beauty—and surely the most careless phase. Care means thought and effort, but even as we approach Phase 15 "thought is disappearing into image; and in Keats, in some ways the perfect type, intellectual curiosity is at its weakest. . . ." The historical period that corresponds to this phase is that of the Italian Renaissance between 1450 and 1550. Yeats particularly mentions Botticelli, da Vinci, Mantegna. Now Mantegna and the Quattrocento are evoked in an impressive poem, "Her Vision in the Wood," in which we have an image of thoughtless thought, a procession of something like the careless muses.

Dry timber under that rich foliage,
At wine-dark midnight in the sacred wood,
Too old for a man's love I stood in rage
Imagining men. Imagining that I could
A greater with a lesser pang assuage
Or but to find if withered vein ran blood,
I tore my body that its wine might cover
Whatever could recall the lip of lover.

And after that I held my fingers up,
Stared at the wine-dark nail, or dark that ran
Down every withered finger from the top;
But the dark changed to red, and torches shone,
And deafening music shook the leaves; a troop
Shouldered a litter with a wounded man,
Or smote upon the string and to the sound
Sang of the beast that gave the fatal wound.

All stately women moving to a song
With loosened hair or foreheads grief-distraught,
It seemed a Quattrocento painter's throng,
A thoughtless image of Mantegna's thought—
Why should they think that are for ever young?
Till suddenly in grief's contagion caught,
I stared upon his blood-bedabbled breast
And sang my malediction with the rest.

That thing all blood and mire, that beast-torn wreck,
Half turned and fixed a glazing eye on mine,
And, though love's bitter-sweet had all come back,
Those bodies from a picture or a coin
Nor saw my body fall nor heard it shriek,
Nor knew, drunken with singing as with wine,
That they had brought no fabulous symbol there
But my heart's victim and its torturer.

What interests us now is the third stanza, and especially its
fifth line. The muse, as Yeats remembered when he was given
the Nobel Prize, is young, and because young need not think.
She is careless—as here the stately women, so lost in the in-
toxication of their singing, seem blind to the agony in their
midst. "Why should they think that are for ever young?" In a

passage of *A Vision,* written about the same time as the poem, Yeats contrasts the "never-ceasing care" of statues of Roman senators with the ease of Greek sculptures. "Those riders upon the Parthenon had all the world's power in their moving bodies, and in a movement that seemed, so were the hearts of man and beast set upon it, that of a dance. . . . What need had those young lads for careful eyes?" Here is the same question in the same form, even in the same rhythm, though one is in prose. Thoughtlessness is proper to youth and to the phase of perfect beauty.

III

But when did Yeats take up with the careless muse? Not certainly in his earliest work, in which passion, so fierce and vibrant later, is neurasthenic, careworn. *Restless, sick, dreary, weary, fretful, pale, grey, dim, waning, mournful*—these were among his favorite words at the time. More than once the human child is urged to come away from a world more full of weeping than he can understand. The muse of the soggy handkerchief saw several volumes through the press; it was not until *In the Seven Woods* (1904), published when Yeats was almost forty, that there are signs of a break with her. He begins to cut himself short when the complaints grow lengthy:

> but enough,
> For when we have blamed the wind we can blame love.

And in "Adam's Curse" he expresses a paradox we will see again and again in the later poems: proper carelessness (as Cicero had observed) is a kind of care, and the verse of the careless muse, like the beauty of a woman, is the result of much hard work done privately.

> "A line will take us hours maybe;
> Yet if it does not seem a moment's thought,
> Our stitching and unstitching has been naught."

Six years later in *The Green Helmet*, his trifling with the casual muse has become serious indeed; he is almost committed to the baggage. The tone of mockery is quite new; the form it takes is disdain of the populace and popular taste, indifference to any event, provided the soul maintain its integrity. If it does, he asks defiantly, "Why should I be dismayed?" Hardly a question he would have asked earlier, with reasons for dismay on every side. But now he begins to profess indifference toward much that had troubled him before: toward love, toward politics, and even toward his own work. He begins to have words of praise for Dionysus. Laughter is heard for the first time in the world of his poetry—laughter that would have been so out of place in the misty air of the earlier work, except for the fey, unearthly laughter of the Sidhe. And he was coming to a new conception of language, as "wrought of high laughter, loveliness and ease"—exactly the tone of the careless muse. The poem in which this line occurs, made up of three questions and nothing else, is typical of the casual new style: no statement, no commitment. Up to now there had not been much questioning in his poetry, but suddenly the laurel wreath is fairly hooked together with interrogation marks. "No Second Troy," for example, is made up of nothing but four questions. Of the twenty-one poems in this collection, exactly one third end with a question mark, whereas only two or three poems or the hundred published before had done so.

Another negligence first shown at this time is a forgetting, or rather a not bothering to remember, this or that. Yeats also begins to use various phrases of indifference, like impatient gestures sweeping aside details: "Let all that be . . ."; "What matter . . . ?" "Enough if. . . ."

And into this book his first horseman comes galloping— that figure of the reckless and noble rider who is the opposite of merchant and clerk. We will hear the thunder of those arrogant hooves often throughout the greater poems, and when the curtains are finally drawn on the great drama of Yeats's passion, they will close upon a horseman against the sky.

IV

Why then, when Yeats was about forty-five, did his poetry take on a new life, a reckless life of arrogance and disdain, of laughter at times derisive, at times exultant? Circumstances that might have broken a man less tough had much to do with the change. In 1903 he heard that the woman he had loved in vain for nearly twenty years had made an unworthy marriage. During the next five or six years he wrote only one lyric; "his fists," says one of his critics, "were tightly clenched."

Disillusioned too by public events in Ireland, he remembered Goethe on Irish jealousy: "The Irish seem to me like a pack of hounds, always dragging down some noble stag."[2] Three times Yeats was in at the death of such a stag, and he never forgot. When, in his twenties, he saw the destruction of Parnell, he had no style capable of dealing with the "dramatic exit of the heaven-born leader"; he wrote only a bad poem whose title, complete with dash and exclamation mark, was "Mourn—And Then Onward!" But the theme of the proud hero dragged to ruin for a woman's sake recurs in his work, to culminate in the strange and violent "Parnell's Funeral" of forty years later.

In 1907 he raged again at the Irish, who had rioted against *The Playboy of the Western World.* Two years later Synge was dead. Not long after, the third blow came when Lady Gregory's nephew offered his great collection of French Impressionists to the city of Dublin provided it would build a suitable museum—and the city refused. The people, it seemed, did not want great leadership, did not want great drama, did not want great art—and for each of these rejections Yeats lashed out with a savagery that settled at last into contempt. More and more he expressed indifference toward what most people thought, toward his own past efforts, and finally even indifference toward his own indifference:

> We too had many pretty toys when young:
> A law indifferent to blame or praise

V

But the gestures of disdain had a theoretical sanction as well: they followed from Yeats's theory of the very nature of reality. The phenomenal world symbolized in *A Vision* is irrational because it is a series of unresolved antinomies. The only sound attitude to take toward it is a certain detachment, a certain indifference—or since, for Yeats, perfection exists in the interaction of opposites, a certain indifference together with a passionate concern. More about these opposites later; enough for now to note that his carelessness has a metaphysical or existential character.

Facts that account then for Yeats's new air of carelessness are not far to seek. But since he was a traditionalist who loved "precedents out of beautiful old books," he must have been pleased to find his own theories sustained by, though probably not originating in, Baldesar Castiglione's *The Book of the Courtier*. In *The Bounty of Sweden* Yeats tells how his "memory had gone back twenty years to that summer when a friend [Lady Gregory] read out to me at the end of each day's work Castiglione's commendations and descriptions of that court of Urbino, where youth for certain brief years imposed upon drowsy learning the discipline of its joy. . . ." The summer would have been that of 1904; in 1907 Yeats visited Urbino. There are several longing references to it in his work, two of them in a diary of 1909. And in a poem that complains of the people, he wishes he might have

> climbed among the images of the past—
> The unperturbed and courtly images—
> Evening and morning, the steep street of Urbino
> To where the Duchess and her people talked
> The stately midnight through until they stood
> In their great window looking at the dawn

The allusion, in which for us the important word is "unperturbed," is to the last page of *The Book of the Courtier*, a book that confirmed Yeats in his preference for a beneficent and responsible aristocratic life, and probably also brought into focus for him a something he had been working toward in his own art: the air of elegant unconcern. Two or three quotations will illustrate the kind of thing that must have struck him in Castiglione's book.

> Having thought many times already about how this grace is acquired . . . I have found quite a universal rule which in this matter seems to me valid above all others, and in all human affairs whether in word or deed: and that is . . . to practice in all things a certain *sprezzatura* [nonchalance], so as to conceal all art and make whatever is done or said appear to be without effort and almost without any thought about it. (I, 26)
>
> What eye is so blind as not to see . . . the grace of that cool *disinvoltura* [ease] . . . in many of the men and women here present, who seem in words, in laughter, in posture not to care; or seem to be thinking more of everything than of that, so as to cause all who are watching them to believe that they are almost incapable of making a mistake. . . ? (I, 26)
>
> Consider how ungraceful that rider is who tries to sit so very stiff in his saddle . . . compared with one who appears to give no thought to the matter and sits his horse as free and easy as if he were on foot.[3] (I, 27)

In Castiglione, Yeats could have found many of his other preferences anticipated, but probably what most impressed him was the desirability, in art as in other things, of the nonchalance shown by those "who seem in words, in laughter, in posture not to care," and who thereby give the impression of supreme mastery. All this he has in mind in "Ego Dominus Tuus":

> We have lit upon the gentle, sensitive mind
> And lost the old nonchalance of the hand;
> Whether we have chosen chisel, pen, or brush,
> We are but critics, or but half create,
> Timid, entangled, empty and abashed

In a letter to Dorothy Wellesley long afterwards (May 22, 1936) he wrote: "Those little poems of yours are nonchalant,

& nonchalance is declared by Castigleone [*sic*] essential to all true courtiers—so it is to warty lads & poets."

VI

Passion rather than thought, abandon rather than prudence, defiance rather than conformity, the air of nonchalance rather than any show of effort—from about 1910 on, these were to be the preferences of the careless muse. *Responsibilities*, Yeats's 1914 volume, opens with what T. S. Eliot describes as "that violent and terrible epistle dedicatory . . . more than half a lifetime to arrive at this freedom of speech." Yeats, recalling his ancestors, remembers especially his grandfather's recklessness and what it taught him:

> Old merchant skipper that leaped overboard
> After a ragged hat in Biscay Bay;
> You most of all, silent and fierce old man,
> Because the daily spectacle that stirred
> My fancy, and set my boyish lips to say,
> "Only the wasteful virtues earn the sun"

Not caring about this or that is a major theme in the book. "The Three Beggars," for example, is a fable to show that men who least desire get most. In the poem a king offers a thousand pounds to whichever of the beggars can first fall asleep within three days. They scheme and bicker, manage to do everything except that one thing they too much desire. The moral is clear to an old crane who has been standing by:

> It's certain there are trout somewhere
> And maybe I shall take a trout
> If but I do not seem to care.

But with the mention of this ode to indifference, suppose we drop our book-by-book scrutiny for a broader survey of the later work.

"Because there is safety in derision . . . ," the safety of disengagement, Yeats often has recourse to it. One section of "Nineteen Hundred and Nineteen" is all mockery: the first three stanzas in turn mock "the great," "the wise," and "the good," and in the fourth Yeats turns on himself: "Mock mockers after that." More than once he looks with derision on himself when young.

> When I was young
> I had not given a penny for a song
> Did not the poet sing it with such airs
> That one believed he had a sword upstairs

and the later "The Circus Animals' Desertion" casts an even more disenchanted eye on the earlier preoccupations of his muse.

As she became younger, she also became more laughter-loving, though never, I think, comic. She may have learned to laugh from Castiglione's ideal of those who "seem in words, in laughter, in posture not to care," as she may have learned from him to desire, as the supreme achievement of a great house, a "written speech Wrought of high laughter, loveliness and ease." Yeatsian laughter: a joyous and whole-hearted acceptance of experience, of the worst it can offer, and particularly of death itself. His jaunty heroes "have lived in joy and laughed into the face of Death," as he says in "Upon a Dying Lady," surely one of the most undaunted of deathbed sequences. With such laughter, gay and terrible, a man meets his fate: in an exultant surrender of personality to the great vortex of being, the spirit of the gyres. There is more of such laughter in *Last Poems* than elsewhere; it rings out even more strongly as the poet himself draws near to death. As souls pass on the backs of dolphins to the shores of another life, in "News for the Delphic Oracle,"

> The ecstatic waters laugh because
> Their cries are sweet and strange

In "Lapis Lazuli" there is gaiety in both the oriental philosophers and the tragic heroes of the west.

Laughter, like song and the dance, is a carefree Dionysian release quite beyond logic. So, preeminently, is drunkenness, which comes in for its share of praise. Drunkenness, that state of apparently heightened nonrational perception and participation, is for Yeats, as for some of the mystics, a metaphor for blessedness. So too are various deprivations: blindness, deafness, dumbness:

> Those men that in their writings are most wise,
> Own nothing but their blind stupified hearts.

Helen's poet, he never forgets, was a blind man.

Other Dionysian forces, antirational and imprudent if hardly nonchalant, are extolled: lust (Hanrahan's "horrible splendor of desire"), rage, folly, frenzy (called sometimes "blind," sometimes "drunken"), and indeed madness itself. For the wasteful virtues, and much that Yeats most cherishes, are in the eyes of the world a kind of madness—the literal and figurative senses of the word run together. "All that delirium of the brave": were the Irish heroes mad because they gave their lives for their country as one might for love?

> You'd cry, "Some woman's yellow hair
> Has maddened every mother's son":
> They weighed so lightly what they gave.

To this rapture of madness one is conducted by love, beauty, poetry, music, wine. Yeats writes of "eyes that beauty has driven mad," and poetry and alcohol have the same effect:

> And certain men, being maddened by those rhymes,
> Or else by toasting her a score of times

Such considerations led him to say of his own art, "If I triumph I must make men mad." Such drunken madness is that of Crazy Jane, who really has a superior kind of knowledge, that of the deep-considering mind which has known much and looked into the very heart of things. Indeed, madness in this sense is the sum of human knowledge:

> I shudder and I sigh to think
> That even Cicero
> And many-minded Homer were
> *Mad as the mist and snow.*

Frenzy, fury, folly, madness—these are to be invoked rather than deplored. Yeats expresses the hope on one occasion that a beloved friend will be visited not by satisfied conscience but by "that great family . . . / The Proud Furies each with her torch on high."

For what straightness, what sanity is possible in the world of "that dolphin-torn, that gong-tormented sea"? Yeats liked all crooked, zigzag, spinning things; he was fascinated by the "great labyrinth" of another's being. He liked gyres and spires and winding stairs—is perhaps the only reader who might have given the unexpected answer to George Herbert's, "Is all good structure in a winding stair?" In general he preferred vagrants to settled citizens; professed to admire all sorts of wild, purposeless activity: "an aimless joy is a pure joy."

Since true wisdom is "a something incompatible with life," it is not surprising that Yeats comes out frankly at times for ignorance: "all knowledge lost in trance / Of sweeter ignorance." Hence he is careless about details, sometimes forgets or professes to forget, often with fine poetic effect:

> Hanrahan rose in frenzy there
> And followed up those baying creatures toward—
> O toward I have forgotten what—enough!

On one occasion, in speaking of the reckless horseman Robert Gregory, he matches the rider's deliberate indifference with an indifference of his own:

> At Mooneen he had leaped a place
> So perilous that half the astonished meet
> Had shut their eyes; and where was it
> He rode a race without a bit?

Forgetting: a dismissal of the unworthy, a kind of disdaining. In *Estrangement* Yeats recalls the night an Irish mob was rioting against Synge's *Playboy*: "No man of all literary Dublin dared show his face but my own father, who spoke to, or rather in the presence of, the howling mob with sweetness and simplicity. I fought them, he did a finer thing—forgot them."

The ethical counterpart of careless memory is indifference to past conduct; Yeats, who came to believe that the soul's "own sweet will is heaven's will," thought that only passionate moments should be preserved in that great storehouse of communal memories, the Anima Mundi. But remorse, as the beginning of judgment, is of the intellect and therefore suspect. Conscience too is a hindrance; if the great lover Hanrahan has ever failed to win a woman, he must blame "some silly over-subtle thought / Or anything called conscience once"—the last word implying that Hanrahan has matured beyond conscience. To the heroic poets whose integrity he praises in "The Grey Rock" he says: "You . . . unrepenting faced your ends." And in old age he grieved, "Repentance keeps my heart impure."

VII

And yet, to return to "Her Vision in the Wood": "A thoughtless image of Mantegna's thought." Beyond the thoughtless, always thought; beyond the careless, always care. Always the insistence on measure, precision, craftsmanship:

> Irish poets, learn your trade,
> Sing whatever is well made

For the poet whose nonchalance we have been finding everywhere is at the same time one of the most earnest of craftsmen. This would have seemed no contradiction to Cicero, with his *neglegentia diligens*, and still less so to Yeats, who believed that a quality finds fulfillment in its opposite. Crazy Jane gives expression to one of his deepest convictions when she cries:

> "Fair and foul are near of kin
> And fair needs foul . . ."

Yeats was at once careful and careless, careful to seem careless; out of the tension between these opposites arise some of the finest effects of his art. In a little poem called "The Dawn" he speaks of "the careless planets in their courses"; careless, perhaps, but moving with mathematical precision, as Yeats himself did when he wrote. He once praised Lady Gregory's house as one in which "passion and precision have been one"; to a friend he insisted that "the very essence of genius, of whatever kind, is precision." And when H. J. C. Grierson sent Yeats his new edition of Donne, Yeats observed that "the more precise and learned the thought, the greater the beauty, the passion."

The effect of nonchalance was achieved with a labor that Yeats found "very great," as he tells us more than once. "Metrical composition is always very difficult to me, nothing is done upon the first day, not one rhyme is in its place, and when at last the rhymes begin to come, the first rough draft of a six-line stanza takes the whole day." And: "When I wrote verse, five or six lines in two or three laborious hours were a day's work, and I longed for somebody to interrupt me. . . ." He wrote little or no free verse, preferring the tougher stanza forms, of which he worked in a great many. "Leda and the Swan," which so shocked his typist that, breaking into tears, she refused to copy it, is in that most respectable of forms, the sonnet. Carelessness, in short, is another of the famous masks; behind it always is the frown of the scrupulous muse.

This is no surprise if we remember what company the careless muses were keeping:

> World-famous golden-thighed Pythagoras
> Fingered upon a fiddle-stick or strings
> What a star sang and careless Muses heard

Pythagoras: science no less than music. When Yeats quoted the whole stanza in a letter to Mrs. Shakespear (September 24, 1926), he said, "Pythagoras made some measurement of the intervals between notes on a stretched string." Stately Pythagoras, tall Pythagoras, who as passion and precision appears twice amid his choir of love in the poetry of Yeats, is intellect, calculation, number, measurement. This we see most memorably in that remarkable late poem, "The Statues." Much of Yeats's curious system supports the poem, but what it means, in brief, is that the scientific measurements of Pythagoras made possible the proportions of a sculpture and the expression of a beauty which the Greeks came to see in human beings; it was the spirit of precision and clarity rather than the Greek fleet which repulsed the Persian menace. The poet concludes by calling on the Pythagorean spirit to save Ireland from the confusion of modern values. Yet in "The Statues" the products of the Greek sculptors are called "calculations that look but casual flesh"—casual but calculated, as Castiglione's nonchalance comes from a care and effort cunningly concealed.

VIII

How Yeats took care to seem careless in matters of technique is a rewarding study. In diction, obviously he worked from the literary to the colloquial and conversational, but these always at concert pitch. He would have agreed with the author of *On the Sublime* that "a low word often reveals much more than an ornamental one; it is recognized from our daily life, and the familiar is that much nearer to carrying conviction." What the critic said about certain passages in Greek would characterize some of Yeats's work: they "graze the limits of vulgar and uncultivated speech, but are not uncultured in their expressiveness." Yeats himself wrote: "In later years I learnt that occasional prosaic words gave the impression of an active man speaking. . . . Here and there in correcting my early poems I have introduced [such] numbness and dullness . . . that all might seem, as it were, remembered with indifference, except some one vivid image." The colloquial, offhand tone is heard not only in the language of Crazy Jane and the wild old wicked man or in the apparent irrelevance of the refrains; even in some of his loftiest passages Yeats may seem to saunter carelessly close to the limits of vulgar speech.

Other effects are more subtle. In a typical lyric of Yeats, a number of obstacles are set up for the poet. Every line has its metrical obligations; it rhymes with the following line or the one after that; the lines generally move in units of four. But with what ease, with how strong and unbroken a stride, the long sinewy sentences, sometimes only one to a poem, take these hurdles!

Rhyme itself is handled more and more airily. Not for any lack of ear; in the earliest work, the rhymes are invariably pure and perfect, at times wearily so. The first poem of the *Collected Poems* has not a single oblique rhyme in its fifty-odd lines: *dead-fed-head, joy-toy, world-whirled,* etc. But in *Responsibilities* (1914) everything is different. In the twenty-two lines of the dedicatory epistle we find such rhymes as *four-poor, blood-stood, cast-crossed, board-stirred, man-sun, sake-book.* Six off-rhymes, some quite far off. The percentage is even higher in later poems. But the discords are used with skill: how numbly *book,* supposed to rhyme with *sake,* thuds down in

> *Pardon that for a barren passion's sake,*
> *Although I have come close on forty-nine,*
> *I have no child, I have nothing but a book*

Far more expressive, this off-key rhyme on a crucial word, than full rhyme could have been. From the time of *Responsibilities* on, Yeats is cavalier with rhyme: always aware of it, he makes the perfunctory bow in its direction, but with no deference whatever. He is the master, rhyme the servant. (A curious footnote: until about 1904, nearly always the word *love* is rhymed perfectly, for the most part with *above.* But after his own love had been embittered, the rhymes on *love* are habitually off-rhymes: *stuff, strove, off, enough,* though the *love-enough* rhyme is never used in the sense that there is or has been enough love.)

Yeats may have been confirmed in his later preference for off-rhyme by some remarks of Giuliano in *The Book of the Courtier*: "in music . . . it is a great mistake to place two perfect consonances one after the other, for our sense of hearing abhors this, whereas it often enjoys a second or a seventh which in itself is a harsh and unbearable discord. And this is due to the fact that to continue in perfect consonances generates satiety and gives evidence of a too affected harmony" (I, 28).

A studied nonchalance is apparent too in the handling of rhythm. From the beginning Yeats had a mastery of traditional effects and sometimes improved on them, as in "The Lake Isle of Innisfree" (published in 1890), with the suppression of a syllable energizing the fourth foot of the fourteeners, or as in "He Remembers Forgotten Beauty" (of five or six years later):

> When my arms wrap you round I press
> My heart upon the loveliness
> That has long faded from the world

If we remember that this is basically the same meter as that of so many singsong little iambic tetrameters, we can appreciate a rhythm brilliantly expressive: in the first line the stringent spondees that make this perhaps the firmest embrace in poetry; the skipped beat of excitement in the second line; the spondee of extent of time in *long fade*, followed by the pyrrhic drop-off that further distances the *world*. Yeats permits himself no liberty in number of feet, but every liberty in their management. Freely as the stresses are handled, there is always discipline beneath the freedom: every line is unmistakably a four-stress line. He is not often as irregular as in the last line of "The Second Coming": "Slouches toward Bethlehem to be born." This carries the disintegration of the iambic pentameter about as far as it can go without leaving the ruins unrecognizable. But even here the apparently haphazard rhythm is built on a careful meter, whether one takes the line as headless with a pyrrhic in the fourth foot or resolves it in one of the other possible ways. A striking example of the jaunty but expressive rhythm overriding the rigid meter is

"The Fisherman," published in 1916. The poem employs a three-stress iambic line, and yet out of its forty lines only three are regular. Of all the variations, only once does the same combination occur in two lines running. Yet high-handed as the treatment of meter is, the variations are meaningful. A healthy rhythm, like the heart, has its reasons for quickening or lagging—unlike a metronome, whose rhythm never changes, whether we blow it kisses or look daggers.

Nearly always Yeats works in fixed stanza forms, or he carries couplets or an *abab* pattern quite through a poem. But at times, with what may seem negligence, he drops a line. This can be exciting to those who care about the trifles from which, as Michelangelo is supposed to have said, comes the perfection which is no trifle. Take as simple a poem as the early "The Lover Mourns for the Loss of Love" (1898):

> Pale brows, still hands and dim hair,
> I had a beautiful friend
> And dreamed that the old despair
> Would end in love in the end:
> She looked in my heart one day
> And saw your image was there;
> She has gone weeping away.

The first four lines are a common *abab* quatrain; the next three lines take us through three-fourths of another quatrain—and leave us there, our expectation vaguely unsatisfied, waiting for something, curtailed of the expected resolution which in our reading of thousands of quatrains had never failed us. But the poem is about loss; even in its form it suffers the bereavement. By its form as much as by the words, and far more subtly, it dramatizes that bereavement. But, with a calculation even about trifles, the line that might have been left unrhymed is given a rhyme from the preceding quatrain.

Another example: in "The Grey Rock" (1913), for one hundred and twelve lines the ear has been habituated to *abab: trade-cheese-remade-please, fashion-breath-passion-death.* Then, when the expectation is firmly grounded, we come upon:

The bitter sweetness of false faces?
Why must the lasting love what passes?
Why are the gods by men betrayed?

First the sour rhymes of *faces-passes,* an unexpected couplet. Between them should have been the rhyme for *betrayed,* but *betrayed* hangs there forever without its rhyme, as if vibrant in a great silence. Then, having brought off his coup, the poet goes back to *up-sound-cup-ground.*

IX

Once he had made the acquaintance of the careless muse, Yeats was faithful to the end. She is nowhere more present than in the eleven-line finale of "Under Ben Bulben," written only a few months before his death.

Under bare Ben Bulben's head
In Drumcliff churchyard Yeats is laid.
An ancestor was rector there
Long years ago, a church stands near,
By the road an ancient cross.
No marble, no conventional phrase;
On limestone quarried near the spot
By his command these words are cut:

Cast a cold eye
On life, on death.
Horseman, pass by!

The first five lines are offhand, almost brusque: merely "an ancestor," "a church," though we know that Yeats was fiercely proud of his ancestors and cherished the details of their history. The directions about the burial have the tone of indifference, impatience, as if he cared nothing for conventional pomp and wanted as little as possible done. And yet he gives a firm command: it must be *this* kind of stone, *these* words exactly. The final image of the horseman is all indifference, detachment, aloofness—or rather, the deliberate air of these.

For, as Frank O'Connor has said, Yeats was no detached observer of life. He was an impassioned participant, but the air of nonchalance is what his muse demanded. Here every rhyme except the very last is cavalier, an arrant off-rhyme. Yeats omitted an original "Draw rein, draw breath" that preceded the last three lines and would have made them a symmetrical quatrain. Whether or not there is significance in the fact that *death* is not even deigned its rhyme, there is surely significance in the choice of a last word that resolves the series of dissonant rhymes in a perfect harmony. As poetry this epitaph would have pleased the careless muse, but we cannot forget that Pythagoras too had a hand in it.

The poets, we said near the beginning of these observations, take delight in disorder because it is charming in itself, contemptuous of minutiae, true to nature, and eloquent of emotion. After his earliest poems Yeats was less interested in charm for its own sake. But high-handed and passionate he always was; more and more he came to believe in a universe at loggerheads with itself. He had other reasons too for august indifference: he had lost a sweetheart, though he had found a book; he had left a country, though he had sailed the seas; he had turned, like those giants of the past, into old clothes upon old sticks to scare a bird. But at least he had heard the careless planets singing and seen the heaven disheveled:

> I dreamed as in my bed I lay,
> All night's fabulous wisdom come,
> That I had shorn my locks away
> And laid them on Love's lettered tomb:
> But something bore them out of sight
> In a great tumult of the air,
> And after nailed upon the night
> Berenice's burning hair.

Notes

1. All quotations from the poetry of Yeats are from *The Collected Poems of W. B. Yeats,* edited by Richard J. Finneran (New York: Macmillan, 1983), and are reprinted by permission.

2. Yeats did remember the Goethe quotation, but his memory had remodeled it to his liking. What Goethe really said to Eckermann (April 7, 1829) was, as translated by Frank Tuohy in his *Yeats* (New York: Macmillan, 1976), 141: "The Catholics squabble among themselves but they are always prepared to make common cause against a Protestant. They are like a pack of hounds, snapping out at one another, but the moment they catch sight of a stag they herd together and attack." I am grateful to Linda Howe for pointing this out.

3. From *The Book of the Courtier* by Baldesar Castiglione, translated by Charles Singleton (New York: Doubleday, 1959), reprinted by permission.

The Classicism of Robert Frost

It is almost four decades since Gorham Munson hailed Robert Frost as "the purest classical poet of America today"; almost three since Dudley Fitts bade the ancient writers make way for him. *Cedite Romani scriptores, cedite Graii.* Classical, then— but in which of its many senses? Pater thought classicism rested on the principle of authority rather than liberty. But Frost, who delights in swimming against the current, shows little deference for received ideas: Edward Thomas called his "North of Boston" one of the most revolutionary books of modern times; Amy Lowell said he used classic meters in such a way as to set on edge the teeth of traditional poets.

Frost is not classical, surely, by virtue of adherence to any doctrine. Nor is he a classicist according to his own definition: "one who knows all the Greek irregular verbs." For himself, he would rather have touched a few stones the Greeks left, he admitted, than have a two-year explication of their significance. All a poet needs is to sample "the virtue of a thing; just enough alcohol or money or love or apples. . . ." Yet the man who studied Latin and Greek at Harvard, who read Vergil's *Eclogues* under the farmhouse lamp, who guided his daughter through Caesar and the *Aeneid,* and who in 1938 was offered a post in the Latin Department at Harvard had considerably more than a sampling of the classics.

Frost is joking in his definition; perhaps Yvor Winters is joking too in saying that Frost "is not classical in any sense which I can understand." Or the subtle critic may have over-

From *Saturday Review,* February 23, 1963.

looked some of the commonly accepted meanings of the word. I find Frost classical because his view of existence is tragic (more classical, then, than romantic), and because— obviously—his work has certain affinities with Greek and Latin poetry.

By the tragic view I mean that which sees human nature, wonderful as it is, as limited. What the limits are we cannot always say, but if we transgress them, willy-nilly we may chance on worse than Theban horrors. A few lines from Hulme's famous essay are interesting here because the very phrasing is like Frost's: "The classical poet never forgets this finiteness, this limit of man. He remembers always that he is mixed up with earth. He may jump, but he always returns; he never flies away into the circumambient gas."

> However it is in some other world
> I know that this is the way in ours.
>
> I'd like to get away from earth awhile
> And then come back to it and begin over.
> . . . Earth's the right place for love:
> I don't know where it's likely to go better.

The first two lines are from "In Hardwood Groves," an early poem about an existence in which suffering and death are the very conditions of life. Life is cruel: Frost has gloried in the admission more than once; he has written more than one poem "too cruel" for his public readings. He has stared into the darkness and terror that encroach on the little clearing of our lives, has seen the mysteries reason cannot cope with. "It had to seem unmeaning to have meaning," God says darkly to Job in "A Masque of Reason." Probably Frost's most scary image for the idiot violence of nature is in "An Old Man's Winter Night," in which the sounds of the outer dark suggest

> nothing so like beating on a box.

Against the gloom man pits his wit and courage; Frost, though aware of the odds, is never defeatist about the outcome. *Amor fati:* he is even in love with the struggle.

Unlike the learned poets, who leave such a thick trail of classical crumbs that a greenhorn can follow their cultural safaris, Frost as reader is not easily tracked. He is not given to classical allusions, nor addicted to mythology. It is up to the poet himself, he insists, to make up his own quotable lines.

Though a "good Greek out of New England," his own temperament and many of his favorite ancients are Roman. In Theocritus he may have noted the realistic speech, not of the bucolic poems, but of the urban mimes. Yet there is little here (except for the colloquial verve of XV) that he could not have found in Vergil's *Eclogues,* one of the two works from which he admitted first hearing "the voice from the printed page." He admired the courage with which Lucretius confronted without illusion the empty spaces of our existence. Probably from Catullus he picked up the "Hen Dekker Syllables" of "For Once, Then, Something" (a leading Frost authority has been fooled into calling the classical lines "irregular"). Probably Frost found Horace the most congenial of the Romans, both for the colloquial *Sermones* and for the tight lyrical strophes so like some of his own stanzas. "Vides ut alta stet nive candidum" is pure Frost in Latin. And may not Latin syntax, perhaps Horatian syntax, have had something to do with such a line as

Back out of all this now too much for us?

But what Frost seems to have found chiefly in the classics was confirmation rather than guidance. If the classical manner had not existed, he might well have invented it.

Form, restraint—these are what he prizes. Form: both in poetry and discussion Frost has stressed his concern for it. "Let chaos storm! . . . I wait for form." According to Sidney Cox, he declared, "My object is true form—is, was and always will be—form true to any chance bit of true life." For form is meaningfulness discerned in the chaos of existence. Faced with tragedy, Frost said later, we make a little form and we gain composure. Hence his fondness for metaphor, which knots together the loose ends of life. Chiefest of the things he has said about poetry "is that it is metaphor, saying one thing and meaning another, saying one thing in terms of another."

Together with form: restraint. The classicist works by inspired makeshift, making do with the simplest means at hand rather than giving way to the anything-goes extravagance of the romantic. Few of the great poets have had as simple a vocabulary as Frost: "We play the words as we find them. We make them do." Whole poems are almost monosyllabic, sometimes eerily, as in "The Hill Wife," sometimes portentously, as in "Neither Out Far Nor In Deep," which Lionel Trilling sometimes thinks "the most perfect poem of our time"—yet so plain the diction that "reflect" and "vary" are the most sophisticated words. A sonnet on the effect of Eve's voice on the song of the birds ends with what a younger poet thinks—in its context—"perhaps the most beautiful single line in American literature."

> And to do that to birds was why she came.

I like to fancy that by some ape-at-typewriter miracle a novice had chanced on the first thirteen lines of the sonnet, and sits deliberating with his Muse. "What I want to say now is: and to do that to birds was why she came. But how should I say it in poetry? How about

> E'en such her scepter o'er th'aëreal folk?

Or, more modernlike,

> Fair air's high scions' pure imperatrix?"

Frost's simplicity is never flatness; his language crinkles with what he has called the play of the mind, the little twists of thinking.

> Always the same, when on a fated night
> At last the gathered snow lets down as white
> As may be in dark woods. . . .

Or the sawdust,

> Sweet-scented stuff when the breeze drew across it.

"Stuff" has Elizabethan overtones; "drew" makes the breeze like a fine silk the sawdust clings to. Our novice might have had the breeze "like trailing silk," but it is typical of Frost's classic economy that he can insinuate a metaphor without stating it. One of the best examples is in his early and otherwise unimpressive "My Butterfly":

> The gray grass is scarce dappled with the snow;
> Its two banks have not shut upon the river.

Again we can imagine our novice brooding: "ice closes over the river like . . . like . . . crystal portals? King Winter clangs / His crystal portals o'er the finny chamber?" But in Frost the whole metaphor is carried by the plain word "shut."

When a metaphor is stated, Frost does not drop it for another.

> He is that fallen lance that lies as hurled,
> That lies unlifted now, come dew, come rust,
> But still lies pointed as it plowed the dust.

At the end of the sonnet the dead soldier is still a fallen lance. The less skilled poet we know so well would have been all butterfingers with the image, perhaps writing:

> He is that mangled lance, by lightning blasted,
> He is that ship, in time's Sahara quelled.

Frost's favorite figure of speech is synecdoche, in which the part is put for the whole—or vice versa. But for Frost never the vice versa: he speaks of the figure always as the part for the whole. Notes a student took quote him as saying, "Always, always a larger significance. A little thing launches a larger thing."

If there are readers who think that Frost writes about little things, it is because they do not see what the little things are launching; they fail to follow the synecdoche. And if they think his means are straitened, they might reflect with Valéry, who, though so different from Frost, has said so many of the same things:

> Life itself goes on only in a framework of terribly narrow conditions . . . my hand has five fingers . . . an arbitrary number: it is for me to find some freedom in the exercise of this hand, and the most agile and adroit actions . . . will be due only to the consciousness of that limitation and to the efforts I shall make to supplement by art and exercise the small group of *given* means.

The classicist knows very well that his hand has five fingers; he learns to adapt them. The romanticist brags he has seven.

Daedalus on Crete

James Joyce and Ovid

           ita Daedalus implet
innumeras errore vias vixque ipse reverti
ad limen potuit: tanta est fallacia tecti . . .
Daedalus interea Creten longumque perosus
exilium tactusque loci natalis amore
clausus erat pelago. "Terras licet" inquit "et undas
obstruat, at caelum certe patet: ibimus illac!
omnia possideat, non possidet aëra Minos."
Dixit et ignotas animum dimittit in artes
naturamque novat. Nam ponit in ordine pennas,
a minima coeptas, longa breviore sequenti,
ut clivo crevisse putes: sic rustica quondam
fistula disparibus paulatim surgit avenis.
Tum lino medias et ceris adligat imas,
atque ita compositas parvo curvamine flectit,
ut veras imitetur aves. Puer Icarus una . . .
cum puer audaci coepit gaudere volatu
deseruitque ducem caelique cupidine tractus
altius egit iter. Rapidi vicinia solis
mollit odoratas, pennarum vincula, ceras.

                        Ovid, *Metamorphoses* (VIII, 166–226)

T. S. Eliot speaks of the contemporaneousness of all literature, and particularly of how a new work can shift and realign the values of the past: a new poem is a new light on all

---

From *Dedulus* [sic] *on Crete: Essays on the Implications of Joyce's* Portrait (Los Angeles: Immaculate Heart College, 1956).

earlier poems; it shows us new possibilities of poetry by showing us the new achievement. It would be difficult for a modern reader to come across the figure of Tiresias in Homer or Sophocles or Ovid without finding him more significant for his role in *The Waste Land*.

> I who have sat by Thebes below the wall
> and walked among the lowest of the dead.

It would be difficult for him to return to the Helen of Homer or Euripides or Marlowe without remembering what she was for a great poet of our own time, William Butler Yeats:

> Why, what could she have done, being what she is?
> Was there another Troy for her to burn?

In *Portrait of the Artist* we come across another of these refluences, as we might call them: again the lines of an ancient writer take on a new meaning, catch fire anew from the work of a modern. I am thinking of Ovid's lines on Daedalus, from the eighth book of the *Metamorphoses*. Joyce studied Ovid: in the *Portrait of the Artist* he tells us how he was taught to construe him "in courtly English, made whimsical by the mention of porkers and potsherds and chines of bacon." One story particularly impressed him: that of Daedalus, the fabulous artificer; it impressed him so deeply that he gives that name to his rather harsh depiction of himself as artist and young man. He also gives unmistakable salience to the Daedalus myth by setting as epigraph at the head of his *Portrait* the ninth line from the Ovidian passage above.

The mere use of an epigraph from another writer, another century, or another literature sets up a comparison: it establishes a sharp point of contact between two realities and invites the reader to seek others. It brings another dimension into the poem or novel that employs it; it suggests that one is to be on the watch for analogies.

If after reading *Portrait of the Artist* we return to Ovid's lines about Daedalus, we find them enormously enriched. They have become, as Dante said of his *Divine Comedy,* polysemous: we find levels of meaning everywhere: Crete has become Ireland, the labyrinth and its monsters have become the streets of Dublin and the adolescent mind. Suppose, in this suggestible way, we look back at Ovid. This device, this artifice, ought to be a double-action one. We find Ovid enriched, and in the enriched Ovid we find forms and patterns meaningful for Joyce.

The first lines that reverberate with Joycean overtones are the lines about the construction of the labyrinth.

> ita Daedalus implet
> innumeras errore vias, vixque ipse reverti
> ad limen potuit: tanta est fallacia tecti

"So Daedalus fills the countless ways with [wandering] error, till hardly he himself can find his way back to the door." We may feel that *error* (the nominative form), which means "wandering" as well as "deception" or "error," itself vibrates between its two or more meanings. Stephen Dedalus too fills the streets of Dublin with his wanderings, in search of pleasure, or while threshing out a problem, or merely observing; his mind goes this way and that, trying to unriddle clew by clew the universe perplexing him, working himself into a maze from which he extricated himself only by unusual resolution.

> Daedalus interea Creten longumque perosus
> exilium . . .

"Daedalus, meanwhile, loathing Crete and the long exile. . . ." Historically, Crete and the Minoan civilization suggest something urbane and graceful (though not without its shadows). In what remains or has been reconstructed of the palace of Minos we can still see the frescoes of the charming girls a French archaeologist called the "Parisians," the gay frescoes of leaping dolphins, and in the museum the ivory statuette of the acrobat still balanced with lovely precision. Mythologically, however, Minos is a darker figure and his court a sinister one—probably because Greeks of another strain wrote the mythology. Dante draws on it for images of horror, and those who know Racine will remember the hair-raising lines in which Phèdre speaks about her family:

> O haine de Vénus! ô fatale colère!
> Dans quels égarements l'amour jeta ma mère!
>
> Ariane, ma soeur! de quel amour blessée,
> Vous mourûtes aux bords où vous fûtes laissée!
>
> (O hatred shown by Venus! o fatal rage!
> In what bewildered ways love hurled my mother!
>
> Ariadne, my sister! wounded with what a love
> you died on the shores where you were abandoned!)

Pasiphaë fell in love with a bull and had the form of the animal constructed in metal so that she might enjoy her monstrous love. And who made this horror? Daedalus. When Stephen Dedalus speaks of the monster in his thoughts is he remembering that his fabulous artificer was a maker of monsters, as well as of wings and images? Dante took Pasiphaë as a symbol of dreadful love; Stephen Dedalus tells us that he studied Italian to read Dante seriously. He can hardly have been unaware of the part Daedalus played in the shocking story.

"Daedalus . . . hating the long exile. . . ." Here in our multiplex reading of Ovid, we find an apparent reversal of pattern: by silence and cunning Daedalus plans to escape from exile to his home; Stephen Dedalus longs to go into exile. Or, like his Greek namesake, he is already in exile: not at home in Ireland, not at home with his family or with his church, seeking a place he *can* feel at home—is his going abroad really a going into exile or is it more of a homecoming?

The same paradoxical relationship between the Greek Daedalus and Stephen Dedalus is found in the words that follow:

tactusque loci natalis amore

"Touched by love of his native land"—could we say that of Stephen? Yes, in more ways than one. First, in the sense that his native land is the artistic or spiritual climate he seeks, the conditions under which he will feel at peace—wherever he is—the *locus natalis* of the artist. Also, more literally, in that he loves Ireland, but in the way that Dante loves Florence: Stephen Dedalus is never so hard on Ireland as Dante is on the city he loved so deeply and yet could excoriate with frightening violence:

> Godi, Fiorenza, poi che sei sì grande!
>
> (Rejoice, Florence, since you are so great!)

There is a similar fierceness in the two exiles, Dante and Joyce.

> "Terras licet" inquit "et undas
> obstruat, at caelum certe patet: ibimus illac!
> omnia possideat, non possidet aëra Minos."

"Though he blocks me by land and sea, there's still the open heaven—and that's the way we'll go. Minos may possess everything else; the sky he doesn't hold." Stephen too is blocked by land and sea, by grossness and insularity, by a corrupted world, by the Minos-monsters of his own mind, but one way of escape is offered: flight, the flight that escapes and the flight that soars—a flight inspired by and hastening toward epiphanies, those "sudden spiritual manifestations," those sudden openings of the heaven, such as Stephen experiences in his vision of mortal beauty.

> . . . et ignotas animum dimittit in artes

"And he directs his mind into unknown arts." There is some bitterness here, to think that the ancient art of poetry should be an *ars ignota* in Ireland.

> naturamque novat . . .

To renew nature, to make nature all over again, to make a new kind of existence, to reorganize a chaotic world, to make out of clods a spiritual beauty—this was the greatness of Joyce's vocation as he conceived it; this is what he was doing in forging "the uncreated conscience of my race."

. . . Nam ponit in ordine pennas

The polysemous reader, worrying the "in ordine" into a rather different meaning, will pounce gleefully on these words about arranging the feathers in order—for what are feathers but quills, pens? and what is Stephen doing in the *Portrait* but putting his pen in order, making ready the instruments of his literary adventure? We remember Ezra Pound's "We have kept our erasers in order."

"So once the rural flute," Ovid continues, "was built up of reeds each slightly larger than the one before it." For our purpose it is a felicitous coincidence that Ovid sees the wing Daedalus is constructing as a musical instrument. For Joyce too the way of flight was the way of the muses, the way of song. Daedalus shapes and flexes his wing "ut veras imitetur aves"—to imitate that of real birds. And we find implied here, by symbol, an esthetic theory of mimesis, of art as an imitation, but an imitation of reality. Poetry is "imaginary gardens," writes Marianne Moore, and she puts the words in quotation marks in later printings of the poem, "imaginary gardens with real toads in them."

The musical instrument seen as the wing of a bird also suggests the propensity Joyce's images have for the world of winged things. Daedalus, his ideal, is a bird-man; later, in his vision of mortal beauty, the wading girl seems a rare sea-bird. All through *Portrait of the Artist* we hear the beating of wings overhead.

The last four lines of Ovid's passage shift the emphasis to Icarus, the young son of Daedalus. If Stephen is a Daedalus-figure he is also an Icarus-figure. Probably we notice in the *Portrait* "a hawklike man flying sunward above the sea." In the framework of the myth this is a highly ironic reference: an image not so much of triumph as of death. For in the myth the sun is a destructive force; it melts the wax that holds the wings together and precipitates Icarus into the sea in which Brueghel paints him vanishing. In the last four lines we may also choose to find a characterization of the artist as a young man: "the boy begins to delight in his daring flight and turns away from his guide, and fascinated with a lust for the sky, goes higher and higher"—until wax melts and the wings fall apart.

In many ways, then, Ovid's Daedalus myth serves Joyce for a pattern of confinement and escape. He too found himself living—"living and partly living"—where he could not feel at home, in a labyrinth, shut in by an ocean, the seas and the lands blocked, corrupted; an escape possible only by way of his private heaven. His Crete was first of all his home, with its increasing sordidness, a Micawber of a father he could not admire, a mother he pitied but hardly seemed to love, a dying sister he never felt he knew. In *Stephen Hero* he had a sympathetic brother he could at least talk to; the rigorous art of *Portrait of the Artist* refuses even this distraction.

His Crete was also his country, whose confused aspirations, whose wild and rather futile patriotism, whose attitudes and temperament repelled him: Yeats often felt the same and might have been speaking for Joyce when he wrote, early in his career (in "The Dedication to a Book of Stories Selected from the Irish Novelists"):

> the barren boughs of Eire,
> That country where a man can be so crossed;
>
> Can be so battered, badgered and destroyed
> That he's a loveless man . . .

More Joycean are the bitter lines of "September 1913":

> What need you, being come to sense,
> But fumble in a greasy till
> And add the halfpence to the pence
> And prayer to shivering prayer, until
> You have dried the marrow from the bone?
> For men were born to pray and save:
> Romantic Ireland's dead and gone,
> It's with O'Leary in the grave.

A letter Yeats wrote to Lady Gregory puts this even more harshly: "I described Ireland, if the present intellectual movement failed, as a little greasy huxtering nation groping for half-pence in a greasy till, but did not add, except in thought, 'by the light of a holy candle.'"

Joyce was largely indifferent to the patriotic movements of his time; likely enough he found them false and sentimental. Thomas Davis's Young Ireland Movement, which was in reaction against the Scottish-inspired utilitarianism of Daniel O'Connell (Yeats's "old rascal") emphasized imagination and passion. It held that the peasantry was mystically in touch with the Irish past, and that in them, Ireland had a repository of traditional values. If this could be ignited, it was thought, all Ireland would flare up. The peasants, however, realists with a worried eye on tomorrow's potatoes, never did rise to an understanding of this idealism; they preferred to throw stones and handfuls of mud at such figures as Mitchel when he told them of the aspirations that ought to be theirs. Yeats himself admired the peasants in a rather misty poetic way, imagining in them the characteristics that Matthew Arnold thought he saw in the Celtic character: charm, grace, mysticism, dreamy feyness. Actually, the ancient Irish literature had been realistic, satiric, ironic—far from having the pre-Raphaelite languor that Yeats ascribed to it. Yeats's romantic attitude is one Joyce scorned; the peasants, for him, stood for nothing significant. He never became, as Ezra Pound said, "an institution for the promotion of Irish peasant industries."

He was confined, also, in what seemed to him the Cretan darkness of an uncongenial religion. Family, homeland, and religion were of course not separate trammels for Joyce; we see only too well how inextricably they were entangled in the episode of the quarrel over Parnell that ruined the family Christmas dinner: here religion, politics, and family bring violence into the home at what should have been a time of peace and goodwill. Again we are reminded of Yeats, the savage stanza of 1919:

> We, who seven years ago
> Talked of honor and of truth,

Shriek with pleasure if we show
The weasel's twist, the weasel's tooth.

Stephen as a child saw the weasel's tooth in his own home. "He'll remember all this when he grows up," says Mrs. Riordan—and how well he did remember! Already the boy had taken sides: "Stephen looked with affection at Mr. Casey's face . . . he liked to sit near him at the fire, looking up at his dark fierce face. But his dark eyes were never fierce and his slow voice was good to listen to." And when Mrs. Riordan's fanaticism goads Mr. Casey into shouting something he well may not mean, "No God for Ireland! We have had too much God in Ireland. Away with God!" how was a child to know he may not have meant it? As Mr. Casey stands there "scraping the air from before his eyes with one hand as though he were tearing aside a cobweb," doesn't Joyce see him as a kind of angel of truth? The allusion to Dante seems clear enough: the angel who rescues Dante and Vergil comes waving the mists of error from before his face:

Dal volto rimovea quell'aere grasso,
menando la sinistra innanzi spesso;
e sol di quell'angoscia parea lasso.

(He brushed away that dense air from before his face, often moving his left hand in front of him; and only because of that trouble seemed weary.)

William York Tindall has said that if *Portrait of the Artist* ended around the retreat it would be "the great Catholic novel." This seems to me a judgment dubious in the extreme. Stephen is certainly "supersaturated," as his friend says, with Catholicism. He has the Catholic sense of sin, as Yeats observes in a letter, and far as his revolt may have gone he never lost it. The autobiography of William Carlos Williams tells of a party in Paris in the twenties at which Joyce was present. One of the guests, a little high on white wine, proposed a toast, "Here's to sin!" Joyce looked up suddenly. "I won't drink to that."

I think we might risk an exaggeration and say that Stephen Dedalus (if not James Joyce) didn't give up Catholicism, he just never quite understood what it was. What we see in *Portrait of the Artist* sounds like some elaborate variety of puritanism: with its priests with no-colored eyes and heads like skulls, who think the unjust punishment of a probably oversensitive boy is a good joke, with its retreats that have two sermons on hell and none at all—though one is announced—on heaven; a religion in which all is the fear and nothing is the love. The religion of the *Portrait* is strange too in that Stephen doesn't seem to feel that God, creator and sustainer, has anything to do with the world of mortal beauty. When "the wonder of mortal beauty" is epiphanized in the girl by the sea, Stephen thinks many things, but, great analyzer and integrater that he is, he does not think of God in connection with this beauty. His fervent "Heavenly God" does not seem to me prayerful in intent.

However truly or falsely Stephen saw it, he feels the church is part of his Cretan confinement—this and his home and his country mock him with hollow-sounding phantom voices that mean nothing. Cretan too is the riot of his own mind, the monstrous thoughts, "the expense of spirit in a waste of shame."

This is Stephen's situation, and from this situation he chooses to flee. For to have chosen *this* home, *this* country, *this* misconceived, misunderstood religion would have been a destruction of what Stephen felt was his truest being and truest end. It was not a choice, for him, between art and morality, but rather between two moralities; in *Stephen Hero* more often than in *Portrait of the Artist* Joyce insists on the morality of his choice. It was not a selfish one: he wished to express his nature freely and fully for the benefit of a society which he would enrich. "I wish to bring to the world the spiritual renewal which the poet brings to it"; to remake nature, as Daedalus had remade it.

Art was no easy way out. It was not so much an escape from something as it was a deliberate confronting and coping with what was to be an arduous way of life. Most people, we read in

Stephen Hero, want to make money, have a good job, get married and have a home; they are impelled to these ends, says Stephen, by passions direct if menial. From these ordinary people with their ordinary ambitions Stephen violently separates himself: "I seek a *bonum arduum.*" His end, like that of Daedalus, was arduous in a double sense: it was difficult and it was lofty. How arduous it was we see in *Stephen Hero* and *Portrait of the Artist.* Joyce's awareness of the sacrifice and the glory involved in his quest is shown in the very name his hero is given, that of the first martyr; the sacrifice and the glory are implied too in the "Bous stephanephoros" and "Bous stephanomenos" with which his school friends playfully taunt him: he is the bull bound for the sacrifice, crowned and garlanded for the solemn rites.

Once Stephen has made his choice, we see in everything he does the preparations for the flight, the making of the wings. All the discussion of esthetic matters which for a casual reader might seem so chill and sluggish is animated here by its tremendous importance: what it is is a kind of theory of flight for Joyce. He wants to escape, but he wants an intellectually sound method of escape. "By thinking of things you could understand them," he had said as a boy. Taken out of the *Portrait,* the esthetic theories might have no particular originality or force; in it, however, they are tremendously vitalized by the tension of the narrative, just as philosophical, historical, and scientific discussions are vitalized in Dante—coming out of passion and drama they are expressed with a vigor and immediacy that speculation for its own sake might do without. It hardly matters that they are sometimes misinformed: "Aristotle has not defined pity and terror," says a cocksure Stephen who apparently has not read the *Rhetoric.* More important is their relevance to his life and situation: all around him he sees kinetic theories of art: art *for* something, for country, for church. So he insisted that art should be static; yet surely he had in mind a kinetic intent for his own art, and certainly it was kinetic in effect, this art that lifted him from the earth and carried him across oceans wider than those of any atlas.

First for Joyce was the theory of flight; the next step, to

continue our metaphor, was the gathering of the feathers. In collecting the materials out of which he would construct his wings, Joyce subjected reality to relentless scrutiny. Walking about the streets of Dublin, he was always observing—"observing" is almost too passive a word for the intensity with which Joyce would seize on what he saw and wring a meaning out of it. Always he was on the watch for what he called his "epiphanies," those "sudden spiritual manifestations, in speech or gesture or intuition." It was the duty of the man of letters to receive these with extreme care, even with something like reverence, for these were the sacraments of his calling.

At the same time he was gathering other feathers, some dingy, some lustrous; he would find a place for all of them when he came to the making of the wings. He has images for the ugly:

> He ate his dinner with surly appetite and when the meal was over and the grease-strewn plates lay abandoned on the table, he rose and went to the window, clearing the thick scum from his mouth with his tongue and licking it from his lips. So he had sunk to the state of a beast that licks his chaps after meat . . . His soul was fattening and congealing into a gross grease."

And for the beautiful:

> Her slate-blue skirts were kilted boldly about her waist and dovetailed behind her. Her bosom was as a bird's, soft and slight, slight and soft as the breast of some dark-plumaged dove.

The metaphor itself is a sort of epiphany; an awareness of a relationship not perceived before; it throws light in two directions and catches a meaning that may have eluded us.

Stephen had a rich store of images; he had other treasures as well. One kind he describes as follows:

> He drew forth a phrase from his treasure and spoke it softly to himself:

> —A day of dappled seaborne clouds.—
> The phrase and the day and the scene harmonised in a chord.
> Words. Was it their colours? He allowed them to glow and
> fade, hue after hue: sunrise gold, the russet and green of
> apple orchards, azure of waves, the greyfringed fleece of
> clouds.

He was sensitive to the whole being of words, their color, their
sound, the cadences they took in combination. How skillfully
he used them we see on every page of *Portrait of the Artist*—
where the art in all these matters goes far deeper than a
casual reading shows. Take the two following passages. In the
first the sound of the words is dull and lifeless, without a
ringing *i* sound or an elate *a*. In the exhilaration of the second
passage these vibrant sounds are everywhere.

> The squalid scene composed itself around him; the common
> accents, the burning gasjets in the shops, odours of fish and
> spirits and wet sawdust, moving men and women.

> He was unheeded, happy, and near to the wild heart of life.
> He was alone and young and wilful and wildhearted, alone
> amid a waste of wild air and brackish waters and the seaharvest
> of shells and tangle and veiled grey sunlight and gayclad light-
> clad figures of children and girls and voices childish and girlish
> in the air.

Such were the materials Joyce assembled, with years and
years of patient culling, to make the wings that would take
him on his epical flight—a flight tragic and beautiful, in
which he was to see the earth and the sea and the sky as no
human being had seen them before. And we also, through
one man's heroic consecration to a *bonum arduum*, see a new
heaven and a new earth: for what his vocation (so often re-
ferred to as a priestlike task) achieved was in some small mea-
sure the redemption of nature.

T. S. Eliot

Greatness in Moderation

Published in 1963 on the occasion of T. S. Eliot's seventy-fifth birthday, the *Collected Poems 1909–1962* shows only trivial changes in already published work. A period tidies up the syntax toward the end of "Gerontion," though there is something to be said for the earlier flurry of words. The line "Views of the Oxford Colleges" has lost its "the." Those cat things are omitted. Sweeney himself must have set up the Greek: there are four brutal errors in as many lines.

A handsome volume, *Collected Poems* represents the work of half a century. During that time Eliot has loomed above our landscape like an Everest, his crags and glaciers crawling with explicators who have chipped their way to the top, or sometimes, dazed by the rarer air, gone clear beyond the top and on into the "circumambient gas." Eliot himself warns us against ranking contemporary poets: the most we can say is that they are genuine. Well, he is genuine: no molehill. If asked what contemporary poets he outranks, we would have to say: just about all of them.

It is true he has written nothing quite so thrilling, to my mind, as "Le cimetière marin"; nothing so richly varied, so deeply thought and felt as the *Duineser Elegien*. If he can hold a candle to Yeats, some would find it a rather pallid one. Frost concealed as profound an art with greater artistic cunning,

A review of *Collected Poems 1909–1962* from *Saturday Review*, October 19, 1963.

and, using less, did more. Stevens, Cummings, Thomas, and probably others, though their eminence is less imposing, have written finer single poems. Even on a diamond jubilee, it would be vain to pretend that Mr. Eliot is without defect. "There is a large class of persons," he once said, "including some who appear in print as critics, who regard any censure upon a 'great' writer as a breach of the peace . . . or even hoodlumism." If we find his own achievement straitened, he has anticipated us with mention of his "meagre poetic gifts." Distinguished in many fields, he should perhaps be considered more writer than poet, more man of letters than writer. We might even describe him as he described Matthew Arnold: "in some respects the most satisfactory man of letters of his age."

As such, he will not be dishonored if we suggest that his preeminence is neither of such kind nor so great as his idolaters believed. My impression has been that he is less respected among poets than among nonpoets, those who seek not literature but certain impurities that may be found with it: culture, or religion, or the social sciences.

Ezra Pound, sending "Prufrock" off to Miss Monroe, called Eliot "the only American I know of who has made what I can call adequate preparation for writing. . . . It is such a comfort to meet a man and not have to tell him to wash his face, wipe his feet, and remember the date (1914) on the calendar." And, in 1914, "Prufrock" must have seemed a bright and trenchant manifesto. News from where people were living. Or partly living.

But it has not been 1914 for a long time now. The question is: how does Eliot look among the immortals, to whose company he has been promoted? A little drab, perhaps, next to his favorites. A little prim next to Dante. A little colorless next to Villon, or Donne, or Marvell, who did not have world enough; next to Blake or Baudelaire or the wild old wicked man; next to Valéry who, facing his brilliant void with no consoling creed, could still cry out "Debout! Dans l'ère successive!"; or next to Rilke, who transcended the worst in a glory of *Jubel und Ruhm*.

If the range of experience is between ecstasy and agony, with boredom at the center, Eliot has hovered midway. When he vacillates it is downward; if not in shantih-town he haunts the dumps and doldrums. What we miss is the exhilaration of great poetry, which, even if it deals with what is weary, stale, flat, and unprofitable, even if it calls on us to absent ourselves from felicity or leave all hope behind, persuades us that we are larger, more alive than we thought. But we hardly enter Eliot's world without shrinking a bit, without being aware of carbuncles and falling hair, without drawing our coats a little closer about narrowing shoulders. There are wistful visions of a loveliness out of reach, lost or renounced or adrift on allegory. There is much antique charm in "Ash Wednesday," much luxurious music in the telltale anaphoras of "Prufrock," many images bright as lenses, though most of them diminish rather than magnify. The very things that depress Eliot, Yeats sees as a splendid challenge. The one prepares "a face to meet the faces that you meet"; the other exults:

> Put off that mask of burning gold
> With emerald eyes.

The one, in an account of the gifts reserved for age, concludes with

> the rending pain of re-enactment
> Of all that you have done, and been; the shame
> Of motives late revealed . . .

The other glories:

> I am content to live it all again
> And yet again . . .

When Eliot quotes St. John of the Cross, he quotes only what is negative; one would never guess that love and ecstasy were St. John's goal, nor that what he saw in the world was the shimmer of infinity. Exhilaration, a sense of increased life, is the theme and effect of his work. So with all great poetry, even the most tragic. Eliot, however, woos the lugubrious. I am closer to his beliefs, if not their spirit, than to those of Wallace Stevens, yet "Sunday Morning" involves and enchants; Mr. Eliot's devotions tend to obtrude and exhort, buttonholing us with "Redeem the time" and so forth.

Even in hell Dante found nobility. But how many handsome characters can we recall from the whole range of Eliot's poetry? Yeats's great lover Hanrahan is a hero; Sweeney, squatting on his hams, is a slob; Yeats, thinking of a woman, notes "the fire that stirs about her, when she stirs"; Eliot detects in Grishkin a catlike smell and makes a joke about breasts. Perhaps such is his triumph: his world of grotesques is "distorted to scale," as he said of Tourneur's; it constitutes in its intensity a unique vision of life, possibly something like a "mystical experience" of human mediocrity as seen against the eternal splendors.

Nor does Eliot's technique quite exhilarate. He is a fine metrist, musical if rarely exciting; for all his freedom, he sounds more like Debussy's metronome than like a human heart. We miss the rough-and-tumble between meter and rhythm that we get in Donne, or, differently, in Frost. His diction is not stirring; it is merely impeccable; a certain lack of character is shown by the fact that it translates so easily. We can imagine "Let us go then, you and I . . ." without loss in any of several languages, as we cannot imagine "Suddenly I saw the cold and rook-delighting heaven . . ." or "Back out of all this now too much for us. . . ."

Is "Prufrock," written fifty years ago, really the "portrait satire on futility" that Pound thought? Or something else? Perhaps a dramatic lyric of the swooning psyche, half-relishing, in those sensuous rhythms and langorous sentences, its own self-immolation? Whatever it is, it made sense against the hated "cheerfulness, optimism, and hopefulness" of the nineteenth century. It makes sense today: anyone who has "taught" the poem knows it as a bonanza to students who little expected such fun. If a poem is indeed, as Valéry said, a machine made out of words, this is a sleek, ingenious, fine-running contraption. It has a few bugs (it shrinks people), but it comes equipped with many shiny inventions. Consider that most celebrated image of modern poetry, as Donne's compass image is the most celebrated of his school:

> the evening is spread out against the sky
> Like a patient etherized upon a table.

An evening pale, still, hushed like a thing asleep. But to Prufrock's neurotic sensibility not naturally asleep. No "sweet dreams and health and quiet breathing." Asleep as Prufrock's will was asleep—for he projects his moods on nature as we all do. A morbid and enforced sleep, a paralysis with the prognosis unfavorable. Eliot had to find a visual image *like* the sky; he had to find one true to his state of mind and way of seeing; had to find it in modern life, not in the tradition. It had to be in key with the laboratory image of the bug pinned to the wall, the anatomical slide of the nervous system. What he finds is perfectly apt: simple, shocking, with that sense of surprise that Poe, as Eliot reminds us, demanded of poetry. "Prufrock" indeed gives pleasure. Yet if it represents the "greatest emotional intensity of our time," as Eliot says it is the poet's business to do, the worse for us.

And what of "The Waste Land," for decades one of our favorite parlor games? The poet himself ridiculed the "bogus scholarship" of the "Notes" which keep us from reading it as the moving poem it can be. Since Eliot gave the cue, everyone gets into the act. (Anyone noticed that every word in

> The barges drift
> With the turning tide
> Red sails

occurs on the first page of *Heart of Darkness*? etc.) "April is the cruellest month . . . ," one remembers how different—aha!— Aprille was for Chaucer, and how, for Malory, just as flowers burgeon in spring, so "every lusty harte that ys only maner of lover . . . buddyth, and florysshyth in lusty dedis." Ironic contrast. Or one turns to Frazer's sonorous periods on "the spectacle of the great changes which annually pass over the face of the earth," and sniffs at those who go south in the winter or call for a closed car if it rains. Even enemies of the poem must concede its propaedeutic value. But it has more: there are wryly beautiful growths on the sandflats:

> Out of the window perilously spread
> Her drying combinations touched by the sun's last rays

Lines no less richly "poetic," no less evocative, than

> Charmed magic casements, opening on the foam
> Of perilous seas, in fairy lands forlorn.

I would even defend the logic (not the poetry) of Eliot's breaking the language barrier at the end of the poem, particularly since, by evoking the insane Hieronymo, he admits that his own seems a voice not only out of cisterns and exhausted wells, but out of the madhouse itself. Imagery is vivid, diction simple, rhythm persuasive. Why then regard the poem as the Rosetta Stone of our civilization? Why go picking over its picturesque desert, nose to the ground, intent on "meaning"? Why not take it merely as the scary incantation it ought to be? The commentators, all over the place, make it hard for us. And the poet does too, for the reproving figure of "Mr. Eliot" is perhaps his most convincing creation. With that sharp-nosed ghost at our shoulder, it seems *lèse-majesté* to read for fun, even though he said—said it himself!—that the first function of poetry is to give pleasure.

"Earnest, earthless, equal, attuneable"—the opening of Hopkins's sonnet describes "Ash Wednesday," again best taken as incantation. A key to its defect is in the opening echo—a translation of Cavalcanti, dying in prison: "Because I have no hope of ever returning to Tuscany, little song, go to my lady and say . . ." The original is about a girl and a place; Eliot uproots the line, floats it in ruminative goo, plays with its meaning, makes it rhyme with a tag from another poem. The girl is gone and the earth is gone; we are left dangling in the vast inane, perhaps musing on Eliot's remark that "A man does not join himself with the Universe so long as he has anything else to join himself with."

The same slackened grip on the physical shows in "Four Quartets." Eliot has become a self-disparaging Prufrock on Parnassus; what is a critic to do when a poet shrugs: "The poetry does not matter"? Much of it comes, here, from an almost disembodied voice. There are no people in this floating world: some dancing wraiths who speak Middle English, a corpse in the river, Krishna and Arjuna, a composite ghost out of Dante. What few concrete objects there are lie askew in a cold aspic of abstractions. Instead of finding his image, his "objective correlative," instead of *trattando l'ombre come cosa salda* (treating the shades as if they were a solid thing), Eliot reverts to what may have been the manner of his Ph.D. thesis: "It seems, as one becomes older, that the past has another pattern, and ceases to be mere sequence—or even development: the latter a partial fallacy, encouraged by superficial notions of evolution, which becomes, in the popular mind, a means of disowning the past." This is the kind of writing that Gerontion, with his failing senses, might have managed; no way of printing it makes it "poetry." Or Eliot is slackly adjectival: within eight lines *tumid, cold, unwholesome, unhealthy, faded, torpid, gloomy.* How slowly he moves can be seen by looking at

> The river is within us, the sea is all about us;
> The sea is the land's edge also, the granite
> Into which it reaches, the beaches where it tosses
> Its hints of earlier and other creation . . .

and recalling Yeats:

> Once more the storm is howling, and half hid
> Under this cradle-hood and coverlid
> My child sleeps on. . . .

"To get *beyond poetry,* as Beethoven, in his later work, strove to get *beyond music,*" Eliot once said, is "the thing to try for."

The quartets, in trying to go beyond poetry, beyond humanity, have simply gone apart from both. This longing for beyondness is quixotic: like wishing to live without a body. Music is already sensuous, if it exists. But language can send us directly to abstraction; it is no more spiritual for being colorless. Still, for those who find it possible to be happy with their feet off the ground, the quartets are probably the best abstract ruminative verse ever written.

Ours is an age, Eliot tells us, of moderate virtue and of moderate vice. Recalling certain horrors of the time, and certain men and women who defied them, we may refuse to share this opinion. But if Eliot's appraisal of his lackluster age is a just one, he may well have provided that age its appropriate spokesman: a great poet, yes, but a poet of moderate greatness.

Screwing Up the Theorbo
Homage in Measure to Mr. Berryman

John Berryman's homage to Anne Bradstreet, three hundred years ago touted (by her brother-in-law) as The Tenth Muse Lately Sprung Up in America, has been as highly acclaimed as the work of the poor lady herself. Many readings over many weeks have left me of many minds about it: it seems magnificent and absurd, mature and adolescent, grave and hysterical, meticulous and slovenly. Critics whose judgment I respect more than my own have heaped it with superlatives; their retinue is an honorable one, and I am quite possibly wrong not to be among them.

What kind of poem is this? To start with the trifles that, in Michelangelo's saying, make perfection: Berryman's fifty-seven stanzas have normally an eight-line pattern that, as in *The Wreck of the Deutschland,* has a final alexandrine riming with the first line. Hopkins allows himself only three rimes and observes them rigorously; Berryman, in his slacker stanza, takes four, and will settle for identical rime, oblique rime, or assonance. Whereas Hopkins does not once shirk the obligations of the form, Berryman sometimes evades them, especially toward the close of the poem, where there are stanzas that accept the challenge of the rime not more than half the time. Occurring where they do, the many unrimed lines seem a sign of flagging interest or concern rather than a deliberate unravelling such as we find in "After Apple Picking." Even so, this is a live and dramatic form, with lines of

A review of *Homage to Mistress Bradstreet* (1956) from *Prairie Schooner* 32 (Spring 1958).

three and four stresses climaxed by a pivotal couplet in pentameter, and with a three-stress line that poises the final alexandrine. There are fine effects too: the dominant and ambiguous "still," a key word in the poem, riming with itself (like "cristo" in the *Divina Commedia*) in the first stanza, in a significant stanza halfway through, and again in the final stanza; the shrill rimes of the tortured stanza 19; the unrimed "howl" dissonant at the end of stanza 21.

Though the stanza recalls Hopkins, the rhythm is not particularly "sprung"; if we want a term we might fancy it, with its slabs of spondees and bergs of reversed feet, as "jammed" or "floe'd" rhythm. At times Berryman takes us for a fine, teeth-rattling ride over the trochees, but in general this is a grave, still, crabbed rhythm, occasionally so free that he can insert whole lines of Anne Bradstreet's verse or even prose without noticeably disturbing his pace. So in stanzas 7, 13, and 14. The last three lines of stanza 8 are a prose quotation adapted to the stanza by transposing pentameter and alexandrine. Without the élan, vigor, or confidence of sprung rhythm, this rhythm is excellent for certain cramped grating effects of its own.

With it the diction is in harmony: tense, nervous, crabbed, agonized, by turns numb and hectic. There are majestic lines:

> Outside the New World winters in grand dark
> white air slashing high thro' the virgin stands

lines of strange and evocative charm:

> Succumbing half, in spirit, to a salmon sash
> I prod the nerveless novel succotash—

lines that might have been written by Tourneur:

> One proud tug greens heaven

or by Webster:

> "Mother,
> how *long* will I be dead?" Our friend the owl
> vanishes, darling, but your homing soul
> retires on heaven, Mercy . . .

(cf. *The White Devil*,III iii: "What do the dead do, uncle? . . . When do they wake?") Particularly in the talk with or about children there is sweetness and grace. But too often there is a grim working of lips and jowls: stretches of god-awful jawbreaking blether. Language is lashed sadistically, racked and hip-sprung, broken on the wheel. Why, for a small example, is the folk-lilt of "Jack-in-the-pulpit" crushed into "Jack's pulpits"?—a phrase for the chunky tongue and the tin ear. Sometimes English is written as if it were Latin:

> so were ill
> many as one day we could have no sermons

or worse:

> Jaw-ript, rot with its wisdom, rending then;
> Then not.

There are too many gobbets of undigested Hopkins:

> I can *can* no longer. . .

(cf. Hopkins's "Cry *I can no more.* I can . . .") or

> Consuming acrid its own smoke. It's me

(cf. Hopkins's "Bitter would have me taste; my taste was me") or

> Shy, shy with mé Dorothy

There are passages that sound like Hopkins in slow motion:

> He to me ill lingeringly, learning to shun
> a bliss, a lightning blood
> vouchsafed, what did seem life. I kissed his Mystery.

We might use as a text for meditation: "It is not in the least likely that a truly great style can seriously oppose itself to the basic form patterns of the language" (Sapir).

But what most puts me off in this remarkable poem is the fable—so strained that any summary of it sounds like burlesque. And this largely because it runs counter to common sense, which, as Hopkins wrote when shown "a strained and unworkable allegory" by the young Yeats, "is never out of place anywhere, neither on Parnassus nor on Tabor nor on the mount where the Lord preached." The "poet" of the poem—and it should not be assumed that this figure is the author or any mask or persona of the author—contemplates Anne Bradstreet and her environment; he finds her, like himself, a rejected figure that the world "unhands." They belong therefore—these two in their "lovers' air"—somehow to each other. Anne begins to speak of the hardships of the voyage and the settlement, of her poetry, of her turning away from God who as a corrective awarded her the smallpox, of her marriage to "so-much-older" Simon Bradstreet, of her child-bed woes, her illnesses and ennuis. Abruptly the poet addresses her in Shelleyan tremolos: he and Anne, soul mates and body mates, belong in bed together. Touched and flattered, she savors to the full the glamor of this sexy evil. She invites him to touch her smallpox scars, exclaims with pleasure when he does. She is both abandoned ("Kiss me") and prim ("That once"). He responds to her "talk to me" by calling to her attention the New England spring, all damply burgeoning with fertility symbols, "Ravishing, ha," she admits, but yet forbidden. "I am a sobersides; I know." Then resorting to throaty italics: "I *want* to take you for my lover," though it's "madness." The poet, after an appeal to some Byzantine icons, makes a kind of Dowsonish general confession. She protests with solicitous indignation. They discuss religion. She is increasingly carried away by a temptation increasingly sexual and therefore (it is hard to say whether poet or poetess is, *au fond,* more Calvinistic) increasingly "a black joy." Women, and she among them, are almost helpless before the tyranny of sex:

> a great male pestle smashes
> small women swarming toward the mortar's rim in vain.

About to yield, she resorts to a last desperate prayer which saves both:

> torture me, Father, lest not I be thine!

In this swart poem there is much sex but little love (except parental love): even God works by "torture" rather than, as in Hopkins, by the sudden thunderbolt that dazzled Paul or the "lingering-out sweet skill" that won Augustine. But with this prayer we leave the panting sexual hothouse and, in one of those flashing transitions which are among the marvels of the poem, are in the world of slipshod domestics and prattling children. These grow up, Anne's father dies, she herself, "ill-er . . . oftener," grows old and dies; and the poet, materializing again to see her interred, meditates on the methods of modern war and our cooling planet. His valedictory addresses her as "a sourcing   whom my lost candle like the firefly loves."

Confronted with these events, I cannot suspend my disbelief long enough to take these lay figures seriously. And I cannot help wondering about the nature of Mistress Bradstreet's attraction for the poet. It is not the fact that she too is touched with the sacred fire; he cannot conceal the contempt he feels for all her "bald abstract didactic rime" that he reads "appalled." What he seems to be making is the appeal of lonely men in shirt-sleeves: he, the real poet, and she, so much manquée, are in the same melancholy barque, cast adrift by an unappreciative world. In herself she seems not a very cogent figure of the poet as exile, this Tenth Muse, "a woman honored and esteemed where she lives."

And though the historical "sourcing" of the poem should be irrelevant, I cannot forget it. If the historical Anne Bradstreet was not "unhanded" by her world, still less was she unhappy in her husband and in need of extramarital consolations from a ghostly poet who barges in like the young man carbuncular. Anne's most passionate rimes were written to her husband:

> If ever two were one, then surely we.
> If ever man were lov'd by wife, then thee;
> If ever wife was happy in a man,
> Compare with me ye women if you can.

But the poet is understandably cool toward a lover bound to Anne by so bourgeois a tie; he accuses "so-much-older" Simon (who was about twenty-five when he married his teenage bride) of being unsympathetic to her literary labors. The accusation has no particular basis; it seems that even Anne's own father, a hornier-handed puritan than Simon, himself wrote verse.

The poet's passion for the body of his poetess is strange too in that (in spite of some lovely lines on her lost beauty) he prefers to dwell on physical aspects not normally the object of desire: her disease, her "cratered" skin, the cracking vertebrae, "wretched trap," and unruly colon of her childbed experiences, her retchings, her broodings on her naked body, her "pustules snapping," her rheumatic joints, her "body a-drain," her dropsical arm and wrecked chest, her hangnails and piles. *Oh Beatrice, dolce guida e cara!* The poet describes his beloved much as Dante describes the figure of nauseating sin or the punishment of certain damned souls. (It is revealing to compare Beatrice and Anne Bradstreet as *figurae*.) Though the beliefs are irrelevant (or almost so) to the success of the poem it seems to me that here he is pumping a bit too glumly for his bias, so that what we get is a sort of depressing propaganda for the view that the flesh is evil: the qualm of love the poetess longs for is described as being like the qualm of smallpox. Even the beauty of flowers becomes dangerous and forbidden: "Ravishing, ha, what crouches outside ought." The historical Anne, puritan or not, has a more franciscan attitude; she can write of the beauty of nature:

> Rapt were my senses at this delectable view
> . . . .
> If so much excellence abides below,
> How excellent is He that dwells on high,
> Whose power and beauty by his works we know
> . . . .
> That hath this underworld so richly dight.

The nervous puritanism of this "homage" is evident if we compare Berryman's description of the voyage with actual records of the passengers—not as a literary judgment on the poem but as a key to its mood. The poem has it that

> By the week we landed we were, most, used up.
> Strange ships across us, after a fortnight's winds
> unfavoring, frightened us;
> bone-sad cold, sleet, scurvy; so were ill
> many as one day we could have no sermons;
> broils, quelled; a fatherless child unkennelled; vermin
> crowding and waiting; waiting.

John Winthrop's *Journal* tells a different story. The "strange ships" were friendly, but even before that was known "It was muche to see how chearfull and Comfortable all the Companye appeared, not a woman or Childe that shewed any feare." The weather was cold, yes; but they had warm clothes and the sense to put them on. Though it was windy and rainy, Winthrop often mentions, with something like exhilaration, "a fine gale," "a handsome gale," "a merrye gale in all our sailes." Even when the storms were at their worst "through Godes mercye, we were verye Comfortable, and fewe or none sicke . . . mr. Philipps preached twice that daye." The sermonless day prominent in the stanza above was immediately after their departure; it seems to have been quite exceptional. "It hathe pleased the Lorde to bringe vs hether in peace . . . we had a Comfortable passage," Winthrop wrote his son. The arrival seems to have been a delight: "faire sunneshine weather, and so pleasant a sweet ayre, as did muche refreshe vs, and there came a smell off the shore like the smell of a garden." A few days later they supped ashore "with a good venyson pastye, and good beere." From the poem this is all censored out—the cakes and ale, the venison and beer—by a lugubrious puritan selectivity; one would never guess that, as Morison says, "there was plenty of fun aboard." In Berryman's stanza everything is tense, numb, shivering, painful. There is no reason the world of a poem, even of a poem about a historical figure, should reproduce the historical world—the point of my comparison is to indicate how the poem is conceived: in the key of *dour*.

When not hunched on his gloomy soapbox under the cadaverous raven, Berryman can perform brilliantly. Witness how he brings to vivid life the Henry Winthrop episode, so drably described in the records: "The very day on which he went on shore . . . walking out . . . to view the Indian wigwams, they saw on the other side of the river a small canoe . . . none of the party could swim but himself; and so he plunged in, and, as he was swimming over, was taken with the cramp, a few rods from the shore, and drowned."

> And the day itself he leapt ashore young Henry Winthrop
> (delivered from the waves; because he found
> off their wigwams, sharp-eyed, a lone canoe
> across a tidal river,
> that water glittered fair & blue
> & narrow, none of the other men could swim
> and the plantation's prime theft up to him,
> shouldered on a glad day
> hard on the glorious feasting of thanksgiving) drowned.

And with what deftness he has worked into the texture of the poem hints from the work of Anne Bradstreet herself (these not identified in the Notes):

> Motes that hop in sunlight

is suggested by one of her verse letters to her husband:

> every mote that in the sun-shine hops.

And stanza 40:

> I pare
> an apple for my pipsqueak Mercy and
> she runs & all need naked apples, fanned
> their tinier envies.
> Vomitings trots rashes

is a reminiscence of lines on Childhood in *The Four Ages of Man:*

> My quarrels not for diadems did rise
> But for an apple, plum, or some such prize

. . . .
> What crudities my stomach cold hath bred
> Whence vomits, flux, and worms have issued

The pleasant lines in stanza 42 about wiggling out a child's tooth seem suggested by a line in the same Bradstreet poem. The strange line in stanza 51

> and holiness on horses' bells shall stand

which the Notes refer simply to Zech. 14:20 is actually Anne's rephrasing of the biblical line near the end of her *A dialogue Between Old England and New.* A number of such little authenticities will unfortunately be lost on most readers. One of the neatest is the combined botanical and astronomical allusion of stanza 31, quite in the manner of Bradstreet's *The Four Seasons,* in which every month is tagged with its proper zodiacal badge:

> Venus is trapt—
> the hefty pike shifts, sheer—
> in Orion blazing.

As for the Notes themselves—one wonders. A few are shifty-eyed: the poet's sudden amorous irruption prompts the following:

> One might say: He is enabled to speak, at last, in the fortune of an echo of her—and when she is loneliest (her former spiritual adviser having deserted Anne Hutchinson, and this her closest friend banished), as if she had summoned him; and only thus, perhaps, is she enabled to hear him.

Preposterous prose; I assume the author, ashamed of the shabby trick he is pulling here, is burying his blushing face in folds of evasive style. Anne Hutchinson her closest friend! This is the kind of impious fraud that drugstore historical fiction goes in for. Is there any reason for thinking that Anne Bradstreet, who lived at Ipswich during the few years the brilliant and tragic Anne Hutchinson (*there* is an Anne to conjure with!) was at Boston, ever met her "closest friend"?

The Note on "brutish" in stanza 42 is mistaken: it is not "her epithet for London" but for Sodom (which does not stand for London). London, in the passage the Notes point to, is "stately" and "our great Britain's glory." A trifle, but if the author thought it was worth having a Note about—? For the rest, the Notes are a bit chic: a reference to Klee, to Baron Corvo, to movie serials, to Fuchs's collections of engravings, and so forth.

In summary, I myself cannot see this as a great poem, though it has magnificent passages. Its successes and failures are dramatized by the first and last stanzas. The grave melody of the first is impressive, unforgettable. But in the last the sense of strain necessary to inflate this flaccid myth, the awareness of having nothing, ultimately, to say about it leads to the contortion and flabbiness of the utterly unmemorable last lines, which the dubious syntax, the shady Dante allusion and the archaic vocabulary do nothing to shore up. Throughout the poem I find this alternation of strength, gravity, even nobility with a shrill hectic fury, a whipped-up excitement, a maudlin violence of *mal protesi nervi*. A suitable invocation for the bad passages would be the lines of Francis Quarles, one of Anne's favorite poets:

> Rouse thee, my soul, and drain thee from the dregs
> Of vulgar thoughts; screw up the heighten'd pegs
> Of thy sublime theorbo four notes higher

In part Berryman's gallant failure (a better thing than many tidy successes in the magazines) is related to his double focus: purportedly concerned with Anne Bradstreet, his poem is really about "the poet" himself, his romantic and exacerbated personality, his sense of loneliness, his need for a mistress, confidante, confessor. One might think there would be more satisfactory candidates for this triple role among the living. Myth too is common sense, offspring of flesh and blood; Berryman, in his dealings with lovesick ectoplasm, has too little human reality to sustain his myth—screw up the sublime theorbo as he will.

The Poetry of Sylvia Plath
A Technical Analysis

What I offer is something in the way of a technical analysis of the poetry of Sylvia Plath. Amid much high talk of culture and poesis and metaphysics, I come, many will think, in a humble capacity: a sort of podiatrist among the brain surgeons, clutching my little bag of timeworn axioms from Michelangelo and Goethe and Valéry, now and then grabbing and brandishing one defiantly. "The artist who is not also a craftsman is no good"—Goethe. "Trifles make perfection, and perfection is no trifle"—Michelangelo.

It is true that Sylvia Plath was struck by a lightning from the spirit. But it is also true that she had spent much of her life forging speech of a metal to conduct the lightning without being instantly fused. There is little that can be said about how to get struck by lightning but a good deal that can be said about how to forge a resistant metal.

We might begin by saying to young writers: Forget *Ariel* for a while; study *The Colossus*. Notice all the stanza forms, all the uses of rhythm and rhyme; notice how the images are chosen and related; how deliberately sound is used. It is no accident, for instance, that there are seven identical drab *a*'s in ". . . salt flats, / Gas tanks, factory stacks—that landscape . . ."[1] Remember that *The Bell Jar* tells us she "wrote page after page of villanelles and sonnets," and this in one semester of one class. Perhaps for writers this is the gist of the Plath case: without

From *The Art of Sylvia Plath,* edited by Charles Newman (Bloomington: Indiana University Press; London: Faber and Faber, 1970).

the drudgery of *The Colossus,* the triumph of *Ariel* is unthinkable.[2]

As a teacher, I speak from experience. How many poets are there, now in the mid-1960s, on the shaggy campuses of the land we love? Maybe 50,000? 200,000? More, certainly, than at any time in the history of the world. Being a "poet" is the young folks' thing these days: they get that look and slap down on paper the holy thoughts no elder ever thought, and troop around in their poet-clothes, nonconforming exactly like the milling thousands in their peer group, and, man, it's beautiful! Only they don't work much. Spontaneity, they think, that's where it's at. Write it like it is. Cries from the heart. But Sylvia Plath, in some prefatory remarks for a recording, dismissed such indulgence with acidity:

> I think my poems come immediately out of the sensuous and emotional experiences I have, but I must say I *cannot* sympathize with these cries from the heart that are informed by nothing except, you know, a needle or a knife, or whatever it is. I believe one should be able to control and manipulate experiences, even the most terrifying, like madness, like being tortured . . . and should be able to manipulate these experiences with an informed and intelligent mind.[3]

Control, manipulate, informed, intelligent, mind—these are the key words, for our present purpose. It does not follow that a poem never "comes" easily (though this is rare); but it comes only along circuits laboriously prepared, generally for years in advance.

My plan is to discuss the work of a good contemporary poet in terms of those things which have made up the physical body of poetry in all times and places, and which indeed never change. Things which could be illustrated from any of the great poets of our tradition: Sappho, Catullus, the Archpoet, Bernart de Ventadorn, Villon, San Juan de la Cruz, Goethe, Leopardi, Valéry, Rilke, or the English and American poets we presumably know better. One of the more frivolous ways of judging poetry is in terms of contemporary significance. Looking at the works of the ten poets I mention, I am struck by how timeless, how undated, their essential quality is. San Juan de la Cruz refers at most once to the exciting events of his day. A poet long ago loved a girl for the same reasons we still do:

> ἐρατόν τε βᾶμα
> κἀμάρυχμα λάμπρον ἴδην προσώπω[4]

or perhaps because, in a metaphor,

> sa beutatz alugora
> bel jorn e clarzis noih negra[5]

As she grows old the lament is still "Quelle fus, quelle devenue!" (What I was, what [I've] become!—Villon). Any might have brooded with the confessional Archpoet, "In amaritudine loquor meae menti" (In bitterness I speak to my mind), or stared upon skies that were "Gestaltenreiche, bald Gestaltenlose" (Rich in [cloudy] shapes, soon with none at all—Goethe), or found the night "Dolce e chiara . . . e senza vento" (Sweet and clear . . . and without wind—Leopardi). No matter what the language, all this is really where it's at.

Poetry, if it is anything, is a real voice in a real body in a real world. The world does not change as much as we think; and the body, with its voice-producing mechanisms, changes probably not at all. The timeless excellence of Sylvia Plath lies in what she has in common with such poets as I have mentioned (though I am not saying that she is of their rank): the sense of language and of metaphor; the throat-produced sounds of her poetry; the physical rhythms that invigorate it.

Metaphor (I use the word here to include simile and all metaphoric ways of seeing) was for Aristotle "by far the greatest thing . . . which alone cannot be learned; it is the sign of genius." Some contemporary theorists are against it, although to reject metaphor is not only to enervate poetry but to do violence to the human mind and the way it works.

The qualities of a good metaphor would seem to be two:

when A is compared to B, B is a thing at first sight surprisingly (and delightfully or shockingly) remote from A; and B is a thing at least as common, as available, as A. Or probably more common, since the purpose of metaphor is to see more clearly.

Sylvia Plath seems to me more brilliant at metaphor than others popularly grouped with her as confessional poets. In her two books[6] almost all of the metaphors are on target, having the excellences I mentioned (and often a third I can only suggest now: A is not only like B in one salient respect, but also picks up a supercharge of meanings proper to B but impregnating A also, as in the *smile-hook* image below). In *The Colossus* we find "The pears fatten like little buddhas"; a corpse is "black as burnt turkey"; "Sun struck the water like a damnation" and "Everything glittered like blank paper"; dead moles are "shapeless as flung gloves . . . blue suede" and they have "corkscrew noses"; a dead snake lies "inert as a shoelace" and the maggots are "thin as pins"; burnt wood has the "char of karakul." In *Ariel*, it is said of a newborn baby that "Love set you going like a fat gold watch," and of its voice, "The clear vowels rise like balloons." Family smiles in a photograph "catch onto my skin, little smiling hooks." The snow of Napoleon's retreat is "marshalling its brilliant cutlery"; a swarm of bees is "A flying hedgehog, all prickles."

She also shows a total control of the figures she uses. This is a matter of attention and tact: how soon can one drop a metaphor, or dissolve it for another? Bad writers sometimes superimpose images so carelessly that we get an amateur's double exposure, with grotesque or comic results. Even good writers nod.

Sylvia Plath shows a more conscientious commitment to her images. "Hardcastle Crags" begins:

> Flintlike, her feet struck
> Such a racket of echoes from the steely street,
> . . . that she heard the quick air ignite
> Its tinder and shake
>
> A firework of echoes . . .

"Flintlike," she begins; therefore the street is "steely" and the air a "tinder" that can "ignite" a "firework." Four stanzas later she is "a pinch of flame," and in the last stanza there is "Enough to snuff the quick / Of her small heat out." Beginning as flint, she ends as "mere quartz grit." In "The Colossus," an early sketch for "Daddy," imagery of a fallen statue is sustained throughout. This knitting or girdering of images is everywhere in *Ariel:* the underwater or water imagery in "Tulips" is only one of the more obvious examples. "Getting There" is all metaphor; "Daddy," "Lady Lazarus," and "Fever 103°" are richly and consistently figurative.

The sound of words—any page of Sylvia Plath shows her preoccupation with it. *The Colossus* shows a concern almost excessive, unless we see it as a preparation for *Ariel.* Sound is an element of poetry tricky to talk about, sense and nonsense here being so close together, and the line between so fine and wavering. The chapter on words in Herbert Read's *English Prose Style* makes sense: he believes that "vocal appropriateness" is "perhaps the most important aspect of the problem of style as determined by the choice of words." Precise meaning is not enough; words have a body as well as a mind, and sometimes the body matters more. Many poets would agree with Valéry that the poet's "inner labor consists less of seeking words for his ideas than of seeking ideas for his words and paramount rhythms." Many would not agree: Look, they feel, I can't be bothered with these trifles when I've got these Important Things to Say. Rather like the hurdler complaining that the hurdles interfere with his stride.

Words are more expressive when they are somehow like what they mean: fast or slow or gruff or shrill, or produced by mouth and lip movements that mimic the dynamics of rejection, say, or the prolonging of a caress. That is why Catullus has given probably the best kiss in literature in his "Illo purpureo ore suaviata (Having kissed [his eyes] with that bright mouth [of hers])," in which not only are lip movements appropriate, but, in Latin prosody, the two round *o*'s coming together fuse as one. These are effects beyond mere onomatopoeia—which we can find too in Plath when it is called for, as in "Night Shift," perhaps an exercise in the manner of "Swarte smekyd smethes." Her factory has less clangor, a more "muted boom":

> though the sound
> Shook the ground with its pounding.

There is much deliberately ugly sound in "Night Shift," especially in the way words reecho noises from a preceding word: "A metal detonating / Native, evidently . . . indefatigable fact." More interesting than such onomatopoeia are those words whose sound is an analogy for, a little charade of, their meaning: *smudge* is smudgy to say: *globe* is a roundness in the mouth; *sling* hisses and then lets go. The thousands of hours Sylvia Plath spent with her thesaurus must have considered words as embodiments. And considered what happens when they go together: poets have a tendency to stay in the same key of sound, to set up patterns in it, so that what they write has a more unified and tougher texture than casual speech. Speech is a tweedy fabric; verse is a twill. Or poets work to avoid repeating a sound, when the repetition is meaningless, or meaninglessly ugly.

Look at any page of *The Colossus,* and you see expressive repetitions and patterns: "greased machines," "gristly-bristled," "wingy myths," "cuddly mother," "clumped like bulbs," "lambs jam the sheepfold." In "Mushrooms," "Our toes, our noses / Take hold on the loam . . . Soft fists insist on / heaving the needles. . . ."

Generally we can see a reason for such effects: in "clumped like bulbs" and "lambs jam" the sound itself is clumped or jammed.

Often Sylvia Plath repeats a sound several times: "Drinking vinegar from tin cups." Now we can get very arch here and talk about "a thin metallic acidity puckering the lips"; but the most we can say sensibly is that the repetitions of the *in*-sound are sort of tinny. Tin cups do go *click* or *clink* rather than *clank* or *clunk.* If we say that the bird that "flits nimble-winged in thickets" has his five short *i*'s to suggest quickness, we have Plato with us: he too held that the short *i* is the quickest of the vowel sounds. It is easy to find monotony dramatized in "daylight lays its sameness on the wall," and to find a sense of unpleasant enclosure in "This shed's fusty as a mummy's stomach." And there are any number of lines somehow like what they mean: the great sow that is

> Mire-smirched, blowzy,
>
> Maunching thistle and knotweed on her snout-cruise—. . .
>
> ("Sow")

or the texture of rocky soil in

> What flinty pebbles the ploughblade upturns
> As ponderable tokens . . .

in which the *ond* of *ponderable* must have encouraged the *godly* and *doddering* of the line that follows.

Sound effects in themselves are trivial, and facility with these will never write a poem. It can temper the metal, but it cannot provoke the heaven into striking. As it did strike in several of the *Ariel* poems. Sound effects here are less obtrusive than before; more subtle, more sparing, more saved for where they matter. But they are here: "Square as a chair," "strips of tinfoil winking," "starless and fatherless, a dark water." There are many in the bee poems: "were there not such a din in it" and "the unintelligible syllables." In "Lady Lazarus" there are such things as "the flesh / The grave cave ate." "Lesbos" opens with a vicious hiss. But "Nick and the Candlestick" is the real showpiece for sound:

> I am a miner. The light burns blue.
> Waxy stalactites
> Drip and thicken . . .

And what a contrast between the brilliant chill of

> Christ! they are panes of ice,
> A vice of knives

and the pulpy warmth of these words to a baby:

The blood blooms clean

in you, ruby.

A sound-device even more compelling in *Ariel* is the kind
of rhyme used. There is something really new here, though it
is not easy to do anything new with a device so time-worn and
so primitive. Primitive: children and simple people love it; so
do composers of folksongs authentic or pseudo. Only some of
our more cerebral theorists, who write as if they had no
bodies anyway, pish-tush it with prudery.

The rhymes we find in *The Colossus* are already at an ad-
vanced stage of their evolutionary history. We can assume
that hundreds of earlier poems had exhausted, for the time,
the poet's taste for full rhyme; it is with real surprise that we
come across, in "Snakecharmer," *breast-manifest-nest.* By pref-
erence she rhymes more atonally. The same vowel sound but
with different consonants after it: *fishes-pig-finger-history;
worms-converge.* Different vowel sounds but with the same fi-
nal consonant: *vast-compost-must; knight-combat-heat* (this is her
most characteristic kind of rhyme in *The Colossus*). Unac-
cented syllables going with accented or unaccented: *boulders-
wore; footsoles-babel.* She considers all final vowels as rhyming
with all others: *jaw-arrow-eye* (perhaps suggested by the
Middle-English practice in alliteration). Or she will mate
sounds that have almost anything in common: *ridgepole-tangle-
inscrutable.* The ties become so very loose that it is not always
clear when they are intended. *Depths-silver-there*—can these be
rhymes? They occur at the end of a poem in terza rima, which
has been clearly in rhyme up to this triad. In "Suicide Off Egg
Rock" the final words of the twenty-four lines each pair some-
where—in her fashion—with another, but the pairings are not
immediately caught by the ear in such a list of end-words as:
*drizzled, flats, landscape, of, updraught, damnation, into, tattoo,
children, spindrift, wave, gallop, sandspit, blindfold, garbage, for-
ever, eyehole, brainchamber, pages, paper, corrosive, wastage, water,
ledges* (the list is interesting as diction). Rhymes like these mean
more to the writer than to any reader, who will miss many of
them. One feels that Sylvia Plath had an obsession with rhyme,

felt poetry *had* to have it, but at times made her compliance a token one. She knows the poems rhyme, even if we do not. Should we call this "token-rhyme"? Or "ghost-rhyme"—since it is like a revenant never completely exorcised? Or are all these things trifles to ho hum away? It is clear that to her they were not.

In *Ariel,* the use of rhyme is very different. In some poems it is ghostlier than ever. But more often it is obvious: rhyme at high noon. The same sound may run on from stanza to stanza, with much identical rhyme. "Lady Lazarus" illustrates the new manner. The poem is printed in units of three lines, but the rhyme is not in her favourite terza rima pattern. Six of the first ten lines end in an *n*-sound, followed by a sequence in long *e,* which occurs in about half of the next twenty-two lines. Then, after six more *n*'s, we have *l*'s ending eleven of fourteen lines; and then several *r*'s, leading into the six or more *air* rhymes that conclude the sequences. Almost Skeltonian: the poet seems to carry on a sound about as long as she can, although not in consecutive lines. "Compulsive rhyme," we might call this, for it seems fair to see it as deeper than a mere literary device, and as somehow related to needs of the exacerbated psyche. Most of the poems after "Lady Lazarus" rhyme on in this way (although the tendency is much fainter in "Berck-Plage"). "Lesbos" is bound together by compulsive rhyme, broken here and there by couplets that recall Eliot— and indeed this poem is her "Portrait of a Lady," and her "Prufrock," with even the breakers "white and black." In "Daddy" the compulsion to rhyme becomes obsession. Perhaps never in the history of poetry has the device carried so electric a charge. Breathing love and hate together, it coos and derides, even more insistent at the end of the poem than at the beginning, so that form refutes what content is averring. Over half of the lines end in the *oo* sound, and of these nearly half are the one word *you.* This is rhyme with—and for!—a vengeance. The bee poems string together the same sort of compulsive rhyme: eight of the last ten lines of "The Arrival of the Bee Box" end in long *e.* The extremely devious and intricate rhyme-work of *The Colossus,* then, has led to something almost excessively simple, something we might find monotonous if it were not so deeply significant.

All I have said about rhyme has implied something about stanza form. She writes almost always in stanzas or stanzalike units. Often in the later poems there is no relation between rhyme scheme and stanza form: each goes its separate way, with a kind of schizophrenic indifference to the other. Just as her rhyme, even when barely there, *is* there, so with the stanza: even when there seems no formal reason for the unit, the poet remains faithful to its appearance on the page. Probably here, as with rhyme, we have a source of discipline that is personal and internal: it is for her, not for us. Of the "pages of villanelles and sonnets" there is nothing in *The Colossus* except one sonnet, in nine-syllable lines. Only four of the poems are nonstanzaic, two of them barely so. There is one poem in rather free couplets. The fifty others are in stanzas of from three to nine lines. Her favourite form is terza rima, which makes up six of the twelve poems in three-line stanzas. In some of these she adds an extra complexity to the terza rima by having the second line short in the odd-numbered tercets, and the first and third lines short in the even-numbered ones, so that the poem seems·to seesaw on the page. Among the longer stanza forms there is much intricacy and variation; she seems to be trying out as many tight forms as possible. "Black Rook in Rainy Weather" even follows the Provençal system of *rimas dissolutas:* each line rhymes with the corresponding lines of all the other stanzas.

In spite of several fine poems, *The Colossus* has the air of being an exercise book. *Ariel* is very different. The stanza forms are fewer and simpler, far more loosely bound by rhyme. Before, there was one poem in two-line units; now there are nine: everything is more concise. Of the nine, none rhymes as couplets; rhyme is present, but in no regular way. Ten poems are in three-line units; two of these look rather like "Sow" on the page, although with shorter lines. But none rhymes as terza rima. The five-line stanzas now have no formal rhyme scheme, although again they are rhyme-haunted. There are only two poems in longer stanza forms (of seven lines), and one nine-line poem about pregnancy (nine-ness:

an earlier pregnancy poem had nine lines of nine syllables each).

And what of rhythm? In *The Colossus*, she seems practising in the rhythms, as well as in everything else. Up until our own time, there have been chiefly two kinds of rhythm in English. The first predominated until Chaucer; it was based on the heavy stress accent native to our language. The line was divided into two halves with two stresses in each (sometimes emphasized by alliteration); it did not matter how many unstressed syllables there were, nor where they were (pronunciation actually limits the possibilities). We find the rhythm everywhere in early poetry:

> Whére beth théy   befóren us wéren?

exactly as we find it centuries later in E. E. Cummings:

> he sáng his dídn't   he dánced his díd

and Sylvia Plath:

> Ìncense of deáth.   Your dáy appróaches.

or

> Beásts of oásis,   bétter tíme.

Ransom discusses it as the "folk line" or "dipodic line"; he finds it in Thomas Hardy

> We stoód by a pónd   that wínter dáy

and uses it as the basis of his own "Bells for John Whiteside's Daughter":

> There was súch speéd   in her líttle bódy

In *The Colossus*, there are ten poems that read themselves naturally, if freely, in the folk line. Perhaps the best are "Suicide Off Egg Rock" and "Blue Moles."

As everyone knows, the other system was brought over from

from the continent by Chaucer. There are still some who resent the foreign importation, although at least three-fourths of the English poetry that matters has been written in it, not without success. The line has five pulsations, and in theory if almost never in fact each pulsation has two syllables, with the second stronger than the first. We find it in Chaucer's

> Hyd, Absolom, thy giltë tresses clere

exactly as in Cummings's

> all ignorance toboggans into know

Unfortunately it is called "iambic pentameter"—dirty words indeed for some theorists today; and a few, like Dr. Williams, have taken after it with some asperity. Basically, iambic is the *lub-dúbb* of the heartbeat, perhaps the first sensation that we, months before our birth, are aware of. Nothing unnatural about that as a rhythm. It has always been common in human speech. Aristotle called it the most colloquial, or speechlike, of the rhythms, the one used most naturally in speechlike poetry because most commonly heard in real speech. R. P. Blackmur once said he had listened to recordings of poetry in thirty-odd languages, and in every one except Chinese could detect the iambic base. I make this defense because the rhythm is some-times attacked today as unnatural. But there are still some, like Sylvia Plath, who would as soon listen to their own heart for rhythms as take dictation from a typewriter. In *The Colossus* she has eight poems in pure iambic pentameter (in the organic, not the metronomic sense), and nearly twenty others that use it freely or in combination with other line lengths. (Why, by the way, *penta*meter? Could it have anything to do with the physiological fact that our heart pulses five times, on an average, for every time we breathe?)

She also has fourteen poems in accentual count (this is a count, not a rhythm)—the system that organizes lines by number of syllables, with no regard for their stress or impor-tance. This is finger-counting, more foreign to the nature of spoken English than Chaucer's imported novelty. People under the stress of emotion may speak rhythmically, but they do not count their syllables. Emotion makes waves in language; the syllables have to pulsate if we are to have a living rhythm. And syllabic count is made up of undifferentiated elements, whereas a stress rhythm has two forces working against each other: not so much the systole and diastole of the accents as the impassioned dialogue between speech rhythm and meter, a dialogue full of anticipations, surprises, and sudden pacts. A tension between such polarities as make up our existence.

It is true that such poets as Marianne Moore and Auden have shaped many of their poems on a grill of syllabics; over these the living rhythms move. And there is always something to be said for exercises in the syllabic line. Once attuned to the accentual, one is easily carried away into a kind of automatic facility, so that the lines "flow" too easily. (It is the prevalence of bad iambics of course that has led its enemies into their blanket condemnation.) Writing in syllabics can be a salutary exercise in countering the sing-song—and this is the importance of the syllabics in *The Colossus*. They tend to be the colder poems: objective, intellectual, descriptive. Passion always brings the poet back to a heart-rhythm, as in "Witch Burning":

> My ankles brighten. Brightness ascends my thighs.
> I am lost, I am lost, in the robes of all this light.

Another advantage of syllabics is that they can be of value to the writer (if not to the reader) as an additional principle of control, a way of making it harder for oneself, of checking (as Valéry thinks we should) the logorrheas of "inspiration." And the syllabic poem can come alive if it has a physical rhythm overriding the finger-count. What speaker of English can hear *as fifteen* the fifteen syllables of a line in "Fern Hill," or would be bothered if Dylan Thomas skipped a couple? Yet we all hear the passionate stress rhythm that overrides them. Something of the sort happens in Sylvia Plath's "Mushrooms":

> Nudgers and shovers
> In spite of ourselves.
> Our kind multiplies:

> We shall by morning
> Inherit the earth.
> Our foot's in the door.

These are five-syllable lines, but what catches the ear is not so much the fiveness as the traditional swing, as old as Homer at least, of dactyls and spondees, with a rest or two.

There is only one syllabic poem in *Ariel,* and it is not one of the better poems. Syllabics seem to have served their calisthenic purpose in *The Colossus;* when the poet comes to write her important work, she dismisses them. In *Ariel,* there is almost no metrical innovation—unless we think of the comma splice and its nervous impetus. But this is more a matter of syntax than of metrics. May I suggest that the best poets are not often the metrical innovators? This they leave for the fussbudgets. It is always easier to invent a new metrical system than to write a good poem in the existing one. New medium: new tedium—was Roethke, that devotee of the nursery rhyme, thinking of this when he wrote "Some rare new tedium's taking shape"?

Far from making meter new, *Ariel* even marks what metrists might consider a severe regression. Apart from the syllabic "You're," everything can be accounted for by the most basic of English rhythms. Frost says that we have "virtually but two rhythms," strict iambic and loose iambic. These, and little else, we find in *Ariel,* often both in the same poem. The loose iambics work toward that most unfashionable of all feet, the anapest (or its mirror-image, the dactyl). Probably not since the Assyrian came down like the wolf on the fold has there been so high a proportion of anapests in an important collection of poems. Not that *Ariel,* in all the ways that really matter, is not a highly original collection. But tampering with the heartbeat of poetry is not a significant kind of originality; all one is likely to get is verbal fibrillation. In *Ariel* at least, the more original and significant the poem, the more traditional the rhythm.

The lines in *Ariel* are by no means always pentameter, although they are so enough times to surprise us. Probably they are heard as pentameter even when not printed so. One example: lines 2 to 10 of "Lady Lazarus" can be spaced, without violence to the cadence, as

> One year in every ten / I manage it—
> A sort of walking miracle, my skin
> Bright as a Nazi lampshade, / My right foot
> A paperweight, / My face a featureless
> fine/Jew linen. / Peel off the napkin / O
> my enemy. Do I terrify?— / the nose

And the poem comes back to that cadence everywhere, particularly at moments of greatest intensity:

> Soon, soon the flesh / the grave cave ate will be
> At home on me / And I a smiling woman

or

> The peanut-crunching crowd / shoves in to see / them
> Unwrap me hand and foot— / the big strip tease

This is much more regular than the opening of Shakespeare's Sonnet 116: "Let me not to the marriage of true minds" which has only one iambic foot in the five.

Many key lines are printed as pentameter:

> And like the cat I have nine times to die . . .
> To last it out and not come back at all . . .
> And pick the worms off me like sticky pearls . . .
> For the eyeing of my scars, there is a charge . . .

"Tulips" is more in the Fletcherian mode: more anapests, more extra syllables:

> I didn't want any flowers, I only wanted
> To lie with my hands turned up and be utterly empty.
> How free it is, you have no idea how free—
> The peacefulness is so big it dazes you

and the conclusion:

> The water I taste is warm and salt, like the sea,
> And comes from a country far away as health.

The poem "Ariel" looks more irregular, but it too never gets far from an iambic base. Much of it could be spaced so that, metrically, it would be no looser than Jacobean verse. "Lesbos," which opens like an echo of Tourneur, is even more regular:

> Where they crap and puke and cry and she can't hear.
> You say you can't stand her. / The bastard's a girl . . .
> She'll cut her throat at ten if she's mad at two.
>
> Even in your Zen heaven we shan't meet.

Look anywhere—the poems of *Ariel* return to a solid pentameter base again and again. Even when they do not, they tend to remain loose iambic, whatever the line length:

> Obscene bikinis hide in the dunes
> ("Berck-Plage")

> Love set you going like a fat gold watch
> ("Morning Song")

> What a thrill—
> My thumb instead of an onion.
> The top quite gone
> Except for a sort of hinge
> ("Cut")

> It is a heart,
> This holocaust I walk in,
> O golden child the world will kill and eat.
> ("Mary's Song")

I quote so much because I expect incredulity. "You mean Sylvia Plath is so *square*?" In *Ariel,* square as a chair, technically. Which is one reason the book seems so original. Except to the shallow and the jaded, the mere novelty is a bore: everything changes, said Valéry, except the avant-garde. And while "Make it new" is very good advice, perhaps "Make it do" is even better. If one has the strength and the resources to do so. But the example of what Sylvia Plath actually achieved is more convincing than any remarks of mine.

In the famous and terrible "Daddy," the iambs are varied with anapests and spondees:

> no not
> Any less the black man who
>
> Bit my pretty red heart in two.
> I was ten when they buried you.
> At twenty I tried to die
> And get back, back, back to you.
> I thought even the bones would do.

"The Bee Meeting" has longer lines of the same units. It is only in the less impressive poems, those more in the manner of *The Colossus,* that we are not likely to be caught into the rhythm: in "Medusa," for example.

Although I have said very little about diction, numerous quotations have probably suggested the point I would make. In *The Colossus* the diction is always distinguished and elegant, but it is a written language more often than a spoken one. More literary than actual. There are lines not likely to come from a human throat:

> Haunched like a faun, he hooed
> From groves of moon-glint or fen-frost
> Until all owls in the twigged forest

("Faun")

But I open *Ariel* and have no trouble hearing:

> I have done it again,
> One year in every ten
> I manage it—

("Lady Lazarus")

or

> Pure, what does it mean?
>
> ("Fever 103°")

or

> Somebody is shooting at something in our town
>
> ("Swarm")

Not every line in *Ariel* passes this difficult voice test, but what we hear almost everywhere is a real voice in a real body in a real world. In *The Colossus,* the voice is often not vibrant; indeed, it is often not her own. Sometimes, as in "Ouija," it is the voice of Wallace Stevens, with "aureate poetry in tarnished modes . . . fair chronicler of every foul declension." In "Spinster" it is the voice of Ransom, and in "Dark House" it is purest Roethke:

> All-mouth licks up the bushes
> And the pots of meat.
> He lives in an old well,
> A stony hole. He's to blame.
> He's a fat sort.

Dylan Thomas is present, and some others. These are marvellous exercises in imitation, and, like everything else she did, prepared her to speak for herself in *Ariel.* Perhaps a writer finds himself only through having tried to be another. "More than half a lifetime to arrive at this freedom of speech," said Eliot of Yeats's 1914 volume. "It is a triumph." Sylvia Plath did not have half a lifetime, but in a few years, in all the ways I have tried to describe, she prepared herself to endure and transmit, if only for a while, the fires of heaven.

Notes

1. "Suicide Off Egg Rock."
2. Since writing this, I have found that Peter Davison has made much the same point in "Inhabited by a Cry: The Last Poetry of Sylvia Plath," *Atlantic,* August 1966, 76–77. He too considers *The*

Colossus "advanced exercises"; and says of *Ariel,* "these poems would never have come into being without the long, deliberate, technical training that preceded them. We can only perform with true spontaneity what we have first learned to do by habit."

3. *The Poet Speaks,* Argo RG 455, London. Sylvia Plath reads "Lady Lazarus," "Daddy," and "Fever 103°," as well as commentary. Other readers are Ted Hughes, Peter Porter, and Thom Gunn. (Recorded October 30, 1962.)

4. "[I would prefer] to see her lovely way of walking and the bright sparkle of her face."—Sappho, Fr. 16.

5. "Her beauty brightens the fine day and lights up the dark night."—Bernart de Ventadorn, "Amors, enquera·us preyara."

6. This essay was written in the late 1960s. "Her two books" were *The Colossus* (1960, 1962, 1967) and *Ariel* (1965).

The Topless Muse

The Benjamin E. Grey Memorial Lecture at the University of Utah, 1968.

I

"Off, off, you lendings! Come, unbutton here," cries the old king, as he rips his clothes off in the foul weather, trying to get down to "the thing itself . . . no more but such a poor, bare, forked animal." In the late fifties and on through the sixties we saw a flurry of unbuttoning, a flurry of insistence that only the bare, forked animal was "the thing itself." No doors were closed in the nudist colony of the arts; a talented young woman poet was able to blazon her faith in the primacy of the bare and forked in these words:

> The authentic! I said
> rising from the toilet seat

A remark that deserves the immortality accorded Praxilla's famous cucumber. This avowal of an epiphany, *ex cathedra*, sums up much of the spirit of those years, and likely enough was thought "holy" by the poet's admirers; "holy" was then a favorite word, particularly when applied to anything that required the removal of clothing for its performance.

It was toward the close of the sixties that I found myself translating "Das Tagebuch," Goethe's long poem about an erotic experience. Thinking it too frank for the moral sensibilities of his readers, he resolved never to publish it. It seems to be one of the poems referred to by Eckermann in his *Conversations* (February 25, 1824): "Today Goethe showed me two remarkable poems, both highly moral in their tendency, but in their several motifs so unreservedly natural and true that they are of the kind the world styles immoral. On this account, he keeps them to himself, and does not intend to publish them." Perhaps "Das Tagebuch" would have seemed "immoral" to Goethe's audience. It would not have seemed so to Chaucer's, and it would not seem so today. A sexy poem, yes; but also witty, warm, healthy, loving—adjectives that do not spring to mind for much of what we call sexy in our time, when, if we hear someone urging "Unbutton here," we can never be sure which orgy of nakedness we are being summoned to: that of the Garden of Earthly Delights, or that of the tangled bodies at Buchenwald.

The moral scruples that Goethe had, his concern for the pieties—however mistaken—of his readers, these have to do with the responsibility of the writer toward his readers. I am concerned not with the moral question but with the esthetic one: the responsibility of the writer toward his material. I am thinking of the good of the poem, and wondering what kind of nakedness, if any, can show the poem off to advantage. Many possible and impossible subjects of poetry have done their striptease for contemporary gawkers, but suppose we turn our spotlight on only a few of them: on the themes of sickness, violence, domestic discord, and—not that I categorize it with these disorders—the matter of sex. We might then wonder if there are not a number of subjects—as Baudelaire noticed there are a number of human bodies—which make a worse and not a better appearance when seen naked.

But in proposing this restriction, are we not putting a limit on the poet's freedom to use concrete detail? And does that not go counter to the advice we continually give our writing students? Be concrete! Be specific! Show, don't tell! It is true that the poet's job is to body forth the form of things unknown, to give them a local habitation and a name. We could easily muster a little anthology in support of the poets' preference for the concrete. Goethe: "I no sooner have an idea than it turns into an image." Blake: "Singular & Particular detail is the Foundation of the Sublime." Ezra Pound: "It is better to present one image in a lifetime than to produce voluminous works." García Lorca: "The poet is a professor of the five bodily senses." Poets involve our full humanity by presenting the intellectual and the emotional in terms of the sensuous; no ideas, said another of them, but in things. With the poet, life becomes a roadway and error a dark wood; lust becomes a leopard, pride a lion, greed a wolf. Hell itself becomes patch after patch of bad acreage. The leopard, the lion, and the wolf, however, are not merely animals; in each we see the qualities each stands for. Frost once said that he never wrote a nature poem; his nature imagery was always nudging us beyond the synecdoche to what it revealed about human nature and the universe. Because poetry, as Frost also reminded us, is a way of saying one thing and meaning another. This is how a poet handles his images: they refer not only to themselves but to something above and beyond. They cast shadows that are longer than they are.

There are images, however, so riveting that the mind cannot wrench itself away from them: so engrossing or so loathsome or so terrifying as what they are that they are useless as metaphors, synecdoches, or symbols for some other thing. Which of us, our eyes wide on a corpse whose throat had just been cut from ear to ear, could diffuse its harrowing actuality by thinking it only a symbol? Lesser realities—the falling leaves of Goldengrove, for example—can serve more powerfully for that. The X that marks the spot may affect our imaginings more poignantly than the body just carried off. When images involve our deepest feelings, too specific a presentation of them may result in emotional backlash. It is all very well for Marianne Moore to show us her little newt "with white pin-dots on black horizontal spaced out bands" or her pangolin with "scale lapping scale with spruce-cone regularity"; we do not have enough emotional investment in newts or pangolins to be overwhelmed by their specificity. What she is showing us is an "awareness of visual patterns," as

228

T. S. Eliot noticed, "with something like the fascination of a high-powered microscope." But writing with that kind of specificity about material more highly charged is not so impersonal—it is more like looking into our neighbor's bedroom window with a telescope.

What the eye presents only too vividly, the mind is not free to imagine. This may be true of certain images of disease and decay: they hold the attention like a basilisk, so that it cannot move on to what the image is trying to suggest. Too close a focus and the background is lost. We are held by the tyranny of the actual. Even the intrusion of realities less ghastly than the funereal one we proposed—indeed, not ghastly at all—can play havoc with a structure of imagery.

So can a bungling recourse to the ordinary. "Imaginary gardens with real toads in them"—that is what Marianne Moore wanted poets to present. But even in telling them to have literal details in their poems she was being figurative. Look closer and you see those are not toads; those are synecdoches. What Marianne Moore wanted were enough samples of actuality to convince the reader that this was indeed the world we live in. Sometimes just a detail or two will do it. The poet's problem is to pick and choose among the multifarious details the universe can offer, and to come up with a few just right ones. One does not improve a poem by throwing a toad or two into it. Keats did not write

> I cannot see what toads are at my feet,
>   Nor what soft incense hangs upon the boughs

No, in that stanza he needed flies. Goethe's ideas turned into images—but into Goethean images, not into the images that might have occurred to anybody. García Lorca called the poet a professor of the five senses—but a *professor,* not a doctoral candidate and much less a dropout. Pound said it is better to present one image than voluminous works, but he did not mean any old image: he meant an image that was fresh, exact, and memorable. The poet has to be very careful what images he selects; it is not enough that they be "authentic." We can also be enslaved by the tyranny of the quotidian.

The characters of Romeo and Juliet, for instance, are real enough for most of us. Yet a whole range of human actualities has been ruled out by Shakespeare. What if Juliet suffered from postnasal drip and a runny nose, conditions that worsened in the night air, so that any time she spent on a balcony was devoted to snuffling and hawking into a phlegm-sopped hanky? What if Romeo had overeaten at the Capulets' party and been subject to noisy discharges of stomach gas?—an innocent enough concomitant of the chemistries of digestion with which humankind has long been familiar. The authentic, in fact.

> But soft! What light through yonder window breaks? (*belch*)
> It is the East, and Juliet (*belch*) is the sun!

There are many kinds of poetry that do not have to be validated by authenticities of that sort. Standing in muck is not the only way of having one's feet on the ground, nor does it give the steadiest footing.

I am not theorizing *in vacuo*. I still have painful memories of writing workshops in the sixties, when down-to-earth authentication was demanded by some of the youthful *scapigliati* of the time. How can I forget the literary aspirant whose only criticism of a poem was, "It's not *dirty* enough!"? How can I forget the other who held that every poem ought to use the word *shit,* or some equivalent, at least once to show that the poet was indeed in touch with the authenticities. Could he have done so, he would have purged and purified all English poetry by retouching it, so that Keats might have begun his ode with something like:

> My heart aches and—aw shit!—a numbness pains
> My sense, as though of hemlock I had drunk

That, he would have said, showed the guy had real feeling.

In the examples that will occur to me, I do not mean to say that the nakedness in itself is not interesting. I only wonder if the interest it arouses is the sort we expect from poetry. There are many kinds of texts that a reader in his human situation will find more gripping than a poem: the Dow Jones averages, a court summons, the account of a scandalous divorce or a shocking autopsy, the directions on a medicine bottle, the insurance policy of a rich relative recently deceased. Certain kinds of frankness in a poem may be equally alluring, but for reasons not essentially related to poetry. And certain stark statements that I think fail as poems may be very powerful documents of another sort.

II

Among these are poems about medical experience. People have always been concerned—and no wonder—with their doctoring. Operations, breakdowns, insanity—these are subjects that compel our attention. In the work of "confessional" poets—not confessional in that they whisper to a priest in a dark stall or to an analyst with his pad and pencil, but to the world at large—there has been a rash of medical detail. It was once said of learned poetry that it smelled of the lamp; it can be said of some of the poetry of our time that it smells of the bedpan. The nakedness we see there is not the nakedness of nature lovers under the sun; it is the pasty nakedness of hospital sheets.

It was not just the ladies who welcomed flocks of visitors into the asylums and operating rooms. W. D. Snodgrass, one of the best poets of the period, asked us to contemplate at some length the harrowing half-life of "A Flat One":

> Old Fritz, on this rotating bed
> For seven wasted months you lay
> Unfit to move, shrunken, gray,
> No good to yourself or anyone
> But to be babied—changed and bathed and fed.
> At long last, all that's done

But the poem is not done; it goes on for seventeen painful stanzas after that one, with much grim imagery of bedsores, catheters, swabsticks, spit pans, diaper pads, red tubes, plugs for the corpse. A powerful piece of writing, which has given Old Fritz an existence beyond his death. But I am not sure the power is in the poetry; it seems rather in the documentary vigor of its graphic medical detail and of its speculations about hospital care for the terminally ill. As poetry, Snodgrass's "Heart's Needle," a sequence about a daughter lost in a painful divorce, is more moving— in part because it leaves veiled in ambiguity the painful specifics of the divorce.

Is the medical history of Old Fritz the most effective way for a poet to deal with illness? We can easily think of poems that have done it differently. George Orwell thought that Hopkins's "Felix Randal" was "the best short poem in the language." Hopkins knew and had attended the blacksmith of that poem; he could have given us the details of the "fatal four disorders" that led to death. But there are no details— not even the names of the disorders. Instead the poet diverts our vision from the sickbed to the splendor of "the great grey drayhorse" the blacksmith had measured his strength against in the days of his pride. One of Ransom's best known poems is "Here Lies a Lady." We are told that "of chills and fever she died," but this is hardly specific enough to be entered in the medical records. We see the "medicos marveling sweetly on her ills," but as readers are given no information that would help in a diagnosis.

One thinks too of Yeats's poem "Upon a Dying Lady."

> With the old kindness, the old distinguished grace,
> She lies, her lovely piteous head amid dull red hair
> Propped upon pillows, rouge on the pallor of her face.
> She would not have us sad because she is lying there,
> And when she meets our gaze her eyes are laughter-lit,
> Her speech a wicked tale that we may vie with her,
> Matching our broken-hearted wit against her wit

There were plenty of medical details available to Yeats, had he cared to inflict them on us. Mabel Beardsley, Aubrey's sister, then in her early forties, had been ill with cancer for six months; in a letter to Lady Gregory, Yeats described his visit to "the dying sister of Beardsley . . . she had had a week of great pain. . . . Just before I was going her mother came and saw me to the door . . . she said 'I do not think she wishes to live—how could she after such agony? . . .' I lay awake most of the night with a poem in my head." But the poem does not detail the pain or the agony; it leaves the ravaged body courteously concealed.

A more intimate experience of suffering prompted Dylan Thomas's "Do not go gentle into that good night." Again, much graphic symptomatology was available. He wrote the poem in 1951, but as early as 1933 a dentist had noticed an ulcer on the elder Thomas's tongue; cancer was diagnosed. The father was subjected to painful and extended treatment with radium needles, his voice was affected by the treatments, he had to resign from his teaching position, saw his salary cut to a small pension. Years of bad health followed; by 1947 he was a semi-invalid, his spirits failing as his health did. A few years later, his heart weakened. By 1952, just before his death, his sight and other senses failed; as Thomas wrote, "He was in awful pain at the end and nearly blind." There are plenty of harrowing specifics here, which a writer given to such listings might have made much of: the ulcer, the needles, the heart trouble, the blindness. But there is not a word about any of this in the poem; no medical history at all. (The "blind eyes" of the poem were entirely figurative when it was written.)

Rilke too had been stirred by the mysterious horrors of terminal illness. *Die Sonnette an Orpheus* owe their existence to the stimulus of such contemplations. They are dedicated to the memory of Wera Ouckama Knoop, the young dancer whose verve and beauty (we see it still in her photo) had fascinated him the few times he saw her as a child. In 1922, on learning that she had died two years before at the age of nineteen, he begged her mother for a fuller account of the illness and death. The mother, who had kept a journal of her daughter's agonizing decline, did send it to Rilke. Deeply moved, he set to work on his sonnet sequence, in which the image of the girl—though she appears in only two of the fifty-five poems—was felt as a presence, the poet said, that "governs and animates the march of the whole sequence." Rilke's attitude toward suffering and his handling of it sent him soaring above the graphic clinical details; the girl is shown not as a patient but as an Orphic image of transcendence. The poet knew well enough about the harrowing physicalities of the case; in a letter he refers to the way her body "changed in some strange way; without losing its lovely oriental look, it became oddly heavy and massive . . . the beginning of the mysterious glandular disorder that was soon to end her life." The mother's journal would have supplied him with more than enough gruesome medical horrors; all are omitted from the poems. In the twenty-fifth sonnet of part one, the onset, remissions, and recurrence of the illness lose their grimness under veils of imagery and in swirls of music. Toward the close of that poem, the allusion to her personified blood, which "drängte verdunkelt" (pressed forward darkened) and "glänzte . . . irdisch" (glistened . . . earthly) is not hematology but symbol. If the poet has in mind paralysis, palpitations, tachycardia, hemorrhages (it has been suggested that his *Sturz* [fall] stands for *Blutsturz* [hemorrhage]), the physical realities of the illness are again lost in the music and idealized under a shimmer of personification, synecdoche, and symbol.

But we need not go so far from home for examples. Sylvia Plath is never content to show raw reality in its rawness, but instead, through metaphor and music, turns it into the surreality of art. The relaxed pentameters of "Tulips," with their imagery of a watery world in nearly every stanza, and with a displacement of focus from the patient to the flowers, show one way in which a poet can handle materials otherwise too painful.

A decision about frankness also has to be made when the spirit has left the body and what the poet is affixing his beam on is a cadaver. Rilke has a poem whose title might be translated as "Washing the Corpse," but in it our eyes are hardly directed to the body itself, as they are in Mantegna's painting of the dead Christ. Most poets show a decent tact in dealing with the dead. When a poet writes

Underneath this stone doth lie

or

> Underneath this sable hearse

we are rarely given any information about the posthumous condition of the corpse, until it has been so sanatized by the passage of the years that the poet dares to show us

> A bracelet of bright hair about the bone

or tell us that

> Here are sands, ignoble things,
> Dropped from the ruined sides of kings

or until the body has been sea changed into coral and pearls. About the transitional state of purulence (except in groundhogs and such) there has not been much comment. Nor have poets been censored, as far as I know, for their prissiness in not displaying this naked truth.

III

Besides the violence that nature inflicts on us in the form of illness, there is the worse violence that we inflict on ourselves. Here too the poet often finds reticence more expressive than a spouting of specifics, and for the same reason: such withholding, instead of freezing our attention on *this right here,* liberates our imagination, which can present events to us more feelingly than even the senses can.

At the narrow pass of Thermopylae, between the mountains and the sea, a few hundred Greek soldiers stood their ground, as they were told to do, against the invading Persians, by whom they were spectacularly outnumbered. What ensued was a massacre; the battlefield would have been a gory sight after the Persians had cut their way through the massed young Spartan bodies. And yet there is not a single bloodstain on the famous distich that Simonides wrote in memory of the fallen:

> Go tell at Sparta, traveller passing by,
> That here obedient to her laws we lie.

Nor did the poet need to evoke the gruesome details of the butchery. Only too many of those he was talking to would have their own memories of a son or a father dead, their own knowledge of what a spear or sword can do to the human flesh one loves. Every good writer, poet or not, knows this: never tell a reader what will leap to his mind without your telling.

But suppose Simonides had described a selection of denuded corpses? Would the impact of the poem have been greater?

> Gore all around, shins shattered, teeth clubbed out;
> Lo! here a body bleeds through many a spout.
> With this, the brain drips clotted out the nose;
> With this—come close and look—the intestine shows . . .

We cannot read far into these thumbnail autopsies without escaping into laughter, derisive or uneasy.

The story of Hippolytus, his body shredded as he was entangled in the reins of his runaway horses, has been told by both Euripides and Seneca. Euripides, in his *Hippolytus,* speaks with reserve about "his dead brow pounded on the rocks, his body bruised." But Seneca, writing for recital to a jaded audience used to gladiatorial brutalities, spares us nothing in his play of the same name:

Chorus: O you his father, arrange in order the scattered parts of his torn body, and fit back the random pieces where they belong. His brawny right arm should go here, his left over there. I can still figure out parts of his left side. But how many pieces are still missing. . . .

Theseus: What is this shapeless, ugly piece, so hacked on every side? I can't say what part of you it is, son, but some part. Here, lay it down, maybe not in the right spot, but anywhere it sort of fits. Is this his *face?*

Is this ghoulish jigsaw puzzle meant to be black humor? It seems not.

But we may wonder if Ovid, abetted by his sixteenth-century translator Arthur Golding, is not being a little tongue-in-cheek in book XII of the *Metamorphoses,* when he throws himself with such gusto into the field-hospital realism, beyond anything in "M*A*S*H," of the battle between the Lapiths and the Centaurs:

> . . . he on the forehead hit
> A Lapith naamèd Celadon, and crushèd so his bones
> That none could know him by the face: both eyes flew out
>   at once.
> His nose was beaten back and to his palate battered flat . . .
> And as [one] spittèd out his teeth with blackish blood, he
>   lent
> Another blow to Amycus, which straight to hell him sent . . .

This is nothing: the writer is just warming up, and goes on with his blow-by-blow account for about three hundred more lines, necessarily increasing in savagery to maintain the crescendo. There are many such gaudy anatomical passages as the one in which Dorylas is done to death: seeing a javelin coming toward him, he raises a hand to ward it off; the javelin pierces his hand and pins it to his forehead: we might say he is crucified on himself. Taking advantage of his plight, father Peleus "struck him under / The middle belly with a sword, and ripped his [guts] asunder." As his intestines trail on the ground, his feet get entangled in them; he trips and dies amid them.

Horrific as this is, it comes too close to the blackest of comedy. Ransom, in "Necrological," gives a more moving description of carnage when he says of the denuded bodies of the casualties:

> Not all were white; some gory and fabulous
> Whom the sword had pierced and then the grey wolf
>   eaten . . .

"Fabulous" is the word that does wonders by releasing the imagination.

Walt Whitman would have known about wounds from his Civil War experiences as a wound-dresser. And yet there is almost no battlefield realism in his *Drum-Taps*, with its vivid glimpses of cavalry crossing a ford, of a bivouac on a mountainside, of an army corps on the march. His poem "Over the Carnage Rose Prophetic a Voice" has carnage only in the title (which is the first line). The poem does rise above it. Only in "The Wound-Dresser" itself is notice taken of actual wounds, but the simple listing does not play up the horror.

Violent as the old ballads are, it is surprising how little they dwell on the sensational incidents. Behind "Lord Randal" is a tale of betrayal and murder at the hands of one the young lord thought his "true love." He has just been meeting her, and yet there is no scene of love or of betrayal. He has just been poisoned, but no symptoms are shown; there is no gasping or gagging, no clutching at the stomach. His dogs, we are told, "swelled and . . . died"—but there is no way the poet, in this poem, would have shown Lord Randal lying bloated on his bed; in fact, there is no deathbed scene. There is the same dramatic reticence in "Edward, Edward"; we are shown a bloody sword, but not the bloody corpse of the murdered father. We are left to guess—though it is not too hard—just what the hellish counsels of the mother were.

Yeats, during the Irish Civil War and later, had his own experiences of violence and bloodshed, and yet the poems give few if any specific details—though *blood* is a common enough symbol in many of his other poems. The experience that may have affected him most deeply was the assassination of his friend Kevin O'Higgins, Vice-President and Minister for Justice, who was murdered by three gunmen on his way to church one Sunday morning. Yeats knew details of the murder, and in a letter mentions the circumstances under which he heard of it. "He was our personal friend . . . and then too his pretty young wife was our friend. . . . We got the news just when we reached the Gresham Hotel where we were to dine and we left without dining and walked about the streets till bed-time." He goes on to tell how he and his wife the night before had had some eerie psychic experience with a phantom motorcar ("You will remember the part the motor car had in the murder") and with ghostly bursts of church music that he recognized later when he heard them at the funeral. For some writers, these are the details that would have made up the poem—these and such other matters as the nature of the gunshot wounds and the pools of blood in which the body lay. They might have used too an actual saying of O'Higgins to his "pretty young wife": "Nobody can expect to live who has done what I have done"—a reference to the firmness with which he had tried to put down civil disorder. But there is none of this—no Gresham Hotel, no phantom car—in the poem which Yeats wrote a few weeks later, with the assassination in mind. In "Death" his speculations are well beyond what the journalist's camera might have shown:

> Nor dread nor hope attend
> A dying animal;
> A man awaits his end
> Dreading and hoping all

IV

Of the kinds of violence we are familiar with, there is none, as Aristotle observed long ago, more tragic than that which occurs within families: violence between those whom bonds of love should hold together. Medea, Othello, and countless other characters we meet in literature have had trouble in the home. A mention of those two reminds us that drama can, and has to, make more use of graphic incident than a poem is obliged to do. The Greeks, it is true, kept the performance of horrors away from the eyes of the audience; a recital of them by a messenger preserved the sanctity of their theater. But on the modern stage we are used to actual weapons and the actual shedding of ketchup.

Outside of the theater, however, suggestion seems to work better; imagination can show events more vividly than the footlights can. In dealing with domestic troubles, some poets seem to forget the power of understatement and intimation; they present the reader with details they ought to send to an advice columnist instead of giving that reader the disagreements and squabbles in all of their shrill, boring reality.

Other poets, more firm of lip, have been more successful. Frost's "The Subverted Flower" is about a misunderstanding between young people—a small misunderstanding, yet one which might have lifelong consequences. A young man has done something, made some advance—we never know exactly what—which has offended a young woman. All we know is that they face each other in a field, she with "her shining hair displaced" and her comb fallen to the ground. The poem begins after the incident has happened; it is referred to only in the symbolism of the flower:

> She drew back; he was calm:
> "It is this that had the power."
> And he lashed his open palm
> With the tender-headed flower

Both, for different reasons, want to forget what happened; the poem collaborates by refusing to specify it, and is the stronger for its reticence.

For a more celebrated and more portentous example, we have the few lines in which Dante has Pia tell her story in the fifth canto of the *Purgatorio*:

> Ricorditi di me, che son la Pia;
> Siena me fé, disfecemi Maremma:
> salsi colui che 'nnanellata pria
> disposando m'avea con la sua gemma.

"Remember me, the one they called Pia. Siena made me; Maremma unmade me—as well he knows, the man who in marrying me put his jeweled ring on my finger." Born in

Siena, Pia was murdered by her husband, who had taken her to his castle in the lonely Maremma. The story was that because he wanted to marry another woman he had Pia thrown out of a window of his castle into the gorge below; she was never heard of again. Pia says not a word about the domestic discord that must have existed; doesn't even say that her husband killed her, but only that he knows well how she died. Delicate touches make the apparently plain statement more moving. She calls herself not Pia but "la Pia," the way others would have referred to her in colloquial Italian, familiarly and perhaps with affection. Besides the tombstone details of her birth and death, she gives us only one specific image: we see her downward eyes on the jeweled ring being put on her hand by the man who should least of any in the world have done her violence. There is much more she could have told us about her marriage. She might have given us the kind of sordid details, as we call them, that turn up in domestic relations courts: "I first suspected that all was not going well with our relationship when he pushed my face into the bowl of spaghetti." Instead, no details. Only the gentleness, the loneliness, the terror, the mysterious death. It is because of what they do not say that her lines have become among the best known in literature.

Dante's Pia is reticent about her own tragedy. Hugo von Hofmannsthal has given us a short poem whose symbolism would seem to cover all possible disagreements between two people whose vivid individualities will not permit harmony between them. His "Die Bieden" might be translated as follows:

The Two

Her fingers bore the winecup in,
Rim shapely as her lip, her chin.
So easy and assured her air
That not a drop fell anywhere.

So easy and assured his hand
—He on a stallion, fiery, young,
Ever so nonchalently swung
Its withers, quivering, to a stand.

Yet when he leaned to take the cup
Her fingers easily held up,
They found it all too heavy there,
With both atremble so, that pair,
That neither hand the other found;
Dark wine ran spattering the ground.

V

At the opposite end of the range of emotions, where rela-
tionships are most loving, the poet has to make the same
decision: how much to tell. If we bring to mind the great love
poems from over the centuries, we find that practically none
have the explicitness we have come to expect in current
fiction.

Sappho is one of the great poets, and love is her specialty.
She is also a poet given to richly sensuous detail. And yet in
the extant poetry she tells us almost nothing about the person
she loves and nothing at all about their lovemaking. She does
tell us, in a poem whose conclusion is missing, how *she* feels:
how in the presence of the one she loves her heart starts to
pound, how she feels chills and hot flashes, breaks into a light
sweat, grows pale, thinks she may faint. But all we learn about
the other person is that she has a nice voice and a lovely
laugh. In her one complete poem ("ποικιλόθρον' ἀθανάτ'
Ἀφρόδιτα . . .") there is not a word about the person she's in
love with; she has kept her name a secret from even Aphro-
dite, to whom she is appealing for help in the turbulence she
feels about some new love—she is clear-eyed enough to be
rueful and ironic even about herself. Another love poem ("οἰ
μὲν ἱππήων στρότον οἰ δὲ πέσδων . . .") begins with imagery
of what other people think is the finest sight on earth: cavalry,
warships, armies. But in her opinion, Sappho goes on to say,
the most beautiful thing of all is the person one loves. She
gives us a name, Anaktoria, but only a line and a half of
description:

τᾶς κε βολλοίμαν ἔρατόν τε βᾶμα
κἀμάρυχμα λάμπρον ἴδην προσώπω . . .

"I would rather see her lovely walk and the bright sparkle of
[play of expression on] her face." And that's all; nothing very
intimate there, except the intensity of the emotion. Whatever
else there was is behind closed doors. Such things, she might
be telling us, are nobody's business—and certainly not the
general public's.

When we turn to Catullus—*enfant terrible* that he is—we
may be in for another surprise. "No poet," says one of his
modern editors, "was ever more unreserved." But this is not
true of the *love* poems, the ones he wrote while really in love,
nor is it true of the poems of regret he wrote as his disillusion-
ment grew and he looked back on the bygone days of hap-
piness. It was only toward the very end, when he knew the
worst about his Lesbia, that he could send those savage "non
bona dicta," but even then he remembered that he had loved
her as no woman would ever be loved again: "amata nobis
quantum amabitur nulla." He tells us how much he loved her
but never how: there is no explicit lovemaking in the *love*
poems of Catullus except for the passionate kisses, of which
he says he can never get enough and which no accountant
could keep track of. He is reserved too, at least by modern
standards, in the poem about the love of Acme and Sep-
timius, and in the lovely marriage songs. I italicize "*love*
poems" because there are a few poems of playful sex, like that
to Ipsithilla, in which he is more outgoing than he ever is in
the poems to the one woman he loved: there are no such
scenes in his poems to Lesbia. Where he is really unreserved is
in the poems of scorn and hatred he wrote about various
contemporaries; in these all barriers are down: there is no
word too frank, too gross, to hurl at them. Or if there is any
grossness he has spared us, some of his recent translators
have added it.

We cannot, in the space we have, ransack the poetry of
Europe and America for examples of love poems in which

243

intensity of feeling goes hand in hand with a refusal to di-
vulge the secret intimacies. If we could, I would begin with a
stanza of Bernart de Ventadorn, to my mind the best of the
Provençal poets:

> Las! e viure que·m val,
> s'eu no vei a jornal
> mo fi joi natural
> en leih, sotz fenestral,
> cors blanc tot atretal
> com la neus a nadal,
> si c'amdui cominal
> mesurem s'em egal?

This might be Englished (though without keeping the same
rhyme through all eight lines) as:

> Life gives—? well nothing quite
> like having day and night
> the one joy mine by right:
> in bed, by window-light
> yourself undressed, a glow
> merry as Christmas snow,
> where we lie fitted so
> we're snug from head to toe.

Much of the charm is in the way the poet diverts us from
frontal contemplation to the symbol of snow at Christmas.

But what about John Donne? we might wonder. Isn't he
pretty explicit about his love for the lady he describes in his
nineteenth elegy, "Going to Bed"? We might begin by saying
that these early works are his Ipsithilla poems, not his real
love poems. But even in these he is not writing "naked poet-
ry"; he leaves his lady neatly dressed in metaphor even while
the literal garments are being shucked.

> O my America! my new-found-land,
> My kingdome, safliest when with one man man'd,
> My Myne of precious stones, My Emperie . . .

(Just as he never strips the topographical coverings from the lady of his eighteenth, "Love's Progress.") Two of the boldest lines of the nineteenth have recourse not to the explicit noun but to the evasive but imaginative adverb:

> License my roaving hands, and let them go,
> Before, behind, between, above, below . . .

The young writer who thought most poems are "not dirty enough" could easily have supplied the anatomical monosyllables that would have filled in the blanks in

> . . . and let them pass
> Over her _____, her _____, her _____, her _____.

Donne knew about such monosyllables too; but he also knew that the use of strong words is the recourse of feeble writers. It was Valéry who said something like that, the same Valéry who went on record against confessional frankness in poetry; that "form of activity that could almost be defined as a perpetual confusion between life, thought, and profession in the one who undertakes it. . . . Some there are who . . . cherish their sufferings so as to write of them, and since the invention of 'sincerity' as valid literary currency . . . a confession is as good as an idea." He then goes on to make his "own confession": "If this system of exposing one's private affairs to the public is called *human,* I must declare myself essentially *inhuman.*"

Such reservations did not keep Valéry from writing his vivid description of girls being made love to (in "Le cimetière marin"), a passage which his explicator Gustave Cohen has called more daring ("plus audacieux") than anything in Baudelaire. Cohen goes further: nothing so gripping or so direct has been written on this subject since Villon.

> Les cris aigus des filles chatouillées,
> Les yeux, les dents, les paupières mouillées,
> Le sien charmant qui joue avec le feu,
> Le sang qui brille aux lèvres qui se rendent,
> Les derniers dons, les doigts qui les défendent

(The keen cries of girls who are tickled ["tickled" is the "literal" meaning; "electrified by caresses" would probably be closer to what Valéry is thinking of], the eyes, the teeth, the dampened eyelids, the charming breast that plays with fire, the blood brilliant in the lips as they yield, the final gifts, the fingers which defend them)

The best writers of love poetry, it would seem, do not invite voyeurs into their bedrooms, nor do they make exhibitionistic displays of the person they love. A little nakedness, at least in poetry, goes a long way—perhaps we need no more than the "naked foot" of the ladies in Wyatt's most famous poem:

> They flee from me that sometime did me seek,
> With naked foot stalking in my chamber

Well, maybe a little more than that synecdoche. The special lady of the second stanza is "in thin array" and her loose gown is slipping from her shoulders as she kisses him. But then Wyatt draws the bed curtains, though presumably the lady's kissing him was not the climax of the evening. Our imagination, if so inclined, can go further than the poem did. Amusing testimony to the power of the imagination is found not only in numerous cartoons but in Peter DeVries *The Mackerel Plaza,* in which a man sits meditating on a girl at a nearby restaurant table: "She was about twenty-five, and naked except for a green skirt and sweater, heavy brown tweed coat, shoes, stockings, and so forth, a scarf knotted at her throat and a brown beret."

We can let this section culminate with what is probably the greatest omitted love scene in literature. It is in the fifth canto of the *Inferno,* when Francesca is describing how her affair with Paolo began. They had been sitting close together, by themselves, reading a romantic tale. When they reached the description of a passionate kiss, they looked at each other, and Paolo, though trembling like von Hofmannsthal's cavalier, was unable to keep from kissing her:

> la bocca mi baciò, tutto tremante
>
> (he kissed my mouth, all trembling)

And then the love scene should come—but none does. Dante says only

quel giorno più non vi leggemmo avante.

"That day we read no further there." What they did do, he does not have to tell us—though no doubt it would have made juicy reading. Whatever it was, they are in hell for it.

Besides the fact that silence can be made to speak louder than words, and that imagination can present reality to us more vividly, or at least more seductively, than the senses can, there are other reasons why the poets have been leery of explicit sex. One difficulty, in English, is in the words they would have to use. The well known and now often printed four-letter words—for four is about what they average—are vocally inappropriate for the delicate nuances they are expected to convey: stubby furtive little words, their hastily grunted vowels cramped in by fricatives and gutturals instead of the more lingering liquids. Valéry's *chatouillées*, now, is caressive as sound; in English it turns into the silly-sounding "tickled." This is by no means one of our sexier words, but it makes the point. The sexy folk words in our language *sound* as if they referred not to making love but to some device used to plug up leaky toilets.

A second consideration is that these same words are heard at least as often in a context of contempt, hate, and objurgation as in a context of affection. Probably oftener; many people reserve them for scurrility. These connotations can hardly fail to carry over when we try to use them in a loving way. Living lips may at times give them tenderness, but it is hard for ink and paper to do so—especially in computerized type. There is bound to be something treacherous about a word that is equally comfortable in the mouth of a rapist or of a lover.

If such words once had any freshness, they had long since lost their virginity by the sixties, when they became something like the poetic diction of that period. Maiden ladies of the preceding century were not fonder of words like *pallor* and *fragile* than the hard-nosed scribblers of our own time were of time were of their pawed-over prizes. Even the shock value was gone; what we might think of as "foul language" is shocking only in a mouth that does not habitually use it. Othello's sudden grossness is so moving because he—unlike Iago—is not given to that kind of talk. But when one habitually speaks in blanks and asterisks there is no longer any surprise, much less shock, in anything one says. In that mouth they are no more a merit than frankness is in a natural blabbermouth.

Another limitation of explicit diction is that the emotional experiences it would describe are, in this field, so nonverbal that it is only with the help of metaphor that they get into language at all. They remain ineffable—no matter how many *f*'s one uses. The difficulty is like that which St. John of the Cross faced with his rather different material: "It would be ignorance," he wrote, "to think that the sayings of love understood mystically . . . can be fairly explained by words of any kind." That is why he thought poetry a better medium than prose for such communications: poetry does not profess to *tell* us anything; it can merely suggest and "by means of figures, comparisons, and similitudes, let overflow something of what [is felt]."

VI

Tell all the Truth but tell it slant—
Success in Circuit lies

These lines of Emily Dickinson might be her advice to poets. Or might be what she had learned from them. To say that poets prefer to tell it slant is another figure for saying that they know it may be better to avoid frontal presentations of the naked truth. They prefer to work as Walther von der Vogelweide does in a poem readers have been fond of for seven centuries now, a poem that will not tell us what exactly happened between the two lovers under the linden on the heath.

Wes er mit mir pflæge,
niemer niemen
bevinde daz wan er und ich

"What he did with me," says the girl, "no one is ever to know—only he and I." They and the *kleinez vogellîn,* the little bird that will never tell. But if not directly in the words of the poem, the little bird does tell us, and so do the flowers and grasses, sweetly crushed where the lovers lay. And so does the passerby later, who, seeing those flowers and grasses, laughs softly to himself. The poet tells it slant.

We have seen some of the many ways poets have taken to do so: imagery, metaphor, synecdoche, symbol, displacement, transcendence. We could find others—such as the way otherwise innocent images combine and take on new meanings, as in Yeats's lines:

"Because I am mad about women
I am mad about the hills,"
Said the wild old wicked man
Who travels where God wills.

Here, by inference, the old man's sexual interests are given the sanction of nature and even of the Almighty. Another way: what is to be said can be diverted from statement into effects of rhythm, as when the iambs stiffen into spondees in Yeats's line about a tight embrace:

When my arms wrap you round I press

Or into the play of our muscles in pronouncing, as, again in Yeats, in the lines about the passionate young kisses:

And pressed at midnight in some public place
Live lips upon a plummet-measured face.

The several puckered *p*'s and *pl*'s mime what they describe. Or what is to be said can be transferred from statement to sound itself, as poets have always known. One of the purest examples of sound bearing the burden of meaning is in Homer—that long ago! In the eighteenth book of the *Iliad,* the sea nymphs have gathered to lament the death of Patroclus. Homer says little about their lamenting, but he lists the names of some thirty of the nymphs, and that list is a mournful wail of nasals, liquids, and long vowels. Their very moans have been translated into name-sounds. As we read poetry we will notice other ways in which the poets find their success in Circuit.

The ancient Greeks were a healthy outdoor people, with no prudery about the human body. So their statues would seem to proclaim: even the gods and goddesses were displayed in a majesty naked enough. But never the Muses; they are shown "in long floating robes, covered by a mantle," as one encyclopedia of mythology assures us. Nor was this enough: we are told too that "they often went abroad clothed in thick mist through which most men could not see."

Of course. But the imagination could see where the eye could not. And how else could we *dream* of them naked?

The Greatest English Lyric?
A New Reading of Joe E. Skilmer's "Therese"

Genuine revolutions in literary taste and theory occur on an average only once every seven generations; therefore it is a source of satisfaction to have myself piloted what may be the most shattering reappraisal in our literature. I am referring—as the world of letters now knows well—to the discovery (made about the time that flying saucers began to be widely observed here and abroad) of that core of inner *is*-ness in the poetry of the long misread, long underrated Joburt Eggson Skilmer, or Joe E. Skilmer as he himself signed his poems. Slighted by serious readers for what seemed the facility of his technique and the pious banality of his thought—especially as shown in the poem known as "Trees"—Skilmer was in reality the perpetrator of an existentialist hoax on a public that prided itself on knowing what was genuine.

For years, many of us had been dissatisfied with the reading generally accorded this remarkable poem—the kind of official reading that provoked academic guffaws in a thousand classrooms. "There is more here than meets thee, eye," I would murmur to myself, teased by a host of ambiguities, of velleities that never quite came clear. It was a question of tone. Perhaps my first breakthrough came when I heard Professor Wrugson O. Muttson reading a line from Pound's "The River-Merchant's Wife: A Letter":

From *Studies in Bibliography,* vol. 20, edited by Fredson Bowers (Charlottesville: University Press of Virginia, 1967).

At fourteen I married my Lord you.

Muttson read the line as if it expressed wifely devotion. But it was obvious to me, as to any especially sensitive reader, that Pound intended the line to be heavily ironic, and that the "tone" might better be represented by something like

At fourteen I married (my Lord!) *you?*

My trouble had been that I was ventriloquizing, putting my own voice into the poem, instead of letting it *read itself to me.* Do not read poems—this became my principle—be read to by them. This approach led to a number of discoveries, of which possibly the most earth-shaking was my article proving that Hamlet's famous soliloquy is not about suicide at all but about his meteorological and alchemical experiments with a number of test tubes (the "retorts" he is famous for), of which the tube lettered "E" seemed the most promising if the most vexatious:

Tube "E" or not tube "E"—that is the quest, chum.
Weather? 'Tis no blur in the mind

But this reading, now officially adopted in the best textual editions, is too well known to need further quotation. I have also found my method of "deep reading" fruitful in the perusal of several thousand lines of *Paradise Lost,* and I suspect that our whole literature will have to be reread in the light of it. However: it was on the basis of this strict principle that I returned to Skilmer's great love poem to Therese Murk of Peoria. Called simply "Therese," or "T'rese," it had too long been thought of as having something to do with "trees"! The misconception arose from Skilmer's supreme irony; he had all too successfully "achieved an overlay," as he liked to say when speaking of the technique of poetry. That is, by a triumph of art he had given a shallow surface glaze, a pretty spindrift, to the profound abysses of the poem—a glaze so *trompe-l'oeil* that many were never able to see beneath it. What the public had been doing was reading only the "overlay"

instead of what he called the "substruct," and what they set-
tled for was something miserably like this:

> I think that I shall never see
> A poem lovely as a tree.
>
> A tree whose hungry mouth is pressed
> †Upon† the earth's sweet flowing breast.
>
> Upon whose bosom snow has lain,
> †And† intimately lives with rain.
>
> A tree that looks †at† God all day,
> And lifts her leafy arms to pray.
>
> A tree that may in summer wear
> A nest of robins in her hair.
>
> Poems are made by fools like me,
> But only God can make a tree.

Sheer banality! (and how far short of Skilmer's own noble
definition of a poem as "a shimmering spitball flung into the
great catcher's-mitt of eternity.") But the poem's *inner*ness,
which my researches have arrived at, is another thing en-
tirely. What I mean to do here is demonstrate the "substruct,"
unit by unit, explicating where I can, though it is doubtful
that any reader, or group of readers, will ever arrive at an
adequate notion of the riches hidden in this most wonderful
of poems.

1.

> *I* think? That I shall never, see!
> Up, owe 'em love. Leah's a tree.

Probably not since John Donne's "For Godsake hold your
tongue, and let me love" has a poem opened with such ex-
plosive élan. "*I* think?" he rages; and in that fury is a ringing
refusal to see life merely in terms of the "cogitations" that
have amazed lesser poets. Here the whole Eliotic tradition of
intellectualized verse is swept cleanly away forever—an

achievement the more remarkable inasmuch as that tradition had not yet come into being. But few poets have had antennae so sensitive, been so unfailing a Tiresias (Therese? Ah yes!) in divining the yet-to-come. Crass indeed is the reader who fails to sense, in the proemial words, the poet's curling lip,[1] or who fails to note the hoot of scorn in the derisive "see" that concludes the line with a vulgarity ah how *voulu*! Almost blatant, this effect; and yet, beneath the brassy fanfare, what delicate counterpoint of grammatical woodwinds in the antiphony of declarative mood to interrogative, an antiphony that becomes harangue when we feel it in terms of the inner dialogue, the colloquy of a soul tormented by an age when all values have turned moot. Yet, as always in Skilmer, violence tempered with amenity: instead of the scowling "will" of resolution, only the disclaiming modesty of that simple "shall."

The second line, opening with courage and defiance, can but deepen the stated theme. "Up!" (cf. the Italian "Su! coraggio!") as the poet, confronting the inenarrable chaos of his world, lifts himself from that slough of despond by the Muses' very bootstrap. Don't *give* love away, he exhorts himself; don't wanton away so rare a substance on the all and sundry. *Owe* them love; do not pay when payment is despised. How much terser these moving words than such romantic maundering as

> When I was one-and-twenty
>   I heard a wise man say,
> "Give crowns and pounds and guineas
>   But not your heart away . . ."

But—oh marvel of art—again the tight-lipped acerbity is softened by one of the loveliest transitions in all poetry. After the corrosive cynicism of the opening, the gentle evocation of biblical womanhood fuses, as in Dante, with the mythology of the ancient world, in a line that sums up the fugacity of all things mortal. "Leah's a tree" indeed; Leah has *become* a tree, has escaped from the aggressor's pursuit, from the weary wheel of being. When Skilmer says "Leah" he is of course thinking of Daphne—the names have three letters (if no more) in common; our poet works by preference in that hallowed *three,* perhaps more meaningfully here than elsewhere, since in his sturdy American dialect *Therese* and *threes* would have been pronounced alike. It is no accident that the number of lines in the poem (12) is easily divisible by three, with none left over. Characteristic too of Skilmer's esemplastic knack is this grafting of image onto image; it is wholly natural that in thinking of the Ovidian Daphne he should conceive of her *a lo divino*—see her not as some mincing pagan, but aureate in the scriptural halo that Dante too looped like lassos of tinsel round her.

2.

A tree—who's hung? Greymouth is pressed
Upon the earth-Swede, Flo Ingbrest.

A tree is indeed a tree, embodies as nothing else the very essence of the arboreal. An image of the world's green beauty—but no less an emblem of its horror. Skilmer's panoramic imagination sees the tree as a death-image, a very gallows with its dismal fruit. Painstaking Dantists ("In our age," the poet dourly quipped, "there are no painless Dantists") may well see here the influence of Dante's Wood of the Suicides.

We have learned little about Flo Ingbrest—Florence C. Ingbrest of 1222 Stitt Street, Des Moines. Her very address is known only because it was found tattooed on the left hip of a sailor washed ashore at Tampa after the great hurricane of '23. It is clear that Miss Ingbrest meant much to the poet, who saw in this simple Swedish girl a power participating so fully in the chthonic matriarchal atavism of the dark earth itself that he calls her simply his "earth-Swede." Her earthy affections, however, were soon alienated by the vague and sinister figure the poet calls Greymouth, a misty shape ominous as any of the ghosts that slink nameless through the early Eliot. Though much research has been done on the unknown Greymouth, little has been ascertained. Dr. Woggs Clurth, basing his argument soundly on the morpheme "rey" in Greymouth, has proposed that he was really Watson King of Canton, the affable rapist; Dr. Phemister Slurk, dispensing with what he derides as "evidence," has suggested that he represents Warren G. Harding, an Ohio politico of the twenties. Cavillings all: Greymouth, whosoever he may have "been" in the world we think of as real, now, through Skilmer's artistry, exists forever in the purlieus of the Muse—slinking, loose-lipped, drivelling, livid with his nameless vice.

3.

Upon whose boozin's (no!) *has* lain
Anne D'Intagh Mittley—lives wi' Thrane.

In the third stanza, sometimes insensitively printed as the fifth, the tragedy grows blacker yet. After Florence C. Ingbrest and a handful of casual flames, the poet sought solace with the Mittley sisters of Boston. Researchers have shown that there were two: Daisy (or "Diz") Mittley, and her much younger sister Anne D'Intagh. It was the younger the poet loved, but again the romance was blighted by a conniving interloper, this time the wealthy Thaddeus Thrane of Glasgow, whose nationality is slyly derided in the dialectal "wi'" for "with." The butt of frequent barbs in the Skilmer corpus, he is here dismissed with a contemptuous phrase. Though his beloved Anne lived "wi'" Thrane at the time the poem was written, Skilmer seems less troubled by this passing infidelity than by her amour with Greymouth—for Greymouth is the true antecedent of "whose." We now learn that he was a heavy drinker—and immediately the mysterious soubriquet is clear. Extensive research has established that *gris* is the common French word for *grey*. But *gris* also means *drunk*. Greymouth then is unmasked as Drunk Mouth. Indeed, so great a guzzler was Greymouth that the loyal Miss Mittley was said, by a witty metonomy (or synecdoche)[2] to have lain not on his bosom but (with a pun that anticipates Joyce by several weeks) on his "boozin's." One almost hesitates to mention that "bosoms" too has its questionable advocates.[3] Be that as it may, one wonders if in all literature the tragedy of four lives has been so harrowingly adumbrated? All one can conjure up for comparison is Dante's

Siena me fè; disfecemi Maremma.

But Dante, with his five and a half words for one life, is long-winded compared with Skilmer, who averages a mere
three words per head, or even less, if one counts the "wi'" as fractional diction. In this grisly aperçu, so true of all humanity, the resources of typography too are put to unexampled use, with the two-letter "no" followed by an exclamation mark that is like a spine straight with moral indignation, and enclosed in the semicircularity of parentheses, like lips rounded in incredulous refusal. But the "no" is uncompromisingly jostled by the assertive *has,* with its harsh aspirate, distorted from honest Roman type into italics, set askew from the vertical: even the letters, means the poet, have *lost their aplomb* before the moral horror. (A textual note: there are those, and their name is legion,[4] who read "Hugh Inta Mittley" in the second line. But nothing in Skilmer's emotional history gives countenance to a suppositious passion for Anne's little brother Hugh, then three years and some months old.)

4.

A tree that *looks* it!—Gawd! Auld, eh?
And Liffs hurl eavey alms, *tout prêts.*

And so it goes. The world-weariness, the melancholy, Skilmer in the depths of his Hamlet mood, or what he himself ruefully called, in the bad German he had learned from "certain ladies" in Milwaukee, "meines Hamletische Gesauerpusskeit." Does even Hamlet, whom so many have called the "Danish Skilmer," have a line so weary, stale, flat, and unprofitable as "A tree that *looks* it"?—in which the poet accepts the humble monotony of things as they are in their weary *haecceitas,* the sad fact that they are only what they are, and so fully *look* what they are, instead of embodying the splendor of their Platonic archetypes. "The interminable pyramidal napkin," broods E. E. Cummings—but how sesquipedalian this in comparison with Skilmer's demotic oomph. And from time immemorial this nauseating sameness—old indeed, and more than old. Probably there is no more plangent understatement in the language than Skilmer's simple but despairing "auld." For the poet, unable to tear his ravaged heart from thoughts of Thrane, glumly Scotticizes: "Auld, eh?" he spits out, thereby more keenly identifying Thrane with all he most distrusts in reality. Cosmic gloom induces wide-ranging speculations: the bard's restless mind hovers around the anthropology he loved so deeply, and from what sad strata of the past he must have disinterred his pregnant and touching lines about the Liffs. A Liff, as we know now, is the baseborn son of a Riff father and a Lett mother.* But even a Liff, born who knows where in semi-savagery, may hurl the alms of charity (as the miserly Thrane never did), alms that shelter us like eaves from the cold and rook-delighting heaven, alms that are always ready, *tout prêts,* to relieve us. In his polyglot technique, Skilmer, as so often, again anticipates the practice of Ezra Pound, his foremost epigone: he uses the French words to imply that even the barbarous Liffs have achieved a measure of urbanity, as compared with certain uncivilized Scots he could mention. The touch of Gallic vivacity brightens, but all too briefly, the poem's Stygian verge. (Again, a textual note: some read "A tree that looks *two,*" and explain it as referring to the illusory nature of perceived reality. Rubbish![5]).

5.

A tree . . . that Mayan summer! 'Ware
Honesta Robbins! Henna hair!

---

*So Professor Nims alleges. There are others who take a less simplistic view. "Liff," as every schoolboy knows, is the way Dubliners refer to the River Liffey, whose waves are here in reference, since one casts alms, or bread, upon the waters. It would seem that Skilmer is alluding to the future *Finnegans Wake* (Anna Livia Plurabelle) which was to be so profoundly influenced by "Therese."—ED. [F. B.]

In explicating this *locus classicus* of modern poetry, it is necessary to bear in mind certain facts about the manuscripts—or "menu-scraps," as Skilmer himself wryly called them. Always a victim of poverty, the poet used to quill his sublimest ditties on the backs of labels laboriously soaked off the bottles of whiskey on which he shrewdly spent what little means the world afforded him. Thousands of these labels have survived, mute testimony to the trembling fingers that treasured them—each bearing only a few words of that great cornucopia of song he willed posterity. (There are also three labels from spaghetti cans, and one from a small can of succotash.) A study of some hundreds of manuscripts shows that Skilmer first wrote "A tree . . . that Aztec summer!"—a reference to the year he spent in Central America with an anthropological expedition. An idyllic year, possibly the happiest of his life, when his natural warmth and high spirits, so often thwarted by dingy circumstance, overflowed with an almost boyish ebullience. Arriving in early May, he had been married there three times by late June—and each time happily. Hence the little idyll about the Aztec summer, found on the manuscript *Old Overholt 202* and certain others. (The spaghetti labels have little authority.) But the definitive reading is to be found on *Heaven Hill 714:* not "Aztec" but "Mayan," a word which Skilmer pronounced with the long *a* of *May.*

"A tree . . . that Mayan summer!"—and there it is forever, the bright leaves bathed in a golden haze of old romance, lost histories. An idyll, yes—but before long Skilmer's domestic bliss was shattered. He was followed to Yucatan by Mrs. Chloe P. Robbins of Ashtabula, a steamfitter's widow. With her came her daughter, the forty-seven-year-old Honesta Lou, whom Skilmer called his "buxom nymph o' siren voice"—she was six feet two, her flaring red hair vivid with purple highlights. It is this vision of somewhat menacing loveliness that is now evoked in lines that recall Coleridge's

> Beware, beware,
> His flashing eyes! his floating hair!

With deft economy, Skilmer laments the timelessness of his plight by using the archaic " 'Ware" for "Beware."

6.

Po' Em's our maid. 'Bye, fools! Like me,
Butt only. Godkin may kertree!

Almost from the beginning, it was clear to a happy few that
what seemed "poem" was really "Po' Em," a poor Southern
girl named Emma or Emily. Her identity long eluded re-
searchers, until Dr. Cecily P. Wunkhead, basing her argu-
ment largely on blood tests, litmus paper, and *Old Crow 1066*
(and rejecting the famous "succotash reading" as spurious)
proposed that the unknown Em was none other than Emily
Dickinson. To show that Emily is the mouthpiece not only for
New England but for all America Skilmer resorts to an
amazingly simple device: he gives her a *southern* voice: proba-
bly not since Praxilla has the ethos of inner dynamic been so
functionally aligned with dialectal specificity.

And why Emily Dickinson? Because she is the American
Muse, ever at our side to lend a helping hand with torch on
him—a servant, she, of servants of the laurel. Po' Em's our
maid, and with our trust in her we can afford to dismiss the
vulgar many, as Skilmer does with much the same testy ar-
rogance that Yeats and Jonson flaunted. Whereas Jonson
needed ten words or so in his

Far from the wolves' dark jaw, and the black asses' hoof . . .

Skilmer does it in two burning words, " 'Bye, fools!" But im-
mediately compassion returns, and he remembers that the
ordinary man, just as he, is only a butt for the slings and
arrows of outrageous fortune. This might have set a-moping
a less resilient bard, but Skilmer recovers, to conclude with a
thundering diapason of *Jubel und Ruhm* such as not even Bee-
thoven has ever equalled: the magnificent "Godkin may ker-
tree!" Godkin: a little god, that least of the divinities in man,
godkin *may*—but how the gala vowel, long *a*, implies lyric
certainty in a word which, heard by the intellect alone, might
seem to allow for doubt. *May* what? He may "kertree"! It is

fitting that the pinnacle of Skilmer's sublimity should glitter in this final phrase of his greatest poem. And how like him to achieve sublimity by means so simple! Here he seizes from its lexical limbo the humble prefix *ker-*, as in *kerplunk, kerplop, kerflooie*. A prefix that only once before in English had assumed nobility, in J. F. Dudley-Andover's sublime translation of Dante's

E caddi come corpo morto cade

as

I plopped kerplunk, as corpses plop kerplunk

Holding the precious *ker-* in the jeweler's forceps of his wit, Skilmer works it into a new thing entirely by fusing it with the unexpected "tree": to "kertree," to burst into flower, into foliage, nay, into very tree itself! One sees the creativity of the universe, the vital breath taking form in a great efflorescence of green, a cosmic sneeze as if the whole sweet growth of April and May, by some cinematic magic, were effected in an instant.[6]

It is around this magical last line that scholarship itself tends oftenest to kertree. "Godkin" in particular has stimulated the finest hermeneutic acumen of our century to new Everests of perception. Professor Fiedler has explored in depth the profound viscerality of "gutkin." The Cambridge School has constructed a breathtaking new theory of the origin of tragedy on the reading "goat-kin." It is hardly surprising that "incentive psychologists" make much of "goadkin." Professor Fitts, citing γάδ- and κύων, finds a fish-dog, or dog-fish, allusion that unfortunately cannot be discussed in these pages. Nor can the suggestion of certain Welshmen, who urge an early form of "gwiddcwyngh." Professor Rákóczi is more to the point in reminding us of what careless readers might forget: "gyödzskin" is a medieval South Hungarian gypsy cant word (though hardly the most common) for a thickish wine made out of half-rotted artichokes: what vistas open here! Only recently Nopançópi Hópail has removed the whole question from the field of linguistic speculation to that of biographical allusion by proposing—how imaginatively!— that "godkin" is "Godkin": E. L. Godkin (1831–1902), who came to America from Ireland when twenty-five, founded *The Nation,* and was a disciple of the Bentham-Mill-Grote school of philosophy.

On the whole subject, however, no one commands more respect than Professor Fredson Bowers, whose monumental fifty-volume edition of Skilmer, *The Fourteen Poems and Certain Fragments,* is promised for 1970 by the Southeastern Arkansas Junior Teachers' College Press. As early as 1962 Professor Bowers wrote: "I wonder if you have thoroughly considered the evidence of *Old Crow 16?* In this version, possibly a trial, 'May' is capitalized and must therefore be taken as the month.[7] If this is so, the possibility obtains that the godkin referred to is the month of May, and hence we can explain the diminutive. After all, in the month of vernal growth there is something godlike in the creative surge of the sap and the burgeoning of the chlorophyll. However, the syntax is then in question. There is perhaps no need to associate 'godkin May' with the 'butt,' even though a month that pretends to be a little god might be a butt for something. I think on the whole we are to take 'godkin May's' activities with approval, not with disapproval. If so, then I suggest that Skilmer, overcome with the wonder of vegetable love and the rites of spring, finds that normal syntax deserts him and is reduced to two paired but mutually discrete exclamations. 'Godkin May!' or: Oh the wonder of it all! And then that exclamation that sums up the plosive force of May, 'Kertree!' "

This is brilliantly reasoned and would seem to be the last word on the subject—but Professor Bowers had not yet done with it. A few years later he decided that the line had further subtleties, which he explained, in bibliographical terms, as follows: "It could be read as a series of ejaculations, rising to a climax. The lack of punctuation appropriate for this reading is of course nothing unusual with Skilmer. That is: only God-kin—the one God—He only. Then, in remembered ecstasy of that Mexican spring, May [and here Professor Bowers shows his grasp of contemporary allusion] just busting out all over, like the bursting sap, the springing leaf, in the ultimate mystical union with Nature, kertree! Thus exclamation points should be placed after each unit. I suggest these are at least alternate readings."

But perhaps these are matters beyond the power of man to determine. However it may be, Godkin may indeed kertree—but it takes a poet of supreme insight to perceive this, a poet able to wrest language from dead strata of the past and ker-plunk it living in the midst of men. But explication is no substitute for the poem. Here, for the first time presented in its ur-textual splendor, is what many* would consider the greatest lyric poem of our literature:

THERESE

By Joe E. Skilmer

I think? That I shall never, see!
Up, owe 'em love. Leah's a tree.

A tree—who's hung? Greymouth is pressed
Upon the earth-Swede, Flo Ingbrest.

Upon whose boozin's (no!) *has* lain
Anne D'Intagh Mittley—lives wi' Thrane.

A tree that *looks* it!—Gawd! Auld, eh?
And Liffs hurl eavey alms, *tout prêts*.

A tree . . . that Mayan summer! 'Ware
Honesta Robbins! Henna hair!

Po' Em's our maid. 'Bye, fools! Like me,
Butt only. Godkin may kertree!

---

*Does this include Professor Ian Watt?—ED. [F. B.]

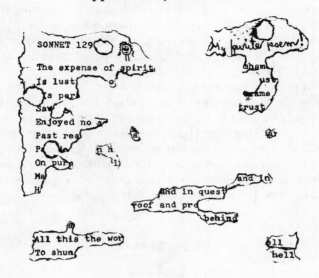

SONNET 129

The expense of spirit
Is lust
s per
Saw
Enjoyed no
Past rea
P
On pur
Ma
H

My fav[o]rite poem!

sham
us
ame
trust

and in
and in quest
roof and pro
behind

All this the wor
To shun

ell
hell

Sonnet 129

These sad fragments, so like the papyri of Sappho preserved
in the hot dry sands of Oxyrrhynchus (in Egypt), were re-
covered, tattered and charred, from a box of hot dry sand at
Luxor (in South Dakota), which had been kept near a wood-
stove in the railroad station for the use of brakemen. Typed
out by Skilmer, the poem is indubitably his, since it bears in
his own handwriting the inscription "My fav[o]rite poem." A
writer as careful with words as our poet would hardly write
"my" if he meant the exact opposite: "someone else's." Even
these poor scraps were preserved only by a lucky chance. Run
through a meatgrinder (luckily coarse) with the daily ham-
burger, the mélange was promptly bolted by a small coon-
hound named Harold, whose stomach as promptly rejected
the unwonted fare, depositing it unceremoniously on the
warm sand by the stove, where the pieces were buried from
sight as the sands shifted in drafts from the opening door.
Fortunately, the very next day a head-on collision killed sixty-
six passengers and tore up a half mile of track. The spur line

was not thought worth repairing; the station was closed, and only an occasional vagrant would stoke up the stove that kept warm the fostering sand. The papyroids are somewhat stained by tobacco juice.

Discovered by an amateur thrill-seeker in 1953, they were entrusted to Professor Koch-Schurr for restoration. Schooled in the methods of J. M. Edmonds (who from a ten-word fragment of Sappho was unfailingly able to reconstruct the lost original, many times as long), Professor Koch-Schurr set to work. He immediately perceived that the key lay in such words as "expense," "trust,"—and, for the poet's attitude—"blame." The poem, he concluded, was therefore an attack on an economic system. "Spirit[s]," in Skilmer's vocabulary, almost surely meant the kind of spirits he knew best. Working from this slim basis of certainty, Professor Koch-Schurr succeeded in restoring the poem to what most scholars will agree is essentially what Skilmer wrote. Here, then, given for the first time to a waiting world, is one of the bard's most significant masterpieces *exactly* as he may have written it—a very fundament of the mighty corpus!

Sonnet 129

The expense of spirits is a crying shame!
Is lust for lucre (money, man!). 'Twould bust
'Is personal nest-egg was 'e Croesus!—blame
Savings & Loans that back the liquor trust.
Enjoyed no sox, sax, sex, soup, soap or sup?
Past reach of average man, the price-tags soar;
Parade on high like bloomy larks. Up up
On purple-fringèd wing, red debits roar.
Ma[d in pursuit and in possession so,]*
Hairy as haystacks, and in quest of grails?
Stand on the roof and proposition Flo?
(What have the little lambs behind: heads? tails?)
All this the worried man can murmur: sell
To shun going broke. Being Broke's like heaven? Like hell.

---

*"Here my inspiration forsook me," laments Professor Koch-Schurr, "yielding only a line flat, jejune, unpoetic—quite without the afflatus of the Sweet Swan of just outside Peoria."

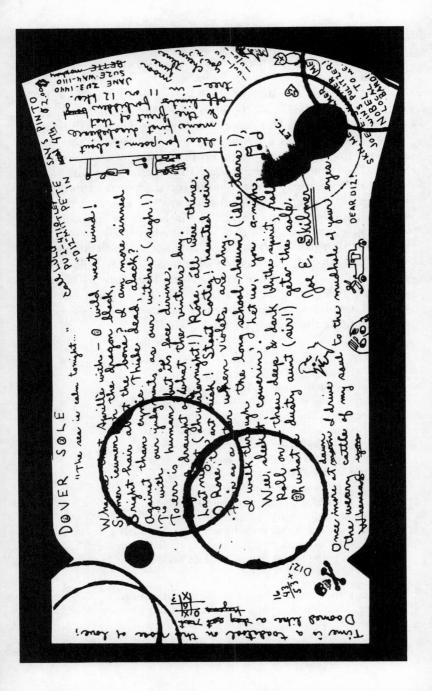

Cutty Sark 711 (*Dover Sole*)

Cutty Sark 711 (fondly called "The Emperor Manuscript") gives us the only known "fair copy" of a Skilmer poem. This precious document, the glory of the British Museum, bears some of the characteristic watermarks found on many of the poet's papers: they are circular and about four centimeters across (roughly the size of a standard "jigger" or "shot glass"). Many things about this touching relic, so rich in humanity, suggest that something fiercer than mere quill of mortal has been here set down. It is little wonder that a leading critic of Belleville (Illinois) has called it "a very Sinai of the spirit."

The text of *Dover Sole* has been extensively studied. Apparently one of the poet's earliest works, it shows a thorough familiarity with the achievements of English poetry up to, and perhaps beyond, his time. Academic critics, insensitive to the workings of inspiration and true creativity, have dismissed it as "derivative" and even "sheer pastiche"!

Almost heartbreaking in their ruined beauty are Skilmer's jottings around the margin—mere luminous inklings of a dawn no sooner bloomed than blasted. Of the haunting "Time is a toadstool on the nose of love," I. A. Leavis-Beehynde has written, "If this is not the finest metaphor in recent European literature, I just don't know what." And surely no poet has ever so summed up the spirit of the American desert, its unpeopled multiscorpioned mirage-bemused vastitudes, the lone charisma of its sandy avatars, as has our poet in his

> Once more at dawn I drive
> The weary cattle of my soul to the mudhole of your eyes.

The numerals and occult code-names on "The Emperor" would seem to be part of a system the secretive poet devised to record his rhythmical inventions. Instead of just saying *ta-dum, da-dum.*

Notes

1. Crudd P. Crass, "Joe E. Skilmer's Uncurling Lip," *LBJ* LX: 167–761.
2. Clementine P. Pugh, "Joe E. Skilmer: Metonomy Si! Synecdoche No!" *EETX* CXL: 930–54.
3. Louis P. ("Lew") Gubrious, "Greymouth: Effeminate Lecher," *PMLX* CLV: 10–656.
4. Lemuel P. and Lizzie X. Legion, "Who's Hugh in American Letters," *ACDC* XI: 1066–1492.
5. Wozlok DeTritus, "Rubbish-Schmubbish: The Ding-an-sich in Late-Middle Skilmer," *RSVP* IX: 51–52.
6. Skilmer's neologism has itself kertreen. One example out of many: Nancy Hale, one of Skilmer's most sensitive readers, has written, "The flowering of New England, that literary outpouring, kertreed everywhere. . . ." *New England Discovery* (New York: Coward-McCann, 1963), 353.
7. Professor Bowers has established elsewhere the fact that Skilmer refused to accept "May" as a girl's name. "You might as well say 'June' is a girl's name," the poet would guffaw. Cf. F. Bowers, "Skilmer and the Non-Nomenclature of Womenfolk," *QED* LX: 7–9.

The Sestina

When T. S. Eliot dedicated *The Waste Land* to Ezra Pound as "il miglior fabbro," he was recalling a passage in the *Purgatorio* (XXVI): Dante, imagining himself working his way up the mountain of Purgatory in the year 1300, comes on the spirit of Guido Guinizelli, the poet of about a generation before, whom he credits with originating the "sweet new style" in which Dante too chose to write. Praised by Dante for his poems, Guido remonstrates: he points to the spirit of a fellow poet as one who

> Fu miglior fabbro del parlar materno

("Was a better craftsman of the mother tongue.") The poet was Arnaut Daniel, whose writing career lay between 1180 and 1200, or just about a century before Dante's own. Arnaut's mother tongue was not Italian, as Guido's and Dante's was; it was Provençal, the romance language spoken in Provence (in southern France) and the regions adjoining. To us today it looks like a play language made up of Italian, French, and Spanish elements, but having, in its masculine endings, something of the brusqueness of English.

The word *fabbro* means not just a skilled workman, but one who deals with obdurate materials. "Blacksmith" is its common modern meaning. Suggestions of toughness are appropriate for Arnaut's technique: we can say of him, as Coleridge said of Donne, that he liked to "wreathe iron pokers into true-love knots." Provençal poetry is sometimes classified as *trobar leu* (easy poetry) and *trobar clus* (closed, obscure, "hermetic" poetry). *Trobar clus* might also be *trobar ric* (rich or precious poetry). Arnaut had the reputation of being among the most *clus* and the most *ric*—master of a more complicated technique than the others.

To judge by his eighteen surviving poems, one way in which this complexity showed itself was in elaborate stanzaic patterns. Arnaut made it even harder for himself by showing a preference for *rimas caras* (rhymes that cost dear)—words that had sounds difficult to find rhymes for. One of his poems has *coblas* (stanzas) of nine lines all rhyming on the same sound. He was especially fond of *rimas dissolutas*, rhymes that would find their mates not in their own stanza but in other stanzas, on sounds that would often remain the same, in corresponding lines, all through a poem of six or more stanzas. Used to the simple rhyme schemes of our own poetry, what are we to make of seventeen-line stanzas with a rhyme scheme like that below, in which the numbers refer to the syllabic count of each line, and the apostrophes indicate that the third and sixth syllables of those lines are followed by an unaccented or "feminine" syllable?

$$a \quad b \quad c \quad d \quad e \quad f \quad g \quad h \quad h \quad i \quad c \quad j \quad k \quad l \quad c \quad m$$
$$3' \; 4 \; 2 \; 6 \; 2 \; 1 \; 5 \; 4 \; 1 \; 3 \; 4 \; 4 \; 2 \; 4 \; 6 \; 4 \; 6'$$

Every line has its answering rhymes in the corresponding lines of all six stanzas, and some are used again in the eight-line envoy that concludes the poem.

Arnaut was not simply filling out a rhyme scheme, as if he were playing some kind of word game. He was also writing a poem around these sounds, composing a musical structure and a syntactical one, "with the words making sense," as Pound says, recalling also that Dante, "the greatest of poets," singled out "L'aur' amara" ("The Bitter Air," whose rhyme scheme is given above) for special praise as a great love poem.

Compared with the form of "L'aur' amara," the form of the sestina, which Arnaut also devised, is almost simple. The name itself means "made out of 6s": a sestina has six stanzas of six lines each and a three-line tornada or envoy, which sometimes is an envoy in the modern sense of someone or something entrusted with a message.

The sestina (in its pure form) does not rhyme; in place of rhyme it repeats entire words. The six end-words of the first stanza will also end the lines in every other stanza, in an order that continually differs in accordance with a fixed formula. If we consider the end-words of the first stanza as 1 2 3 4 5 6, then the order in the second stanza will be 6 1 5 2 4 3. The third stanza will reorganize the end-words of the second according to the same formula—and so on with the other stanzas. In the envoy the six words will all be used, three in midline, three as end-words. A preferred order there returns to that of the first stanza, but one finds other arrangements.

The sestina depends on 6s, but its structural principle has been tried with other numbers. We can have five stanzas of five lines, as (with a two-line envoy) in Alfred Corn's "Audience" (*The Various Light*, 1980). We can have seven stanzas of seven lines. Fewer than five might bring the repetitions too close together; more than seven might push them too far apart. We are all free to make up forms, as Arnaut Daniel did, though they may not have the centuries-old authority and associations of the sestina.

Many have thought that this structure of 6's culminating in a seventh element, the envoy, is not fortuitous. In earlier centuries the symbolism of numbers was felt more strongly and handled more elaborately than today. Six, the product of the first even and first odd number (2×3), was seen as symbolic of the world and of time: Jehovah created the world in six days. Seven stood for completeness, eternity: "And on the seventh day God ended his work . . . and he rested on the seventh day." It has been noticed that the pairings of the mutated stanza (6–1; 5–2; 4–3) each add up to seven. Analogies have been found between this pattern of mutations and corresponding solar and lunar zodiacal signs (many early sestinas seem to make use of imagery of light and darkness, as Dante's does).[1]

And yet there may have been nothing more occult in Arnaut's hammering out of the sestina than his interest in craftsmanship and in a form that he found challenging. He was not inventing a wholly new form; most literary forms evolve from simpler ones that already exist. In the earlier *canso redonda* (circular song), perhaps meant to accompany folk-dancing in a ring, we find something like one of the characteristic features of the sestina: the last rhyme of one stanza is repeated as the first of the next. In a later form of popular poetry, the rhymes of one stanza are repeated, in reverse order, in the stanza that follows. The next step seems to have been taken by Guillem Peire de Cazals, who repeated, in reverse order, not only the rhymes but the identical end-words in a poem of five six-line stanzas with a three-line envoy: almost a sestina. In his poem, stanzas 1, 3, and 5 have the same order of end-words; 2 and 4 the reverse order. Arnaut's poem goes beyond Cazals's in symmetry and ingenuity. Instead of simply reversing the order of end-words, Arnaut repeats them in crisscross fashion, taking them, as Davidson says, "alternately from bottom up and top down," a pattern which scholars call *retrogradatio cruciata*.[2]

A shallow view of the sestina might suggest that the poet writes a stanza, and then is stuck with six words which he has to juggle into the required positions through five more stanzas and an envoy—to the great detriment of what passion and sincerity would have him say. But in a good sestina the poet has six words, six images, six ideas so urgently in his mind that he cannot get away from them; he wants to test them in all possible combinations and come to a conclusion about their relationship. In "real life" we are frequently obsessed by such *gestalten* and keep working them over in our minds. The vital force of a sestina comes from this internal urgency which demands that the poet brood over certain realities—not from the imposition of an external and apparently artificial shape. As Karl Shapiro and Robert Beum have said in their *A Prosody Handbook* (1965):

> The sestina seems not necessarily to be a mere curious exercise or virtuoso showpiece, but at least ideally to be a form designed to encourage and express a meditation or reverie upon certain thoughts or images. If such an obsessive vision or reverie-like impulse does not in fact exist or come into existence as

the poem is written, the six key words will seem unmotivated and the whole poem will turn out to be an academic exercise. The sestina would seem to require the poet's deepest love and conviction, involve his deepest impressions.

Arnaut's end-words are *intra, ongla, arma, verga, oncle, cambra*. They happen to be related in sound, like half-rhymes, but that is not required or usual in a sestina. His words mean *enters, (finger)nail, soul,*[3] *rod, uncle, chamber*. These are the ideas and images he cannot get out of his mind. Loving his lady, body and *soul*, he longs to *enter* her *chamber*, to be close to her as *nail* to finger, but he sees that he may be frustrated by such protective social and familial forces as the *uncle* represents; from that conflict may result violence, given or received: the *rod*. It is clear that some of the end-words are used with a rich ambivalence (sometimes sexual), as we can see in translation. (The first line of his stanzas is shorter then the other lines by two syllables.)

Arnaut Daniel: *Lo ferm voler qu'el cor m'intra*[4]

The resolute desire that enters
My heart, won't give for prying fingernail,
For liar with black tongue—that damns his soul!
Since such I dare not thrash with birch or rod,
Secret at least, none near in shape of uncle,
Joy I'll enjoy, in orchard or . . . her own room.

When memory turns to that, her own room
Where no man—to my grief I say—can enter
(They're worse, the pack of them, than brother, uncle!),
No part of me's not quivering, not a fingernail;
I'm like a truant when he sees the rod,
For fear I've given her less than all my soul.

My wish is body, not just soul!
I wish she'd ease me, secret, in her own room.
My heart's sick, feels it worse than pain of rod,
That where she is her loyal man can't enter.
I'm with her always, snug as skin to fingernail;
Care nothing for rough tongue of friend or uncle.

273

Not even the sister of my uncle
Did I love more, as much even, by my soul!
Familiar as a finger with its fingernail
Is what I'd be (she willing) with her own room.
Love bends me to its might, when once it enters,
Easy as strong men bend a feeble rod.

Since burst in flower the barren rod,
Since from Sir Adam down came nephew, uncle,
So pure a love as in my own heart enters
I can't believe there was, in body or soul.
Wherever she is—in public, in her own room—
My heart won't stir from her the width of a fingernail.

My heart holds, clings like fingernail,
As fast to her as bark does to its rod.
For me she's pleasure's palace, tower—its own room.
I've no such love for brother, parent, uncle.
In heaven a bliss on bliss will flood my soul,
If loving well's what qualifies to enter.

So Arnaut sends his song of "nail" and "uncle"
To pleasure her whose rod rules all his soul,
His one Desired, whose own room splendor enters.

The Italian critic U. A. Canello analyzes the effect of the
form in a description that might be paraphrased as follows.
The poet, as if tormented by certain deep-rooted images,
feels himself revolving them in his mind, looking at them now
one way, now another, each time accustoming himself and the
reader a little more to their hidden harmonies or dissonances.
The first stanza, surprisingly, is without the rhymes the ear is
used to hearing. The second stanza immediately repeats a
word from the first, but the next line repeats one so distant
that the hearer barely remembers it; he is left as if in an
emptiness, deprived of harmony. Gradually the emptiness
fills in as he picks up end-words less distant than in line two.
With each stanza the words become more familiar, but the
combinations are new and surprising. In the three lines of the
envoy he juxtaposes and reconciles the six haunting images at
first in conflict.

The best-known early sestina is the one that Dante wrote,

with Arnaut's in mind. One of his *rime petrose,* or "stony poems," it is addressed to a lady whose heart, the poet complains, is hard as stone. He meditates on the *shadow (ombra)* or darkness of the wintry season in a country of *hills (colli)* and *grass (erba)* which have lost the *green (verde)* of pleasanter days, and on the hard *stone (petra)* which from voice and appearance one would take to be a *woman (donna)*. Like most good sestinas, this one is a study in ambivalence and ambiguity; the key words are used in more senses than they seem to have at first. Images of the landscape and the woman's body fade into and out of each other, like the anamorphic images of surrealism. For Leslie Fiedler, who says he had thought about this poem for years, it is the loveliest of all of Dante's *Rime.* Fiedler, who has done his own brilliant translation of the poem, accompanied by an essay that brings out its structural and symbolic richness, has shown why it is impossible to fully translate.[5] "Donna," which my own translation renders as "woman," really means more than that; it is from the Latin *domina* and means a lady who rules or commands, almost, as Fiedler translates it, a "queen." "Lady," which perhaps comes closest, has, I thought, become too genteel a word for a love poem. Even worse for the translator is *petra,* the old Italian (or Latin) form of *pietra,* "stone." But "Petra" is also the lady's name, whereas we can hardly pretend that "Stone" is a girl's first name in English.

Dante: *Al poco giorno e al gran cerchio d'ombra*

To waning day, to the wide round of shadow
I've come, alas, and come to whitening hills
Now when all color dwindles from the grasses.
Not so with my desire: no change of green,
So sunk its roots are in the ruthless stone
That listens, talks—you'd think a very woman.

But like the season, this incredible woman
Stands frozen there, a bank of snow in shadow.
The heart within her no more melts, than stone
When softer weather mellows all the hills,
Changing them back from chilly white to green,
The time it nestles them in flowers and grasses.

When round her head's a garland of sweet grasses,
Out of my thought goes every other woman!
So trim they mingle, curly gold and green,
That love comes down to linger in their shadow
—Love that enfolds me in those gentle hills
Tighter by far than mortar holds a stone.

More magic power than any fabulous stone
Her beauty has; its pain no herb, no grasses
Have skill to heal. Across wide plains, through hills
I've fled to escape the glamor of this woman.
In vain: from sun so bright no hope of shadow,
No hill, no wall, no wood's deep leafy green.

There was a day I saw her dressed in green,
And such, she would have driven the very stone
Wild with the love I feel for her least shadow.
How I'd have wished her then, in pleasant grasses,
As deep in love as ever man knew woman
—And wished our field were snug among high hills.

But sooner the low rivers ride high hills
Than this young plant, so succulent and green,
Bursts into flame for me, as lovely woman
So often does for man. I'd couch on stone
My whole life long, feed like a beast on grasses,
Only to see her skirt in swirls of shadow.

Whenever now the hills throw blackest shadow,
With her delicious green the one young woman
Hides all that dark, as summer grass a stone.

Dante is sometimes given credit for writing a "double sestina"
in his elaborately structured *canzone,* "Amor, tu vedi ben che
questa donna . . . ," a form taken over by Auden in his "Can-
zone" (1942), by Ashbery in his poem with the same title
(1956), later by James Merrill in the poem which opens the
"&" section of his "Scripts for the Pageant," and by Anthony
Hecht in his "Terms." Though resembling the sestina in its
formal repetition of end-words, Dante's poem is not a sestina.
The unwieldy term *canzonesestina,* suggested by modern edi-
tors of Dante, is more accurate.

After Dante, the most celebrated Italian poet to use the

sestina was Petrarch (1304–1374), among whose 366 poems (mostly sonnets) to the lady he called Laura are several opulent sestinas. One is a genuine double sestina on Laura's death: twelve stanzas, all using the same end-words and following the same pattern of permutations, and a three-line envoy.[6] Among the poets influenced by Petrarch was Lorenzo de' Medici (1449–1492), called "The Magnificent," and author of five sestinas.

A century and a half after Petrarch, Jacopo Sannazaro (1456–1530) included a double sestina in his *Arcadia,* which influenced Sir Philip Sidney when he came to write his own *Arcadia* in the last years of the 1570s. Sannazaro's work, written as early as 1489, published in a pirated edition in 1502 and authoritatively two years later, was more successful than any popular romance today: it was republished on an average every two years throughout the entire century. In its fourth chapter two gentlemen, Logisto and Elpino, complain in alternate stanzas about their unhappiness in love. Their end-words, in translation, are *rhyme, plaint, day, fields, rocks, valley*— pastoral scenery was likely to be a feature of the early sestina. Throughout the sixteenth century countless Italian poets wrote sestinas. It is not surprising that Michelangelo, who preferred to work with difficult materials, was among them.

Though the influence of Dante was always felt, it was enthusiasm for Petrarch and Petrarchism that carried the sestina throughout Europe. In France, however, it met with a cool reception from Pierre Ronsard (1524–1585), the greatest poet of his time, and in many ways an admirer of Petrarch. He and the influential Du Bellay thought it too restrictive a form, one in which the poet had to torture his thought and cramp it into shackles. But a fellow member of the Pléiade, Pontus de Tyard, thought otherwise; his *Erreurs amoureuses* (the first part published in 1549), contained the first two "sextines" written in French. Since French is fonder of rhyme than Italian is, Tyard added rhyme to an already difficult form. His first sextine begins with a stanza rhyming *abcbca;* his second, with *abbacc.* Stanzas that follow preserve the Italian scheme of permutations, so that the arrangement of the

rhymes is different in each stanza. In order to keep his pat-
tern of rhyme, Tyard had to add a fourth line to the envoy.
Since his time, rhyme has been characteristic of the French
sextine, a form which seems not to have attracted their best
poets. In the nineteenth century, Ferdinand, Comte de
Gramont, tried to revive it in his *Chant du Passé* (1854) and his
Sextines (1872), to which he added a history of the form. But
to little avail; his many sextines, rhyming *abaabb,* are forgot-
ten by all but a few scholars. Among the few is Maurice Gram-
mont, of the similar name, whose *Petit traité de versification
française* (5th ed., 1955) describes Gramont's rhyming stanza
and regrets that, since the only merit one finds is that of
difficulties overcome, the poet did not make better use of his
talent. Balzac, however, would have disagreed. He had pub-
lished Gramont in 1840 in his short-lived *La revue parisienne*
and praised the sextines in which, as he said, the poet man-
aged to dance like Taglioni (the famous ballerina) even
though his feet were in irons.

In *The Spirit of Romance* Pound says that the sestina was
"introduced . . . into Spain, I believe, by Fernando de Her-
rera." Herrera, whom the Spaniards have called "el divino,"
lived from 1534 to 1597; his four musical sestinas are proba-
bly the best in Spanish. He was not, however, the first to use
the form. The Spanish sestina has a tenuous association with
our own country. When Queen Isabella, the backer of Colum-
bus, died in 1504, one of the poems to lament that loss was a
"sextina," the first known in Spanish. It was published in the
Cancionero general of Hernando del Castillo (Valencia, 1511).
Others followed. The form enjoyed its greatest vogue in the
second half of the sixteenth century. "Unas sextinas de
pésimo gusto" ("in abominable taste") are found in the *Diana*
of Montemayor (1559) and the *Diana enamorada* of Gil Polo
(1564). Cervantes wrote one for his *Galatea* (1585); Lope de
Vega used sextinas to mark the end of act 1 in three of his
early comedies, as Shakespeare sometimes ended scenes with
a couplet. In his *Arcadia* (1598), like other *Arcadia*s a mixture
of prose and verse, Lope has a double sestina in the Italian
manner. The sestina was also written by Portuguese poets of

the century, including the greatest of them, Camões. Though theoreticians called it "la más noble de todas las estrofas," the poets themselves soon lost interest in it. Cervantes wrote only the one; Lope, who lived until 1635, wrote none after 1604. The great poets Góngora (1561–1627) and Quevedo (1580–1645) ignored it. One may say of the Spanish sestina that after the first years of the seventeenth century it sank almost without a trace.

The sestina came somewhat later into Germany, where the earliest were written by Martin Opitz (1597–1639), the Francophile poet who also knew English and translated Sidney's *Arcadia*. In his pastoral *Schäfferey von der Nimfen Hercinie* (1630), three men compose a sestina in iambic alexandrines with a set of mutations suggested not by the Italian but by the sestina in Spenser's *The Shepherd's Calendar*—and with that mention we come home to the sestina in English. We might wish, however, that the work of August Wilhelm von Schlegel (1767–1845) were more available. Schlegel, in favor of strict rules for the writing of poetry, translated a sestina of Petrarch and theorized about its form, "according to which poetic expression distinguishes itself from [that of] ordinary life as much as possible."[7] A reading of some modern sestinas about "ordinary life" would suggest that he was not aware of its possibilities, though he may have been, as Marianne Shapiro says, "the only brilliant critical mind at work on the sestina during the nineteenth century."

The first sestinas in English were written by Sir Philip Sidney in the late 1570s for inclusion in what is called "The Old Arcadia," as distinguished from the "New Arcadia," the revised but incomplete version published in 1590 as *The Countess of Pembroke's Arcadia*. The first of Sidney's three sestinas, "Since wailing is the bud of causeful sorrow . . . ," is regular, except that the envoy repeats only three of the six end-words. In his third sestina, Sidney introduces rhyme, as Pontus de Tyard had done before him. His first stanza has the common six-line rhyming pattern *ababcc: light, treasure, might, pleasure, direction, affection*. In the following stanzas these words are put through the usual pattern of permutations, so that each stanza rhymes differently. In the envoy the six words occur in the order they had in the first stanza. A glance at his rhyming words enables us to correct one misapprehension: it is not a requirement of the sestina that the end-words be trochaic. The misconception arose because in Italian the lines are hendecasyllabic, ending with an unaccented syllable after the accented tenth since most Italian words end that way: *vita, morte, amore* where we have the monosyllabic *life, death, love*. When Shakespeare ends a line with an extra syllable, as in "To be or not to be, that is the question," he is not ending the line with a trochaic foot.

Sidney's second sestina, a double one, is "Ye goatherd gods . . . ," to many the greatest sestina in the language. It seems to have been the one that most interested Auden, who lodged the sestina securely in the world of contemporary poetry. It may have been William Empson who in 1939 was the first to call attention, in his *Seven Types of Ambiguity*, to "those lovely sestines of Sidney." His scrutiny of the end-words reveals the richness of their ambiguities: "*Mountains* are haunts of Pan for lust and Diana for chastity. . . . *Forests*, though valuable and accustomed, are desolate and hold danger." And so with the others (*valleys, music, morning, evening*). "It is at these words only that Klaius and Strephon pause in their cries; these words circumscribe their world; these are the bones of their situation; and in tracing their lovelorn pastoral tedium through thirteen repetitions, with something of the aimless multitudinousness of the sea on a rock, we seem to extract all the meaning possible from these notions." Empson concludes by finding the rhythm of the poem "magnificent." "And limited as the form may be, the capacity even to conceive so large a form as a unit of sustained feeling, is one that has been lost since that age."[8]

John Crowe Ransom, in *The New Criticism* (New Directions, 1941) speaks with similar admiration of Sidney's "quaint but beautiful" poem, and praises "the way it keeps exploring the character of its local object" and still carries on a progressive dramatic movement. For a more extensive analysis, see Fowler's *Conceitful Thought*, pp. 38–58. Looking for a twentieth-century analogue to Sidney's work, Fowler thinks of Wallace Stevens.

Many poets, in taking up the sestina, like to give some personal turn to the basic pattern. So Spenser, perhaps in emulous admiration of Sidney, whose work he could have seen in manuscript, concluded his August eclogue in *The Shepherd's Calendar* (1579) with a sestina. But he invented a new pattern of permutations. In the second stanza and those that follow, he does repeat the last end-word of one stanza as his first end-word of the next, but he then takes the other end-words in the order they had in the preceding stanza. The second stanza becomes 6 1 2 3 4 5, the third 5 6 1 2 3 4, and so on. Instead of repeating the exact words, Spenser sometimes uses variants that have the same final syllable: *resound, sound; part, apart.* This is a liberty that later writers were to exploit more freely; it has a precedent in Arnaut Daniel, who changed his *ongla* to *s'enongla.*

Barnabe Barnes may also have been vying with Sidney when he wrote five "sestines" for his amorous sequence of nearly two hundred poems, *Parthenophil and Parthenophe* (1593). But he was certainly not imitating Sidney; four of the five are very odd indeed, and the fifth, a triple sestina, takes on Sidney's double sestina and goes it one better. All five are alike in having only three of the end-words in the envoy. "Sestine 1" keeps the regular system of permutations, but instead of being in iambic pentameter (which corresponds to the Italian hendecasyllabic) it is written in rather free three-beat lines—a daring innovation, but, like most of Barnes's experiments, disappointing. "Sestine 2" is more ingenious. Written in four-beat rhyming lines, its first stanza gives us *aabbcc.* The end-word of the last line of each stanza is repeated in the first line of the following one, but instead of repeating the other end-words Barnes substitutes a rhyming word for each, in the proper sestina formation. "Sestine 3" has the regular pattern but is in a strange rhythm, possibly suggested by classical anacreontics. Except for the lines ending in *forests,* the meter is ⌣ – ⌣ – ⌣ – –. "Sestine 4" is a real curiosity. It is an "Echo poem," with the nymph Echo responding to questions put to her. The rhythm represents the classical hexameter, as in Sidney's more successful Echo poem, "Fair rocks, goodly rivers. . . ." An Echo poem in classical hexameters is itself a virtuoso piece, but Barnes does it in the form of a sestina! "Sestine 5," the triple sestina, regular and without eccentricities, is by far the most interesting of the five, a passionate lyric of witchcraft and eroticism, set in an eerie forest at night. Though the end-words are arranged, through eighteen stanzas and an envoy, in the traditional way, they are used in several senses. *Bare*, for example, can mean *naked, carried*, or *bore* (endured). *Wood* can mean *firewood, forest*, or *insane*.[9]

In spite of his one triumph, Barnes's assault on the sestina seems to have left it stunned and reeling. For over two centuries it hardly lifted its voice: there is not a single sestina in the three volumes of the Oxford anthologies that cover the seventeenth, eighteenth, and nineteenth centuries.

It was not until the mid-nineteenth century that the sestina again showed signs of life. When Dante Gabriel Rossetti published, in 1861, *The Early Italian Poets . . . in the Original Meters*, readers found there his translation of Dante's sestina. Friends of Rossetti might have known it long before; some of the versions had been made as early as 1845, and most of them long before the book was published. The rhyming sestinas of the Comte de Gramont (book publication 1854 and 1872) may have caught the attention of Swinburne, who early in 1872 published his "Sestina" in a British magazine; six years later it appeared in his *Poems and Ballads*, second series. In a letter, Swinburne mistakenly professes to have written the first rhymed sestina: his poem begins with an *ababab* stanza. In order to keep his *a*'s and *b*'s from bunching together, however, he kept the sestina pattern only in the first two lines of each stanza. In the same volume, Swinburne follows a similar procedure in "The Complaint of Lisa (*Double Sestina*)" in which the twelve twelve-line stanzas and six-line *congedo* rearrange their rhyming end-words not in the sestina pattern but so that no two rhyming words come together—obviously not a "double sestina" in the way that those of Petrarch and Sidney are.

In 1877 Edmund Gosse published a sestina that begins with an account of the origin of the form:

> In fair Provence, the land of lute and rose,
> Arnaut, great master of the lore of love,
> First wrought sestines to win his lady's heart

Scholars and the literary public were also aware of the sestina. In 1878 Francis Hueffer (the father of Ford Madox Ford), who had come to England from Germany about a decade before, published *The Troubadours: A History of Provençal Life and Literature in the Middle Ages.* Two years later, in a magazine article, he warned that "the sestina is a dangerous experiment, on which only poets of the first rank should venture." Such a challenge is irresistible to all lesser poets, and one guesses that a number of literary folk took up the gage, with results probably no better than Gosse's. But on one occasion a more rugged talent, that of Rudyard Kipling, was also attracted to it. Perhaps he knew of it through Gosse and other lady-and-gentleman poets, perhaps through the pre-Raphaelites. His aunt had married Sir Edward Burne-Jones, the painter friend of Rossetti. At any rate, one July day in 1896 Kipling sat down in his Vermont home and in a few hours completed a perfectly regular sestina that set the form on its heels. Kipling's "Sestina of the Tramp-Royal" is far from "the land of lute and rose"; the monologue of a super-hobo or "king of the road" who wants to experience as much of the world as he can, it speaks in demotic cockney that drops its *h*'s and says "ain't." Kipling's tramp is in spirit like Tennyson's better spoken Ulysses:

> . . . such as cannot use one bed too long,
> But must get 'ence, the same as I 'ave done,
> An' go observin' matters till they die.

Many have considered this upstart sestina (published in *The Seven Seas,* 1896) as one of Kipling's best poems. T. S. Eliot thought enough of it to include it in his *A Choice of Kipling's Verse* (1941).

The sestina burst rambunctiously into the twentieth century with the "Sestina: Altaforte" of the twenty-three-year-old Ezra Pound, which begins:

> Damn it all! all this our South stinks peace.
> You whoreson dog, Papiols, come! Let's to music!
> I have no life save when the swords clash.
> But ah! when I see the standards gold, vair, purple,
>   opposing
> And the broad fields beneath them turn crimson,
> Then howl I my heart nigh mad with rejoicing . . .

It was accepted by Ford Madox Ford for his *English Review* in 1909 (Pound's first publication in a British magazine) and was reprinted in Pound's *Canzoni* in 1911.

Pound's persona in his Browningesque monologue is the Provençal poet Bertran de Born, whom Dante had put in hell for being, as Pound says, "a stirrer up of strife." "I had de Born on my mind," he tells us in "How I Began" (1913). "I had found him untranslatable. Then it occurred to me that I might present him in this manner. I wanted the curious involution and recurrence of the Sestina. I knew more or less of the arrangement. I wrote the first strophe and then went to the [British] Museum to make sure of the right order of permutations. . . . I did the rest of the poem at a sitting. Technically it is one of my best, though a poem on such a theme could never be very important." Though he checked up on the permutations, Pound gets them wrong once and uses only four of the end-words in the envoy.

His poem was suggested by de Born's *sirventes* (a stanzaic poem chiefly abusive or satiric, often political or moralizing) which, in English, is generally given some such title as "In Praise of War." The poet begins with a lyrical evocation of spring:

> Be·m platz lo gais temps de pascor
> Que fai fuolhas e flors venir
>
> (The merry time of spring much pleases me,
> which makes leaves and flowers come)

It goes on to say that the poet also likes scenes of warfare and battle. There is much graphic detail, as of horses running riderless, armies in rout with baggage strewn behind them, corpses whose ribs are pierced by splintered lances with their pennons still aflutter. But the tone is cooler and more objective than in Pound's poem. Bertran says "platz me" (it pleases me) whereas the young Pound's persona goes berserk, as in the last line of the stanza quoted. In Bertran there is no "God damn" or "stinking" or "whoreson" or madness or howling, nor are heaven and hell involved, nor is the sun "blood-crimson." The Provençal word for blood (*sanc*) is not used at all. "Have I dug him up again?" asks Pound. Maybe so. But Bertran, cool pen if hot head, would not have recognized himself in this howling delusionary.

The *sirventes* of Bertran is not a sestina. For his form Pound went back to the source itself, the original sestina of Arnaut Daniel. Pound had an excessive admiration for Arnaut's poetry: "I am quite ready to hold the position that Arnaut is the finest of the troubadours." He tells us that he spent six months of his life translating some fifteen poems of Arnaut, which are in the long study "Arnaut Daniel" in his *Literary Essays*. But he says he did not translate the sestina, "for it is a poor one." "This amazing poem," as Fiedler calls it, is not as bad as Pound says; judging from the two stanzas which he did translate as "A War Song" in his collected *Translations,* he was confused by the syntax. But the form of the sestina caught his attention, "a form," he wrote, "like a thin sheet of flame folding and infolding upon itself." About the same time as he resurrected Bertran, Pound also wrote his milder "Sestina for Ysolt"; later on he was to translate Pico della Mirandola's "The Golden Sestina."

But Pound, like Kipling before him, showed that this literary form could radiate vigor and be used for dramatic purposes. His poem has had its admirers. T. S. Eliot—in 1917—thought it "perhaps the best sestina that has been written in English." (One wonders if he had forgotten the Elizabethans?) Donald Davie speaks highly of it; Guy Davenport refers to "the great 'Sestina: Altaforte.'" But there are probably more contemporary readers who would share Pound's own modest evaluation of his "bloody sestina," as his friends called it—or who might even find it coarse and shrill.

Still, for a couple of decades it was the poem thought of as *the* English sestina, so well known that in the fifties Donald Hall could begin his own "Sestina" with

> Hang it all, Ezra Pound, there is only the one sestina . . .

and go on to wonder if a weakness of the sestina was not its preoccupation with itself.

One can guess that a fair number of closet sestinas were being written by men and women of letters. Of those that emerged, many must have been as vapid as the "Sestina" that appeared in a literary magazine in 1922:

> To thee, O fairest of the world, my love,
> I send the messengers that fly with song,
> And bear their precious gifts from heart to heart

Mediocre talents are irresistibly drawn to forms like the sestina, which offer easy satisfaction in that they seem only forms that need filling out, like an application for a library card.

About two decades after Pound's sestina, the influence of W. H. Auden made itself even more powerfully felt. The first of his half-dozen sestinas was written in September 1931, for "Journal of an Airman," book II of his *The Orators: An English Study* (1932). In the *Collected Poetry* (1945) and later it has the title "Have a Good Time." After the bravado of the young Pound—who at twenty-three was not yet the important poet he was to become—it is good to be back with the easiness of a kind of language we recognize as like our own:

> We have brought you, they said, a map of the country;
> Here is the line that runs to the vats,
> This patch of green on the left is the wood,
> We've pencilled an arrow to point out the bay.
> No thank you, no tea; why look at the clock.
> Keep it? Of course. It goes with our love.

We soon realize that the landscape here is symbolic, a geography of the spirit, which some might even like to call allegorical, uneasy as we are with that medieval category. Probably John Blair is right in suggesting that "they" are our elders, our mentors, presenting us with their view of life, with its neat compartments for "intellect-will-sensation" (*bay, clock, wood*) which the young person will have to decompartmentalize and, in the envoy, integrate, thanks to his vocation or art (the dyer's *vats*). By returning to such symbolism as Dante has used in his sestina, Auden has enriched the possibilities of the form for the modern poet. Though he has kept the regular permutations of the end-words and used them univocally, he has given us a new rhythm instead of the usual iambic pentameter: the four-beat strong-stress rhythm of northern metrics.

Auden's most influential sestina is his second one, which has become one of the most frequently reprinted poems of the period:

> Hearing of harvests rotting in the valleys,
> Seeing at end of street the barren mountains,
> Round corners coming suddenly on water,
> Knowing them shipwrecked who were launched for islands,
> We honor founders of these starving cities
> Whose honor is the image of our sorrow . . .

Written in May 1933, it was published that year in T. S. Eliot's *Criterion* and in Auden's *Look, Stranger!* in 1936. John Fuller thinks it was "a conscious effort to rebuff" Empson's contention, already referred to, that since the age of Sidney it has been impossible to sustain feeling through as ample a form as the sestina. We know that Auden liked Sidney's sestina; when working with John Garrett the following spring on their anthology, *The Poet's Tongue* (1935), he included it, as "Strephon and Klaius," as the final poem. Sidney's first two end-words are *mountains* and *valleys;* Auden's are *valleys* and *mountains.* Auden's iambic pentameter, with its feminine endings and end-stopped lines, is like Sidney's, though Auden's lines begin more rapidly.

Auden later called the poem "Paysage Moralisé"; its method is symbolic, like that of his first sestina, with a kind of "psychic geography" in part derived from Rilke, one of whose characteristic devices, Auden had pointed out, was "the expression of human life in terms of landscape." Auden's theme, the history of man's quest for a happier life and the disillusionment which that quest involves, is dramatized in the symbolism of his end-words.

Auden's other sestinas, less successful as poems, are of technical interest in extending the possibilities of the form and of the content itself. "Kairos and Logos," composed in 1940, is am ambitious attempt at something new: a sestina sequence. But these four theological sestinas on the theme of the incarnation, influenced by Paul Tillich, have not found a host of admirers. Auden invents a new pattern of permutations: his second stanza, and the rest, follow the formula 3 1 5 2 6 4, which, compared with the symmetry of the traditional order, seems arbitrary and ungainly. One particularly misses the immediate emphatic repetition of the end-word that closes a stanza. The envoy of each has two of the end-words per line, but in no particular order.

Sebastian's sestina, in part II of *The Sea and the Mirror* (written between August of 1942 and February of 1944, and published in *For the Time Being* in 1947) further loosens the pattern. Stanzas 2, 4, and 5 mutate the end-words of the preceding stanza according to one pattern: 3 6 4 1 2 5; stanzas 3 and 6 according to another: 2 4 6 5 3 1. The sestina is not of unusual interest.

Though somewhere harvests have been rotting and mountains barren, since Auden's time decade after decade has given us a bumper crop of sestinas. In the pages that follow, we can refer to only a few, cited because of their own excellence or interest or because of some significant mutation in the form itself.

In the 1930s, Louis Zukofsky found a surprising sestina subject for his "Mantis," published in *Poetry* in 1935 and in his *55 Poems* in 1941. In rough-hewn iambic pentameter, it ponders the strange insect out of place in the stone world of the

New York subway. Around the same time, Elizabeth Bishop was thinking about sestinas. Her "A Miracle for Breakfast" was published in *Poetry* in 1937 and in her *North and South* in 1946. In four-beat lines, like those of Auden's first sestina but without their jaunty lilt, it preserves the traditional permutations in the stanzas, but not in the envoy. The year before, she had written Marianne Moore that this sestina "is just sort of a stunt." But it was a stunt she took seriously, as a letter of January 5, 1937, to Miss Moore shows: "It seems to me that there are two ways possible for a sestina—one is to use unusual words as terminations, in which case they would have to be used differently as often as possible—as you say, 'change of scale.' That would make a very highly seasoned kind of poem. And the other way is to use as colorless words as possible—like Sydney [*sic*], so that it becomes less of a trick and more of a natural theme and variations. I guess I have tried to do both at once." (We may wonder if "colorless" is the right word for Sidney's richly emotional archetypes.) Of her own six end-words, the first three are more particularized than Sidney's: *coffee, crumb, balcony, miracle, sun, river*. The last two are more like his; *miracle* is less a thing-word but it is the point of the poem.

When, in the middle 1950s, she came to write her deeply felt "Sestina" (*Questions of Travel*, 1965) about a lonely childhood in Nova Scotia, with neither mother nor father in the house, she again built it around simple but emotional concrete realities: *house, grandmother, child, stove, almanac, tears*. Again in four-stress lines, but more legato and lyrical than those of her earlier poem, this sestina is deservedly one of the best known of the century, and shows how that form can still be used to search the depths of emotional experience.

T. S. Eliot, as Auden's publisher at Faber and Faber and as editor of the *Criterion*, in which "Hearing of harvests . . ." was first published, may have had Auden's sestinas in mind when he wrote the sestina-like poem for part II of *The Dry Salvages* (1941).

When is there an end of it, the soundless wailing. . .

It has six stanzas of six lines each, but instead of end-words repeated in changing patterns it has the corresponding lines of the stanzas rhyming (in *rimas caras*) on the same sound through the first five stanzas, with the original words repeated in the sixth.

Early in the 1940s, Weldon Kees found in the sestina a release for the perturbations and obsessions of his spirit. "After the Trial" appeared in *Poetry* in 1941; "Sestina: Travel Notes," two years later. Both are in *The Fall of the Magicians* (1947) and the *Collected Poems* (1962). His permutations are the traditional ones. "After the Trial," with its memories of Freud and Kafka, departs from iambic pentameter in only a few lines. Far from being a mere stunt, the form encourages deeply felt meditations on its key words and their relationship. To greatly oversimplify, since the words bear more than a single meaning, we can say that problems of *guilt* and *innocence* and the consequent *sentence* imposed by *parents*, others, and the self are seen against a scenario of the significant *rooms* in which actions, past and present, have frozen into a kind of *forever*.

After the Trial

Hearing the judges' well-considered sentence,
The prisoner saw long plateaus of guilt,
And thought of all the dismal furnished rooms
The past assembled, the eyes of parents
Staring through walls as though forever
To condemn and wound his innocence.

And if I raise my voice, protest my innocence,
The judges won't revoke their sentence.
I could stand screaming in this box forever,
Leaving them deaf to everything but guilt;
All the machinery of law devised by parents
Could not be stopped though fire swept the rooms.

Whenever my thoughts move to all those rooms
I sat alone in, capable of innocence,
I know now I was not alone, that parents
Always were there to speak the hideous sentence:

"You are our son; be good; we know your guilt;
We stare through walls and see your thoughts forever."

Sometimes I wished to go away forever;
I dreamt of strangers and of stranger rooms
Where every corner held the light of guilt.
Why do the judges stare? I saw no innocence
In them when they pronounced the sentence;
I heard instead the believing voice of parents.

I can remember evenings when my parents,
Settling my future happily forever,
Would frown before they spoke the sentence:
"Someday the time will come to leave these rooms
Where, under our watchful eyes, you have been innocent;
Remember us before you seize the world of guilt."

Their eyes burn. How can I deny my guilt
When I am guilty in the sight of parents?
I cannot think that even they were innocent.
At least I shall not have to wait forever
To be escorted to the silent rooms
Where darkness promises a final sentence.

We walk forever to the doors of guilt,
Pursued by our own sentences and eyes of parents,
Never to enter innocent and quiet rooms.

"Sestina: Travel Notes," is metrically more free, with as
many tetrameters as pentameters and with a concluding hex-
ameter. It ponders the *voyage* of life and our encounters with
others, the failure of communication, the *silence,* which we
find a *burden* and a *harm* as things and people drift *away.*
What in other hands might be a mere literary form is here,
as in Kees's first sestina, vitalized by the current of personal
urgency.

Quite a few poets have tried out the sestina at the begin-
ning of their careers, found it not to their purpose, and never
returned to it. Elizabeth Bishop is something of an exception
in coming back to it after her early experience with it. So is
Howard Nemerov. In his first book, *The Image and the Law*
(1947), we find his "Sestina I" and "Sestina II." Both are in

iambic pentameter. The first has no regular scheme of permutation; each stanza repeats the original end-words, but at random. The second, like Sidney's double sestina in that it has two speakers, A and B, in alternate stanzas, forsakes the traditional order for a novel one: the second stanza, and following ones, observe a 2 5 3 6 4 1 pattern of rearrangement. We wonder if Nemerov is showing his impatience with the form when in the sixth stanza he has B ask: "Stranger, has this silly game no end?" He does end the poem abruptly after that stanza, with no envoy. Neither sestina is reprinted in his *New and Selected Poems* (1960) or in *The Collected Poems* (1977). We might take it that this is his farewell to the sestina.

But in "Sarajevo" (*The Blue Swallows*, 1967), he did return to it, "varying it," as he says, "to suit my needs." The variations consist of his omitting again the *congedo* and of his repeating the entire first line of the poem—and not just its end-word—in each stanza: "In the summer, when the Archduke dies." In the second stanza it becomes the second line, and so moves down by steps through the stanzas until in the sixth stanza—this time modulated into a past tense and with the midline comma omitted—it gives us the concluding line of the poem.

It was in the 1940s that Malcolm Lowry, while revising *Under the Volcano* and awaiting word from his publisher about its fate, was at work on the long collection of poems he had started years before. One section of it was called "The Cantinas," after the Mexican taverns he had known so well. Like the novel, it dealt with the tempestuous years Lowry had spent in Mexico in the late thirties: years of marital conflict, prolonged spells of drunkenness that had brought him to the attention of the police, and actual incarceration in an Oaxaca jail over the long Christmas holidays. It may seem strange that for experiences so searing Lowry should have chosen the most disciplined and demanding of forms. And yet the best of these poems, in the opinion of most Lowry scholars, is his double "Sestina in a Cantina,"[10] set in "a waterfront tavern in Vera Cruz at daybreak." It is about a struggle against the tyranny of alcoholism; though it ends with an exorcism, the struggle is felt as hopeless: "he likes his horrors." The six end-words are the *dawning* and *sunset* of the drunkard; the *prison* of his compulsion (as well as an actual jail); the *ocean* of possible freedom and escape; the distorting *mirrors* in which the victim sees himself and his world; and the *horrors* of his existence. As in most good sestinas, the words are ambivalent: if dawn and ocean suggest purity and health, they also suggest hangovers and nausea.

The poem is dramatic in structure, with several oddly assorted characters as speakers: Legion, St. Luke (a ship's doctor), Sir Philip Sidney, Richard III (a barman), the early edition of a newspaper, and The Swine that deliver the envoy. The basic allusion is to the Gadarene swine in the fifth chapter of St. Mark's gospel: "Legion" is the name of the devil or "unclean spirit" ("for we are many") that possesses a man until, exorcised by Christ, it (or they) leave the victim and enter a herd of swine, who rush into the ocean and are drowned. The relevance of the biblical account to Lowry's own situation is obvious.

The cameo appearance of Sir Philip Sidney is Lowry's acknowledgement of his influence. Though fond of Kipling, whose sestina he no doubt knew, Lowry had Sidney's "Ye goatherd gods . . ." in mind. His poem, like Sidney's, is a double sestina; its end-words *dawning* and *sunset* parallel Sidney's *morning* and *evening;* its diction and syntax occasionally recall the Elizabethan poet. Richard III is on loan from Shakespeare's play; in I, ii, he ironically calls for a looking glass in which to admire himself, and he concludes the scene with

> Shine out, fair sun, till I have bought a glass
> That I may see my shadow as I pass.

Lowry's Richard echoes these lines with his

> Shine out fair sun till you have bought new mirrors
> That you may see your shadow pass the ocean

For all of the struggle and torment the sestina expresses, the formal requirements are scrupulously met. End-words are used even more rigidly than they have to be; *dawning,* *prison,* and *mirrors* are always nouns, though they might easily have been verb forms or adjectives; *sunset, ocean,* and *horrors* are also unvaried. Lowry seems to have been among the writers who feel that the use of a strict form is one way of mastering otherwise uncontrollable emotions. No sestina seems to have come from more troubled depths; Sidney's "deadly swannish music" has become for Lowry a deadly swinish music in which he comes to grips with his own legion of devils. Unfortunately, in Lowry's own case, the exorcism was of no avail; in 1957, ten years after his poem was published in a Canadian magazine, he rushed into his own suicidal ocean.

Though a testimony to the potential of the sestina, Lowry's poem is not a complete success. Like so many of his poems, as his biographer Douglas Day has noticed, it has the air of being unfinished, even though Lowry reworked his manuscripts through draft after draft over the years. This one, powerful in parts, has lines that are obscure in syntax and ragged in rhythm. The ending may seem particularly unsatisfactory, though admirers of the poem might hold that no satisfactory ending was possible. Success or partial failure, the poem would seem to show that there is no material too harrowing to be handled in a sestina.

The four sestinas of Donald Justice, written from 1952 on, are found next to each other near the beginning of *The Summer Anniversaries* (1960), his first book. The poet chose only two for inclusion in his *Selected Poems* (1979): "A Dream Sestina" ("Sestina: A Dream" in the later book) and "Here in Katmandu" ("Sestina: Here in Katmandu"). The change of titles might imply that the poet came to regard them as exercises in a form. The first is basically in iambic tetrameter. "Here in Katmandu" is much freer, ranging from lines as short as "Comes down" to as long as "Meanwhile it is not easy here in Katmandu." These prose rhythms give a new feeling to the old form; since the end-words do not occur at regular intervals, they are much less clearly sounded—are, in fact, sometimes quite lost in the prose flow of the stanzas. There is no envoy. Of Justice's other two sestinas, "Sestina on Six

Words by Weldon Kees" takes, in their original order, the end-words of "Sestina: Travel Notes" for a further comment on human loneliness. The fourth sestina, "The Metamorphosis," in free trimeters, is original in the way it metamorphoses the end-words: it gives us variations based on sound. Instead of *tavern* six times (there is no envoy), what we have is *tavern, heaven, haven, having, heaving, living.* Instead of *went*, we have *went, wind, wound, whined, wonder, unwound.* This is a process later writers have found suggestive. Having discovered ways of loosening up the line and varying the repetitions, Justice did not return to the sestina.

Four sestinas of John Ashbery were also written near the beginning of his career: three are in *Some Trees* (1956), one in *The Tennis Court Oath* (1962). His first sestina, "The Painter," was inspired, he says, "both by Auden's 'Paysage Moralisé' and the Elizabeth Bishop one about drinking gallons of coffee." "Faust," in the second book, is amusingly closer to Ashbery's mature manner. But none of these practice pieces would rank with Ashbery's best poems. "Poem" is a sestina without punctuation—one way of updating an ancient form. None of the four are in pentameter; most have lines so free of a meter that they might be said to be in free verse. All keep to the traditional pattern of permutation.

Such early examples led Alan Ansen to dedicate his own sestina, "A Fit of Something Against Anything," to Ashbery (*Disorderly Houses,* 1961). Beginning with ceremonious elegance as it recalls "the burgeoning age of Arnaut," Ansen's amusing poem, while preserving the requirements of the sestina, collapses at the close into gibbering shrugs and grunts— as much of the poetry of those years had done. At a time when young poets were rebelling against "that alien order," Ansen has them wondering how anyone could write "that Gestapo sestina."

> Get lost, sestina,
> Go way . . .

But it wouldn't get lost or go away. Ashbery himself returned to it in *The Double Dream of Spring* (1970), in which his "Farm

Implements and Rutabagas in a Landscape" handles the form more engagingly, more in the manner we think of as his own, than the earlier sestinas had done. Here the ancient Provençal stanzas make room for the world of the comic strip: for Popeye, Olive Oyl, Swee'pea, Wimpy, Alice the Goon, and the Sea Hag, who cavort darkly through its permutations.

Other sestinas from the fifties by well-known poets would include Robert Pack's "Sestina in Sleep" (*The Irony of Joy*, 1955), which substitutes a rhyme scheme (in the first stanza *abbcca*, with random changes in the other stanzas) for the usual permutations; William Meredith's "Notre Dame de Chartres" (*The Open Sea*, 1958); and Daryl Hine's "The Destruction of Sodom" (*The Devil's Picture Book*, 1960), in which the poet goes back almost four centuries to the pattern Spenser had invented—or perhaps reinvents it on his own. All three poets like their sestinas well enough to include them in later collections of selected poems.

Early in the 1960s, Richmond Lattimore's "Sestina for a Far-off Summer" became the title poem for his 1962 collection. It evokes the pleasures of *youth* in *summer*, in the *forest*, by the *river*, with memories of young *arms* swimming or rowing, in a time of no *problem*, or only the happy problems of vacationing. The last two end-words are wrenched to grimmer meanings as the adolescents awake to the deadly *problem* of a world at war—"the globe in *arms*."

In England, Roy Fuller jammed rich rhyming into the "Finale" to "Faustian Sketches" (*Collected Poems*, 1962). Beginning with a stanza that rhymed *hell, sky, tell, die, fell, lie,* he put the rest of the stanzas through the regular changes, even though that gave him a stanza that chimed *aaabbb*—a stanza that almost chokes on its own sound. In America, Diane Wakoski took the sestina in an opposite direction—after Justice and Ashbery—in her "Sestina for a Home Gardener" (*Inside the Blood Factory*, 1968); she puts dampers on the end-words by using long proselike lines of uneven length, lines that are mostly run-on, even at the end of stanzas, and with strong pauses within the lines, so that the end-words do not recur with any regularity and are hardly heard when they do, since the voice cannot linger on them. They are further subdued by being rather weak in character and color: *removed, losses, sections, precise, pointed, unfamiliar.* Sandra McPherson has also written a soft-edged sestina in her graceful meditations on birds bathing in a pool. "In a Garden" (in *Poetry* in 1975 and in her *The Year of Our Birth* in 1978) flows around end-words that tend to be abstract and neutral, so unobtrusive that they hardly ripple the current of lines unmeasured by meter and almost never end-stopped.

> I'd just as soon be a skull, among elements that love
> my elements, as teach the thick-skinned and the faint to
>   seize
> life. They should teach me. Everything out of doors knows
> what's good for it, a wordless book on how and when
> to eat and what to sniff at. All compete to bathe,
> dive, hover over, and splash each other
>
> and grow so clean they drink what made some other
> species clean . . .

Here the armature of the sestina has supported the poet even as it concealed itself. It is like form disavowing form, and yet there is no doubt as to the success of the poem.[11] There may be some doubt, though, as to whether this is what a sestina wants to be. The muffling of the end-words seems not in itself desirable. If it were, one could carry the process even further by using such words as *the, of, in, an, to, or*—words that would not be noticed at all in a reading of the poem. But unless the end-words have enough presence and urgency to resonate and *demand* that they be returned, the sestina, as sestina, goes flaccid.

Peter Klappert's "The Lord's Chameleons" (*Circular Stairs, Distress in the Mirrors,* 1975) gave a new look to the sestina without playing down the importance of the end-words. The four-beat lines, often like Marianne Moore's in their vividness, are printed without the usual stanza divisions. Some lines are divided and dropped in midstanza, so that the familiar division into 6s is not visible: we may not know we are reading a sestina. The pattern of permutations is the one which Spenser had introduced in the sixteenth century and

Daryl Hine employed in the twentieth. End-words are also used in a new way as some turn into their look-alikes: *imitation, intimation, intimidation.*

Anthony Hecht preferred to let his end-words be heard in finding the sestina's pattern of recurrence appropriate when he came to write his "Sestina d'Inverno" (*Millions of Strange Shadows*, 1977), in part a curse on winter, in part a poem of endurance and fantasy-escape from a city in which "the one thing indisputable" is snow.

> Here in this bleak city of Rochester,
> Where there are twenty-seven words for "snow,"
> Not all of them polite, the wayward mind
> Basks in some Yucatan of its own making,
> Some coppery, sleek lagoon, or cinnamon island
> Alive with lemon tints and burnished natives,
>
> And O that we were there. But here the natives
> of this gray, sunless city of Rochester

During the 1970s a great many poets were drawn to the sestina—but none more strongly than Marilyn Hacker, who has published about a dozen of them. Her first book, *Presentation Piece* (1974) has seven, all regular, even in the envoys, and all in her own rather free iambic pentameter, which doesn't mind dropping a syllable or two, or occasionally even a foot, that conventional metrics would require. In "Landscape for Insurrection" (several of her sestinas have such feisty themes) we notice how the end-words are used in different senses:

> They stood in the embrasure of a bay
> window . . .
>
> . . . to count the tankers entering the bay;
>
> I'll seed a plot with spices, dill and bay . . .
>
> . . . Dogs began to bay . . .
>
> . . . keeping bugs at bay . . .

The little tingle of semantic dissonance is particularly keen when such words are next to each other, as the second and third *bay* above, or as in and humps up the slopes close to the ground.

Winded again, I only ground
my teeth and kept going . . .

Her second book, *Separations* (1976) has only one sestina,
but many would feel that it is her most unusual and interest-
ing use of the form, which here concentrates what could be a
scene from a racy novel:

La Vie de Château
—a fiction

That morning, she crisply snapped a postcard
next to his cup. "I think this is for you,"
she said. *Bugger! How does that girl
know where I am?* "How does that girl know where
you are? Only my husband and the servants
know you've come here." "And the children."

"Is she in correspondence with your *children?*"
"Hardly." He smiled, rereading the postcard,
accepted through a swath of sun the servant's
proffered brioches, and more steamed milk. "*Are* you
going to explain?" Postcards fluttered from nowhere,
like the too-clever fingers of the girl.

It wouldn't do to think about the girl.
"I think that I'll go for a drive with the children
this morning." "I think that you'll go nowhere
until you explain." It was almost a rude postcard.
Well, quite rude. How *did* she know? How could you
explain one to the other? Now the servants

had left. He couldn't accustom himself to servants,
or didn't like to think he could. The girl
who ironed, dark and thin, an arrogant smile you
wanted to decipher . . . His children and her children
shouted in the orchard. He'd sent *her* a postcard,
of course. She hadn't sniffed him out of nowhere

with a very naked man headed for nowhere
running like hell (the older woman servant
sailed the plates off)—a British Museum postcard

of a Greek vase. "Let's forget that wretched girl.
I thought I'd have Françoise take all the children
swimming, and spend the morning alone with you."

"Yes, lovely, I'd like to spend the morning with you."
Blonde and blue air, a morning for getting nowhere.
Already he regretted the drive with the children,
regretted, really, consigning them to servants
on their holiday. Could they forget the girl
by lunch? He might send her another postcard.

"What are you looking at?" "Nothing. White lace. The
    servant's
apron." "I know where we'll go." Grappling the girl
like children in the dark. He'd send a postcard.

Unlike most of the poets we have considered, Hacker stays
with the sestina after her earliest work. Her third book, *Tak-
ing Notice* (1980), has three. "Tranche Romancière" is again
like a passage of dialogue from a work of fiction. In it the poet
does something new in her handling of the end-words, allow-
ing many to be parts of hyphenated words: *sink, sink-/*ing,
*synch-/*ronize; *count,* ac*count-/*able, *Count-/*ess; *act, act-/*ress,
*act-/*ion, *act*ually (in the envoy). An amusing gimmick, but
probably not worth doing more than once. "Five Meals," rich
in food and wine detail, and with its end-words *leaves, wine,
oil, frosting, butter, coffee,* is a sestina for gastronomes. In
Hacker's sestinas the form is never an end in itself; always its
repetitions permit her to express more vividly the intensities
and shadowings of the subject.

As we look back over the history of the sestina, we see little
if anything that we could confidently call progress. Auden's
twentieth-century sestina is not better than Sidney's sixteenth-
century one. No poet has written a better sestina than Dante.
Little progress, maybe—but no end of change. From the be-
ginning there have been efforts to elasticize the form. Pe-
trarch began by stretching it out double. Pontus de Tyard
bedizened it with rhyme. Spenser and later poets have varied
the original scheme of permutations. Barnes introduced

other rhythms besides the pentameter and played fast and loose with the end-words. In our time, poets have written sestinas in no meter at all; they have tinkered tirelessly with the end-words, subduing their emphasis, muting their sonority, modulating homophones through a shimmer of nuance. The developments have all been toward freedom from what came to seem restrictions. As poets probed and tested, a Brownian restlessness strained and expanded the container. The movement toward freedom has been especially marked in subject matter. Originally a love poem that tended in less talented hands to jell into literary postures, the sestina in our time has come very far from the land of lute and rose. Opening a magazine nowadays we come on a poem like Eric Weil's "The Path of the Headlights" (*Poetry*, May 1980):

> The sticky whir of rubber on the wet road
> Makes tracks past a washed-out barn
> Painted CHEW MAIL POUCH TOBACCO fading in a
>   headlight-
> Swept mist. I can't see very well
> Because of the fog and the windshield wipers
> Screaming at the cars up ahead.

We may be well into such a poem before we realize it is a sestina. A few pages further on in the same issue we find a pair of poems by Jeffrey Skinner which gives us "His Side" and "Her Side" of a passionate quarrel over a husband's infidelity. The husband begins with his side:

> There can be no explanation
> elaborate enough to satisfy your curiosity.
> Don't you see that yet? When the hurt
> has nowhere to go it becomes a kind of hunger,
> a sad relish for lewd detail. And the questions
> lead to nothing, like a series of doors
>
> in a dream.

The wife concludes with hers:

                    All I see is your hand, touching
her there, and there, lifting her
out of some hell, and into my life.
Why? why—that's the only question
I want answered. Why did you damage
a promise I thought went beyond words,

and now is just words? You can't touch
me now without damage: I think of her.
Answer the question, bastard. Don't waste my life.

Tormented as the wife may be, the end-words, in her envoy, are in the traditional order. In both sestinas the end-words are a key to the emotional differences in the attitudes of husband and wife.

This then is where the sestina has brought us. One other matter: since our early mention of mystic numerology, we have had little to say about the relation between numbers and poetry. Some writers have been on the alert for a subject whose very arithmetic might justify their writing a sestina. In "Sestina for Warm Seasons" (*A Time of Bees,* 1964), Mona Van Duyn lets her six stanzas and envoy make graphic the fact that the body renews its physical substance every seven years. Tom Disch begins his "The Thirty-Nine Articles" (*The Little Magazine,* Fall 1977) with

        Ten days ago I turned thirty-eight. If I were thirty-nine
        I'd have lived one year for every line of this sestina

Michael Blumenthal realized he had a sestina subject ("Cheers," *Poetry,* June 1983) when he read this sentence in Wendell Berry's *The Body and the Earth:* "The word health belongs to a family of words, a listing of which will suggest how far the consideration of health must carry us: *heal, whole, wholesome, hale, hallow, holy.*" James Merrill enjoyed playing with sestina numbers in his "Tomorrows" (*The Yellow Pages,* 1967), which begins:

The question was an academic one.
Andrey Sergeyvitch, rising sharp at two,
Would finally write that letter to his three
Sisters in the country. Stop at four,
Drink tea, dress elegantly and, by five,
Be losing money at the Club des Six.

The end-words undergo antic changes: *two* becomes *to, Tim-buctoo, tu* (Italian), *into,* and *too; six* becomes *Sikhs, 1936, 2.6, classics.*

It was after an experience involving 6s that I had my only adventure with the sestina. We had run aground on a sandbar off Beaufort, South Carolina, and as we waited for the tide to come in and float us off I was instructed in the "rule of twelves" and the way it governs the six hours of the changing tide: during the first hour, one-twelfth of the water moves; during the second, two-twelfths; during the third, three-twelfths. During the next three, the fractions run in reverse order. This had to be a sestina.

Tide Turning

Through salt marsh, grassy channel where the shark's
A rumor—lean, alongside—rides our boat;
Four of us off with picnic-things and wine.
Past tufty clutters of the mud called *pluff,*
Sun on the ocean tingles like a kiss.
About the fourth hour of the falling tide.

The six-hour-falling, six-hour-rising tide
Turns heron-haunts to alleys for the shark.
Tide-waters kiss and loosen; loosen, kiss.
Black-hooded terns blurt kazoo-talk—our boat
Now in midchannel and now rounding pluff.
Lolling, we eye the mud-tufts. Eye the wine.

The Atlantic, off there, dazzles. Who said wine-
Dark sea? Not this sea. Not at noon. The tide
Runs gold as chablis over sumps of pluff.
Too shallow here for lurkings of the shark,
His nose-cone, grin unsmiling. *Cr-ush!* the boat
Shocks, shudders—grounded. An abrupt tough kiss.

Our outboard's dug a mud-trough. Call that *kiss?*
Bronze knee bruised. A fair ankle gashed. With "wine-
Dark blood" a bard's on target here. The boat
Swivels, propeller in a pit, as tide
Withdraws in puddles round us—shows the shark-
Grey fin, grey flank, grey broadening humps of pluff.

Fingers that trailed in water, fume in pluff.
Wrist-deep, they learn how octopuses kiss.
Then—shark fins? No. Three dophins there—*shhh!*—arc
Coquettish. As on TV. Cup of wine
To you, slaphappy sidekicks! with the tide's
Last hour a mudflat draining round the boat.

The hourglass turns. Look, tricklings toward the boat.
The first hour, poky, picks away at pluff.
The second, though, swirls currents. Then the tide's
Third, fourth—abundance! the great ocean's kiss.
The last two slacken. So? We're free, for wine
And gaudier mathematics. Toast the shark,

Good shark, a no-show. Glory floats our boat.
We, with the wine remaining—done with pluff—
Carouse on the affluent kisses of the tide.

(The Kiss: A Jambalaya, 1982)

It seems to be the poetry workshop that is the breeding
ground of sestinas today. Every editor of a poetry magazine,
knowing in what abundance they are produced, will some-
times smile ruefully in agreement with Dana Gioia's "My Con-
fessional Sestina" *(Poetry,* October 1983):

Let me confess. I'm sick of these sestinas
written by youngsters in poetry workshops
for the delectation of their fellow students,
and then published in little magazines
that no one reads, not even the contributors
who at least in this omission show some taste . . .

But Mr. Gioia is himself smiling, and knows he is being out-
rageous—having just added to our rich variety of sestinas.

We have seen that many of our best poets have written sestinas early in their careers, but that only a few have returned to the form in their maturity. It is not a form that any poet is likely to use often; once or twice in a lifetime may be enough. But for that once or twice it may be the only form that vibrates in perfect sympathy with the poet's feeling. Meanwhile, it offers a handy kind of calisthenics for the young poet; the hours of exercise spent with it can be not only a pleasure in themselves but a preparation for whatever more spontaneous bursts of genius are to come.

Notes

1. For numerology and other matters regarding the sestina, see Alastair Fowler, *Conceitful Thought* (Edinburgh: Edinburgh University Press, 1975), 39ff.; and Marianne Shapiro, *Hieroglyph of Time: The Petrarchan Sestina* (Minneapolis: University of Minnesota Press, 1980), 10–13.

2. F. J. A. Davidson, "The Origin of the Sestina," *Modern Language Notes* 25 (January 1910): 18–20. For information about patterns that led up to the sestina, see A. Jeanroy, "La 'sestina doppia' de Dante et les origines de la sextine," *Romania* 42 (1913): 481–89.

3. Not "arms," as Pound thinks. His translation renders "qui pert . . . s'arma" (line 3) as "who loose their arms." It means "who loses his soul."

4. Manuscripts of Arnaut Daniel and the editions based on them give variant readings, which would call for various translations. I follow Gianluigi Toja's edition of the *Canzoni* (Florence: Sansoni, 1960). The "barren rod" of the fifth stanza is the Virgin Mary: virginity that flowered.

5. Leslie Fiedler, "Green Thoughts in a Green Shade," *Kenyon Review* 18 (Spring 1956): 238–62.

6. For a consideration of the Petrarchan sestina, see Marianne Shapiro, *op. cit.*

7. Marianne Shapiro, *Hieroglyph,* p. 28, translated from Janos Riesz, *Die Sestine: ihre Stellung in der literarischen Kritik und ihre Geschichte als lyrische Genus* (Munich, 1971), 28: ". . . wonach sich der poetische Ausdruck so viel wie möglich von dem des gewöhnlichen Lebens unterscheiden soll."

8. William Empson, *Seven Types of Ambiguity*, 3d ed. (New York: Noonday Press, 1955), 42–46.

9. *Parthenophil and Parthenophe* has been edited by V. A. Doyno (Carbondale: Southern Illinois University Press, 1971). The triple sestina can also be found in *The Penguin Book of Elizabethan Verse*, edited by Edward Lucie-Smith (Aylesbury, Bucks.: Penguin, 1965).

10. *Selected Poems of Malcolm Lowry*, edited by Earle Birney (San Francisco: City Lights Books, 1962).

11. The poet writes: "The secret of my sestina is that (1) I was angry and so had the momentum to keep going and (2) I thought of each stanza as an *inning* in baseball. So I'd say to myself, 'Now I'm in the top of the 3rd, the bottom of the 5th, etc.'"

UNDER DISCUSSION
Donald Hall, General Editor

Volumes in the Under Discussion series collect reviews and essays about individual poets. The series is concerned with contemporary American and English poets about whom the consensus has not yet been formed and the final vote has not been taken. Titles in the series include:

Forthcoming volumes will examine the work of Robert Creeley, H.D., Galway Kinnell, and Louis Simpson, among others.

Please write for further information on available editions and current prices.

Ann Arbor   **The University of Michigan Press**